# HOW PEOPLE
# CHANGE

## INSIDE AND OUTSIDE THERAPY

# THE PLENUM SERIES IN
# SOCIAL / CLINICAL PSYCHOLOGY

**Series Editor: C. R. Snyder**
*University of Kansas*
*Lawrence, Kansas*

---

---

A Continuation Order Plan is available for this series. A continuation order will bring delivery of each new volume immediately upon publication. Volumes are billed only upon actual shipment. For further information please contact the publisher.

# HOW PEOPLE CHANGE

## INSIDE AND OUTSIDE THERAPY

### EDITED BY

REBECCA C. CURTIS

AND

GEORGE STRICKER

*Derner Institute of Advanced Psychological Studies*
*Adelphi University*
*Garden City, New York*

PLENUM PRESS • NEW YORK AND LONDON

Library of Congress Cataloging-in-Publication Data

How people change : inside and outside therapy / edited by Rebecca C.
Curtis and George Stricker.
        p.    cm. -- (The Plenum series in social/clinical psychology)
    Includes bibliographical references and index.
    ISBN 0-306-43784-8
    1. Behavior therapy.  2. Change (Psychology)   I. Curtis, Rebecca
C.  II. Stricker, George.
    [DNLM: 1. Behavior Therapy.  2. Personality.  3. Psychology,
Clinical.   WM 425 H847]
RC489.B4H62   1991
616.89'142--dc20
DNLM/DLC
for Library of Congress                                         91-2691
                                                                   CIP

ISBN 0-306-43784-8

© 1991 Plenum Press, New York
A Division of Plenum Publishing Corporation
233 Spring Street, New York, N.Y. 10013

Printed in the United States of America

# CONTRIBUTORS

ELLIOT ARONSON, Stevenson College, University of California, Santa Cruz, Santa Cruz, California 95065

BARBARA BENEDICT BUNKER, Department of Psychology, State University of New York at Buffalo, New York 14260

SHEILA M. COONERTY, Department of Psychology, Long Island University, Forest Hills, New York 11375

ALLAN COOPER, William Alanson White Institute, New York, New York 10023

JOEL COOPER, Department of Psychology, Princeton University, Princeton, New Jersey 08544

REBECCA CURTIS, Derner Institute of Advanced Psychological Studies, Adelphi University, Garden City, New York 11530

JACQUELINE J. DELISLE, Department of Psychology, State University of New York at Buffalo, New York 14260

MARVIN R. GOLDFRIED, Department of Psychology, State University of New York, Stony Brook, New York 11794

LESLIE S. GREENBERG, Department of Psychology, York University, North York, Ontario M3J 1P3, Canada

DIANA ADILE KIRSCHNER, Private Practice, Gwynedd Valley, Pennsylvania 19437

SAM KIRSCHNER, Private Practice, Gwynedd Valley, Pennsylvania 19437

OTTO KLINEBERG, Professor Emeritus, Department of Psychology, Columbia University, New York, New York 10022

LEIGH MCCULLOUGH, Department of Psychology in Psychiatry, University of Pennsylvania, Philadelphia, Pennsylvania 19104

ESTHER MENAKER, New York University Postdoctoral Program, New York, New York 10003

RENÉ H. RHODES, Program in Clinical Psychology, Teachers College, New York, New York 10022

CAROL M. RUBIN, Private Practice, 20 Claremont Street, Newton, Massachusetts 02158

JEFFREY Z. RUBIN, Department of Psychology, Tufts University, Medford, Massachusetts 02155

GEORGE STRICKER, Derner Institute of Advanced Psychological Studies, Adelphi University, Garden City, New York 11530

PAUL L. WACHTEL, Department of Psychology, City College of New York, New York, New York 10031

# PREFACE

In the myth of Daphne and Apollo, Cupid fired two arrows: one causing flight from love, the other passionate attraction. Cupid aimed his first arrow at Daphne, a beautiful nymph who loved her freedom; the next struck Apollo, who lusted after Daphne. Daphne, frightened and intent upon virginity, fled Apollo but was unable to run fast enough. When her strength was almost gone, she sought protection in the familiar waters of her father's river. He answered her prayers: Her hair became leaves, and her feet, roots growing into the ground; she was transformed into a laurel tree. Apollo, kissing the sprouting bark, pledged to honor Daphne by placing a laurel wreath on the head of every hero who won a victory. Unable to evade the consequences of the arrow that wounded her, Daphne called upon the river, the creative power of both nature and time—a symbol of fertility, but also of oblivion—to help her survive when her strength was gone.

Daphne's inner triumph in the face of injury is an appropriate symbol for the types of transformation witnessed by psychologists. In his book on symbols, Circlot (1962, p. 173) writes that the crowning of the poet, artist, or conqueror with laurel leaves "presupposes a series of inner victories over the negative and dissipative influence of the basest forces." Further, the tree "denotes the life of the cosmos: its consistence, growth, proliferation, generative, and regenerative processes" (Circlot, 1962, p. 328).

As I reflected upon the contributions to this volume, the image of Daphne's transformation into a laurel tree came frequently to mind. Although the changes that occur in Greek and Roman myths are sometimes violent and rapid, the psychological significance of these "truths of fiction," as Horace Gregory (1958, p. xii) tells us in his introduction to *The Metamorphoses*, is "more convincing than any document or 'case history' can hope to be." Sometimes it is impossible for people in the real world to make changes in their actual life circumstances. Like Daphne, when the obstacles people are facing are assessed and the brute power and cruelty of others are experienced, the most that people can hope to change is their perception of their situation and/or themselves.

Hearing the life stories of patients, I have often tried to imagine how I would have endured the series of abuses that patients had described. I have also wondered how change might take place so that in many of these cases a patient would not try to commit suicide again soon after leaving the hospital. Very rapid transformations are required in such circumstances if patients are to avoid long-term hospitalization. And although the metamorphoses of these people, when they occur, are less dramatic than those in fiction, their extremes of passion are not—for these people are ready to die if their desires remain so unfulfilled.

As a clinician with a background in social psychology, certain questions inevitably arose when I became engaged in psychotherapy. For example, are there any commonalities between theories of individual change and theories of social change? Or, even more specifically, what are the similarities and differences among theories of individual change in naturally occurring settings and theories of individual change in therapy?

With questions such as these in mind, a conference entitled "How People Change: Inside and Outside Therapy" was organized and held at Adelphi University on October 1, 1988. The introduction by Curtis and the chapters by Aronson, Goldfried, the Kirschners, Klineberg, Menaker, Stricker, and Wachtel are based upon presentations at that conference. Morton Deutsch, Harvey Horstein, and Hans Strupp also spoke there, with the Strupp paper published in *Journal of Cognitive Psychotherapy and Research: An International Quarterly.*

Hopefully, the ideas of the contributors will be of use to both scientists and practitioners. And knowing that political and social changes affect the lives of many much more quickly and dramatically than does individual psychotherapy, it is hoped that these ideas will be of use as psychologists and other change agents attempt to help themselves and others make interventions which will lead to a less destructive world.

Sometimes change seems so difficult that many of us believe any efforts to make large-scale changes will be wasted. It is difficult, however, to envision how a society can cope when at least 18% (Brazelton, 1990) to 43% (Blakeslee, 1990) of the babies born in major cities have suffered the effects of substance abuse *in utero* and are possibly neurologically damaged for life. It is important, of course, not to make recommendations with insufficient knowledge, but it is irresponsible for social scientists not to communicate that we know much more about conditions affecting the maintenance and change of human behaviors than was known 100 years ago. Although we are aware that change can be very difficult, we also know that it is possible. And although the pathways of change cannot be mapped out adequately in one volume, we have hopefully left footprints leading in some useful directions.

> To tell of bodies transformed,
> That is my purpose
> Because it is you, O Gods,
> Who create change and art,
> Breathe life into me to further this enterprise
> > (Ovid, *The Metamorphoses*, Book I, lines 1–4a, author's translation)

Rebecca C. Curtis

*Garden City, New York*

## REFERENCES

Circlot, J. E. (1962). *A dictionary of symbols* (J. Sage, Trans.). New York: Philosophical Library.

Gregory, H. (1958). Introduction. In *Ovid: The metaphorphoses* (H. Gregory, Trans.). New York: The Viking Press.

Blakeslee, S. (1990, May 19). Child-rearing is stormy when drugs cloud birth. *New York Times*, pp. 1, 9.

Brazelton, J. B. (1990, September 9). Why is America failing its children? *New York Times Magazine*, pp. 40–42, 50, 90.

# CONTENTS

*Chapter 11*

Barbara Benedict Bunker and Jacqueline J. DeLisle

*Chapter 12*

Jeffrey Z. Rubin and Carol M. Rubin

PART III.   INTEGRATION AND CONCLUSIONS

*Chapter 13*

Allan Cooper and Joel Cooper

*Chapter 14*

Toward an Integrative Theory of Psychological Change
    in Individuals and Organizations:
    A Cognitive-Affective Regulation Model.................... 191

*Rebecca Curtis*

How People Change: A Brief Commentary..................... 211

*George Stricker*

CHAPTER 1

# HOW PEOPLE CHANGE
## INTRODUCTION

### REBECCA CURTIS

> *Be fresh each day like nature itself.*
> Scroll at Urasenke Chanoyu Center, New York

...some (seed) fell by the wayside; and it was trodden down, and the fowls of the air devoured it. And some fell upon a rock; and as soon as it was sprung up, it withered away, because it lacked moisture. And some fell among thorns; and the thorns sprang up with it and choked it. And other fell on good ground, and sprang up, and bore fruit a hundredfold... And that which fell among thorns are they, which, when they have heard, go forth, and are choked with cares and riches and pleasures of this life, and bring no fruit to perfection. But that on the good ground are they, which in an honest and good heart, having heard the word, keep it, and bring forth fruit with patience. No man, when he hath lighted a candle, covereth it with a vessel, or putteth it under a bed; but setteth it on a candlestick, that they which enter in may see the light. For nothing is secret, that shall not be made manifest; neither any thing hid, that shall not be known and come abroad. (Luke 8: 5–8; 14–17)

People, like seeds, develop and change in a great variety of environments. In the natural world some changes are gradual, others sudden. Natural changes involve an interplay of forces, some from within an or-

REBECCA CURTIS • Derner Institute of Advanced Psychological Studies, Adelphi University, Garden City, New York 11530.

ganizational system, some from outside of it. Sometimes the changes occur within the already existing organizational system, sometimes the organizational system itself changes.

Matter and energy are the two ways nature shows itself to us. "Matter is neither created nor destroyed" we thought until Einstein proved that mass can be changed into energy and energy into mass. Now we say "mass energy is neither created nor destroyed." Change in the living world differs from change in the nonliving world in that only animate organisms have the fundamental characteristic of energy change known as metabolism with its constructive and destructive phases we call anabolism and catabolism, respectively. Animal life differs from other life forms in the way in which animals transform energy and in that they move freely from their own energy, rarely held down by roots. Humans make plans for the future, formulate goals, and evaluate alternative strategies for achieving these goals in a way that only other primates can approximate. Among primates, only chimpanzees, orangutans, and people demonstrate the capacity for self-observation leading to self-recognition (Gallup, 1982; Gallup & Suarez, in press). People reflect upon their own thought processes and may become aware of their own state of awareness. They develop theories about the natural world, themselves and the social world, and about their systems of psychological and cultural organization and change.

Changes occur not only in the organizational systems of the natural world but in our theories about these organizational systems. Kuhn (1962) has provided one well-known description about how these theories of the organization of the physical world change. According to Kuhn, advances sometimes are made within an existing paradigm, at other times the paradigm shifts. So psychological change occurs in these ways as well. Sometimes behaviors, thoughts, and feelings are altered within an existing framework, at other times our whole organizational system changes. Our theories of change must account for both types of phenomena.

Even people who believe that human behavior is largely determined by genetics appear to expend energy consciously in shaping the lives of their children, their work environments, and the political systems of which they are members. People certainly differ from animals and other forms of nature in their awareness of their capacity to influence their environments, both physically and socially. Although one seedling sprout may consume more of the ingredients in the soil essential for growth and thereby deprive another sprout, there is no nervous system available in the sprout capable of conscious awareness of the processes of interdependence and influence taking place. People have the potential to become aware of these processes, however, and it is with this potential for increased awareness that the chapters in the current volume were written.

When I think about change, especially individual change, what comes to my mind first is the fairy tale of "Beauty and the Beast," with the images as seen in Jean Cocteau's film of the same title. In this tale, love and acceptance lead to a man's transformation from a beast back into a prince. So it also seems sometimes in real life that an acceptance of the worst in ourselves and others leads to an almost magical metamorphosis of reality or perception.

Such a transformation occurs in the life of Ivan Ilyich in the story by Tolstoy (1886/1967). Two hours before his death, when Ilyich realizes that he has been spiritually dead his whole life, he is transformed by the light of his insight that he has lived his whole life according to an erroneous conviction. The intensity of his pain and suffering appears in fact to have been due to his mistaken belief that his life had been a good one. Without the pain, however, Ilyich's "rebirth" likely would not have taken place. The acceptance by Ilyich that his whole life has been wrong leads to a metamorphosis. As in a fairy tale, the "right thing" to do becomes obvious to him. When he then wonders what has become of his pain, he finds it, but says "what of it?" When he seeks the fear of death to which he was formerly accustomed, in place of it there is light. When he forgives his family, he realizes "he must act so as not to hurt them: release them and free himself from these sufferings" (p. 302). Then, in conclusion he states, "How good and how simple."

These words of Ivan Ilyich are reminiscent of the "Easy Change" in the Book of Changes, the ancient wisdom regarding the release from the cycle of creation and destruction, of birth and death, and of pain and suffering when people become free from "the anxiety as to success or fear as to failure" (Chai & Chai, 1964, p. lxvii). In the Buddhist tradition the aim of life is to be fully born (Suzuki, Fromm, & De Martino, 1960, p. 88). Perhaps this is similar to the sort of psychological birth that occurs to Ivan Ilyich in his final hours.

According to the I Ching, the concept of I, or change, has three important attributes or meanings: (1) ease and simplicity, (2) change and transformation, and (3) invariability (Chai & Chai, 1964, p. xlvii). Elsewhere the I is said to represent production and reproduction (p. xlii), or "the unceasing movement" of the stream of life, "abundant and daily renewed" (p. xli).

According to this Chinese philosophy, the process of transformation is believed to start with the easy and the simple. Things are ever changing and changeable, but their underlying principles are constant and invariable. Although the universe is complex and always changing, "among the complexities simplicity can be found, among the changes something unchanging" (p. xlviii). The purpose of the current volume is to attempt to discern some of these simple invariances without ignoring the complexities of ever-changing and unique situations.

Thus far I have alluded only to examples of individual change. Certainly social change processes need to be investigated as well. This volume will explore how social changes and changes in external realities affect individuals, but will not attempt to give such change processes a full examination. Instead, the focus will remain primarily on individual change, the major domain of psychology and hence the subtitle "Inside and Outside Therapy."

The current volume thus does not attempt to present a comprehensive view of change processes. Omitted are the contributions to understanding this phenomenon made by scholars in religion, education, sociology, anthropology, political science, and other disciplines, as well as contributions from such important areas as developmental psychology and neuropsychology. The volume does not deal with many specific dimensions of the change process. For a theoretical consideration of personality change and ways to induce change, the reader is referred to the volume edited by Worchel and Byrne (1964) entitled *Personality Change*, which also includes contributions by both clinical and social psychologists. The process of change and the patterns of change in psychotherapy are described in many volumes including Rice and Greenberg's (1984) and Mahrer's (1985) works, respectively. Advances in the measurement of natural change processes have been reported recently in Silka's (1989) book entitled *Intuitive Judgments of Change*. Change across the life span and changes in reactions to negative life events are discussed in volumes edited by Callahan and McCluskey (1983) and Snyder and Ford (1987), respectively. Changes in reactions to seemingly paradoxical interventions have been presented by Watzlawick, Weakland, and Fisch (1974).

Instead, this volume focuses on theories and assumptions regarding change in clinical and social psychology. It brings together leading social, clinical, and organizational psychologists to discuss their working assumptions regarding how people change inside and outside therapy. The contributors have been chosen for their outstanding contributions within their own fields and for their knowledge of issues in both clinical and social psychology. Thus, the clinical psychologists are concerned about social change and the social–organizational psychologists are familiar with the therapeutic process.

## THE IMPORTANCE OF UNDERSTANDING HOW PEOPLE CHANGE

At a time when specialization within the field of psychology has grown to the point where many in the discipline find it of questionable value for scientists and practitioners to continue to meet together in one professional association, there are some psychologists whose work and interests continue to span both domains. Largely, I guess, because of the divisions within our profession, clinical and social psychologists rarely speak in the same symposia or engage in the discussion and debate of substantive ideas that regularly occur within each specialty at conventions and conferences. Therefore we have grouped together in this volume what some of the best thinkers in our field have to say about an important topic of interest to several specialties within psychology and other disciplines.

At the present time our planet and its people are faced with serious threats to their continued existence as we know it. With a depletion in the ozone layer, the greenhouse effect, the destruction of thousands of acres of rain forest in South America, the accumulation of tons of garbage and toxic substances from a wasteful style of consumption unprecedented in history by such a large population, and the ever-present threat of nuclear destruction, Daniel Goleman (1989), a psychologist and writer for the *New York Times*, has asked if we are *denying* the gravity of the problems facing our planet and enjoying the *illusion* of well-being normally characteristic of happy, healthy people so well documented by Taylor and Brown (1988). And, as so many scientists have noted, the most difficult problems facing us are now social ones, not technological ones. Are they so difficult to face that we are *denying* their seriousness?

In 1945, Einstein (cited in Lapp, 1964) asserted that "The unleashed power of the atom has changed everything save our modes of thinking and we thus drift toward unparalleled catastrophe." Freud had stated in 1930: "The fateful question for the *human* species seems to me to be whether and to what extent (it)...will succeed in mastering the human instinct of aggression *and* self-destruction" (1930/1946, pp. 143–144). Fortunately, psychologists have gained a great deal of knowledge since Freud and Einstein made these statements.

Let me elaborate on this. We know that the behavior of human beings is less determined by our genes than is the behavior of other organisms. Psychologists in this century have learned much about the social experiences and conditions that make particular behaviors, such as aggression, selfishness, love, and generosity, more or less likely to occur. We know a lot about what leads people to behave, think, and feel the way they do, what leads them to persist in their ways, and how to enable people to change. And psychologists have a vision of life beyond technology, beyond the miracles of science, beyond materialism, beyond limitless consumption and endless indisposable waste—a vision that focuses increasingly on issues of interdependence. Tolman in his (1940/1941) presidential address to the Society for the Psychological Study of Social Issues predicted that American society would cease to be dominated by "economic" man and would be replaced by "psychological man," with the principal dominant needs similar to those described by Maslow (1954) as "higher needs." Obviously, his prediction has not yet come true. Yet I think the scholars represented in this volume hold a vision of such a psychological type of person and a view of how to empower people to become that way.

We know much about the experiences with parents and the types of relationships in schools, in communities, and within and between countries that make it less likely for people to hurt others and themselves in lives of crime, child abuse, substance abuse, negligence of health maintenance, anxiety, depression, and loneliness. We have also made steps, some small, some large, in bringing our vision of a slightly less destructive world into fruition. The desegregation decision in this country is one example in which the work of psychologists played a major role. But we know there is much to do. We know we have had very little impact on our social world. The knowledge we do have about how people change must be articulated more clearly to each other and to the public, and our ideas refined through discussion, our theories further developed, and our hypotheses tested, where possible, in our research endeavors.

The difficulties of understanding and attempting to change human behavior have been great enough to be avoided by many brilliant minds attracted to challenging problems, but the scholars assembled in this volume have thought about it, researched it, written about it, *and* empowered people to change. Nick Cummings (1987) spoke of the distinguished psychologists and psychiatrists, such as Erik Erikson, Karen Horney, and Frieda Fromm-Reichman, called in to help in World War II with the distressing mortality rate for American parachutists, which was the highest in our military. This was because the parachutists would panic when it was time to jump and delay their jump until they had passed the time when it was safest. The psychologists made suggestions to help the parachutists tolerate their anxiety and freely make their leap earlier while it was still safe. Among the suggestions were those to help the parachutists channel their anger.

In this volume we have a similarly distinguished group of psychologists presenting their ideas with somewhat different types of aggression and self-destruction facing the people of our planet. I believe these psychologists suggest some ways to help channel our energies to work in the most productive ways possible to reduce destructiveness to self and others, to avoid catastrophe, and to launch our parachutes while we still have time to land in a safety zone. And perhaps as we drift in the winds, there will be a "paradigm shift" in our outmoded ways of thinking.

## OVERVIEW OF THE CHAPTERS IN THIS VOLUME

Change within the psychotherapy process is examined first. Menaker, a psychoanalyst, presents in her chapter a major challenge to the factor considered most essential to the psychoanalytic theory of therapy, that is, the transference. In the next chapter, Wachtel, an analyst who advocates behavioral and systems approaches in addition to psychoanalytical ones, examines how the external reality which the client has constructed creates obstacles to change in therapy. Five factors common to the change process across therapeutic modalities are discussed in the following chapter by Goldfried who identifies himself most closely with the cognitive–behavioral approach. Affect as an organizing principle and as a crucial component to therapeutic change is the focus of the contribution by Greenberg and Rhodes who have roots in the experiential tradition. This theme is extended and elaborated on by McCullough who examines how exposure to conflictual impulses and the anxiety surrounding them leads to an expression of affect in short-term dynamic therapy and subsequently to alternative ways of acting. That change does not occur in a straight line and is not unilateral is pointed out in the chapters by the Kirschners and Coonerty.

The second section of the volume deals directly with change and the role of change agents outside the therapy session. Aronson emphasizes the importance of the details involved in the change process, regardless of the theory used. He points out the impossibility of teaching a change agent all the possible nuances and contingencies that must be taken into account. The futility of inducing people to change by using congnitive techniques alone is addressed by Klineberg. His chapter also deals with the resistance of people to change their basic worldviews. Although a deep and lasting change can occur through the resolution of conflict, practical realities many times instead necessitate a settlement of issues, as opposed to a "resolution," as the Rubins indicate in their chapter. Bunker and DeLisle provide specific theoretical and practical approaches to individual change within organizations.

The final part of the volume speaks to change and the role of change agents both inside and outside therapy. Cooper and Cooper call attention to the problems that can ensue when external pressures are brought to bear on the change process. Curtis examines in relation to normally occurring self-regulation processes. And, finally, Stricker notes some of the areas of agreement and disagreement in the ideas of some of the contributors.

Although this volume will leave many of the reader's questions about how people change unanswered, it will hopefully lead to more appreciation of some of the processes involved in the psychological transformations that have excited the imagination at least since *The Metamorphoses* of Ovid's day. To the extent that the more readers know about the processes of change and recreation, the more interested they become, this volume will have achieved its major goal.

## THE FACILITATION OF GROWTH, CHANGE, AND GENERATIVITY

There must be an almost universal sense of awe and wonderment at the sight of a newborn baby, a new life that is never simply a combination of two parents but a special (although not always unique) reorganization of genes into a new life. In a world in which nothing anymore appears to be sacred, it seems that the creation of new life at least should hold such status—that is, never to be taken lightly. A similar sense of awe occurs when new life is created psychologically, when a personality organization changes so much that the person hardly seems the same. "She's like a new person," we say. Sometimes the person even looks different physically.

A change in one element of an organization may lead to changes in the other elements of the existing system or to changes in the organization. It is this complete reorganization that occurs in Beauty's Beast and Ivan Ilyich. As our scientific tools shed light on the processes by which new life is created psychologically, our role in this process should not be taken lightly. As the progress of science makes better known the secrets of psychological and social organization, these secrets and this energy, like the powerful energy of the atom, have enormous potential for changing the lives of ourselves and others. But knowledge of these processes unleashes a powerful potential to hurt as well as to help, to destroy as well as to create new psychological life and new organizational systems that will at times change, even dissipate our own.

In spite of our overwhelming ignorance, we cannot live without acting. Let us hope, then, that as the secrets of psychological change are unleashed, we do more good than harm. And, when we are the soil on which some seeds may fall, let us hope that the thorns already growing in our midst do not choke the emerging seedlings.

## ACKNOWLEDGMENT

I would like to express my appreciation to Michael Leippe, Tram Neill, Eugene Roth, C. R. Snyder, and George Stricker for their comments on an earlier version of this chapter.

## REFERENCES

Callahan, E. J., & McCluskey, K. A. (1983). *Life-span development: Nonnormative life events.* New York: Academic Press.

Chai, C., & Chai, W. (Eds.). (1964). *I Ching: Book of changes* (J. Legge, Trans.). New York: Bantam Books.

Cummings, N. (August, 1987). Brief psychotherapy intermittently through the life cycle. Paper presented at the annual meeting of the American Psychological Association, New York, August, 1987.

Freud, S. (1946). *Civilization and its discontents* (J. Riviere, Trans.). London: Hogarth Press. (Original work published 1930)

Gallup, G. G. (1982). Self-awareness and the emergence of mind in primates. *American Journal of Primatology, 2*(3), 237–248.

Gallup, G. G. Jr., & Suarez, S. D. (in press). Toward a comparative psychology of self-awareness species imitations and cognitive consequences. In J. Strauss & G. Goethals (Eds.), *The self: An interdisciplinary approach.* New York: Springer-Verlag.

Goleman D. (1989). What is negative about positive illusions? When benefits for the individual harm the collective. *Journal of Social and Clinical Psychology, 8,* 190–197.

Kuhn, T. S. (1962). *The structure of scientific revolutions.* Chicago: The University of Chicago Press.

Lapp, R. E. (1964). The Einstein letter that started it all. *New York Times Magazine,* August 2, 13–54.

Maslow, A. H. (1954). *Motivation and personality.* New York: Harper & Row.

Mahrer, A. R. (1985). *Psychotherapeutic change: An alternative approach to meaning and measurement.* New York: Norton.

Rice, L., & Greenberg, L. (Eds.) (1984). *Patterns of change: Intensive analysis of psychotherapy.* New York: Guilford.

Silka, L. (1989). *Intuitive judgments of change*. New York: Springer-Verlag.

Snyder, C. R., & Ford, C. (1987). *Coping with negative life events: Clinical and social psychological perspectives*. New York: Plenum.

Suzuki, D. T., Fromm, E., & DeMartino, R. (1960). *Zen Buddhism and psychoanalysis*. New York: Grove Press.

Taylor, S. E., & Brown, J. O. (1988). Illusion and well-being: A social psychological perspective on mental health. *Psychological Bulletin, 103*, 193–210.

Tolman, E. C. (1941). Psychological man. *Journal of Social Psychology, 13*, 205–218.

Tolstoy, L. (1967). The death of Ivan Ilyich. In *Great short works of Leo Tolstoy* (L. Maude & A. Maude, Trans.) (pp. 245–302). New York: Harper & Row. (Original work published 1886)

Watzlawick, P., Weakland, J., & Fisch, R. (1974). *Change: Principles of problem formation and problem resolution*. New York: Norton.

Worchel, P., & Byrne, D. (Eds.). (1964). *Personality in change*. New York: Wiley.

PART I

# PERSPECTIVES FROM CLINICAL PSYCHOLOGY

# CHAPTER 2

# QUESTIONING THE SACRED COW OF THE TRANSFERENCE

## ESTHER MENAKER

As we know, the transference is the sacred cow of the psychoanalytic treatment method. Since I have always been skeptical about sacred cows, I thought it worthwhile to examine this one and to question some of the premises that the psychoanalytic world has taken for granted.

In Freud's work with Breuer (1895/1955) on Anna O., he observed that some of her symptoms, her dreams, and fantasies were elicited by her feelings toward her therapist, Dr. Breuer. While they had a life of their own that originated in her own familial experience, they were then—in the course of her "talking cure"—reflected in the mirror of her relationship with Breuer. Anna O.'s feelings were largely of a sexual nature—a fact that was more disturbing to Breuer than to Freud, for whom sexuality was the primary motivating force in human life. The phenomenon of the projection of emotions that originate with the primary love objects in one's life onto other individuals who are experienced as having similar roles, Freud (1912/1953) called transference. While he was aware that transferences take place in relationships outside of analysis, he was primarily concerned with making use of this general phenomenon for purposes of psychoanalytic cure. It is important to remember that Freud's great discovery was the dynamic uncon-

ESTHER MENAKER • New York University Postdoctoral Program, New York, New York 10003.

scious and its role—because of repression—in the development of neurosis. The major task of treatment was, therefore, the uncovering of the unconscious through the lifting of repression. Since the expression of emotions in the transference reflected unconscious aspects of the patient's ways of loving, or hating, it became an important vehicle for understanding an individual's deeper life. Not that the emotions expressed in the transference were unconscious; on the contrary, they were usually very strongly and consciously experienced, but their origin and significance for understanding an individual's way of relating to others had remained unconscious until they appeared and were analyzed in the transference relationship.

The transference is at one and the same time a phenomenon of memory and an "acting out" in the analysis of these memories in the sense that the feelings toward the analyst—the wishes, longings, fears, angers—are expressed. Thus if an important goal of analysis is the recovery of repressed memories, and it was that for Freud, then the transference in which the feelings are expressed though not acted upon may be seen in a resistance to this process. Yet Freud saw the analysis of the transference as an unusually convincing way for the patient to experience, in the flesh as it were, the validity of the repetition of emotions that originated in very early childhood. The interpretation of the transference—the bringing into consciousness of the connection between past and present emotions—freed the individual's ego to choose other ways of reacting. The bond to the past could be altered; the repetition compulsion need not be in command and balance could exist between the various parts of the personality.

Why should I speak of pitfalls in this well thought out, logical conception of the role of the transference in the cure of neuroses and other behavioral and emotional disorders? To answer that question, let me first return to a discussion of the psychoanalytic situation. The analytic relationship between analyst and analysand is set up (and I am speaking of classical psychoanalysis) in such a way as to reproduce in reality and in actuality certain aspects of the childhood situation of the individual under analysis. The inevitable hierarchy of the parent as protector but inevitably as final authority on the one hand and the dependent child on the other is repeated in the authoritative position of the analyst and the inevitably submissive position of the patient. It might be argued that whenever one person seeks help from another a similar situation exists: the physician and patient; the lawyer and client. To some extent this is true for all transference responses that are apt to occur whenever one individual needs another. There is, however, an important difference between the psychoanalytic situation and other situations in which help is sought. The physician and the lawyer, for example, have something very concrete to offer in response to the expressed need, to the request for help: medical advice, a medical procedure, or legal advice or strategy. The request made of the analyst, on the other hand, is for an emotional response; and this is precisely what the analyst is enjoined *not* to give in the name of maintaining the powerful transference experience for the patient. The analytic situation recreated the unrequited love, on the sexual level, of the childhood experience. But it does more. In childhood there are normally other aspects of loving that the child experiences, such as affection, tenderness, care, and protection. Except in some cases, there are in the analytic situation only very attenuated forms of caring and protection, especially if the analyst is at pains to maintain a so-called neutral stance. By definition and intent the analytic situation is one of abstinence and rejection in the sexual sense, as indeed it should be. Whether it should be so in regard to other forms of loving and relatedness between two individuals in which one is dependent on the other is a moot point.

Nowhere in the clinical application of psychoanalytic theory do its origins and history become clearer than in an exploration of the transference. As is well known, Freud's (1915/1953) theory of repression, his knowledge of the unconscious, derived from his experience with hysterical patients; and he concluded that they suffered from repressed memories of sexual experiences or wishes, more specifically of repressed Oedipal wishes. This insight then became generalized: repressed memories were the cause of psychic illness; the memories were sexual in nature—in fact, they were specifically Oedipal. To the extent that the rejection of the gratification of these wishes when they surfaced in the transference is therapeutic, their evocation by the analytic situation is appropriate. But is the recovery of memories and the making conscious of sexual wishes the curative factor in psychoanalytic treatment? And is the Oedipal complex truly at the root of neurosis?

The word "neurosis" is scarcely appropriate today. For we deal with many different kinds of disturbances and maladjustments of personality that are not primarily the result of repression and very rarely of sexual repression. In this age of sexual expression—at least in the overt behavioral sense—the individuals seeking emotional help suffer from a lack of relatedness, from inhibitions in the ability to love, to feel affection or tenderness. This inhibition results from a deficit in early childhood experience, from a lack of the experience of being loved and accepted unconditionally so that there are insufficient internalizations of previous experience to build a cohesive and integrated personality. It becomes quite clear that the Freudian definition of the transference as a projection of unconscious wishes is inappropriate, or at least limited, in terms of today's patients. What is needed to effect a cure is not the lifting of repression, not the regression to the wishes of an earlier time, but rather the opportunity to grow in a better environment; an environment that can provide through the active participation and relatedness of the analyst a model for how loving, caring, and affirming is done, so that this positive experience of receiving affirmation can be internalized and can become part of the patient's personality for future relationships in which he or she can then be the one who actively affirms others.

I am sure that by now you will have recognized Heinz Kohut's (1977) conception of the transference as a relationship with the analyst that recreates not the original situation of childhood, but creates a new parent–child relationship in which the old deficits in affirmation are not repeated and the opportunity for new internalizations is provided. Kohut made these valuable contributions to our understanding of human development on the basis of his work with narcissistic personality disorders. As his work grew, he, too, generalized about the applicability of his concept of the transference to all persons. Transference has two distinct aspects: What Kohut called the mirroring transference referred to the interaction between analyst and patient in which the deficits in affirmation during childhood are made good; and the idealizing transference in which the patient idealizes the analyst's image and internalizes it. This inner representation of the idealized analyst forms a large part of the patient's value system.

It is important to contrast Kohut's concept of the analytic situation with that of Freud. For Freud it is one in which the ego is to gain strength through frustration and rejection in the transference experience; for Kohut the self is to become cohesive and integrated through the active participation of the analyst in giving to the patient what he or she either lacked entirely in childhood or experienced in insufficient quantity or inappropriate quality. The first is an experience of deprivation; the second, an experience of fulfillment. In each case there are transference reactions. Where then are the pitfalls?

In the first instance in which the premise upon which cure is founded is the lifting of repression and the stance of the analyst is neutral and uninvolved, the pitfall has two aspects: the first lies in the dubious authenticity of the patient's emotions vis-á-vis the analyst; for it is the technical maneuver of unresponsiveness or unrelatedness that artificially induces the patient's extreme emotions of the transference. True, to some extent such emotions are based on expectations that originated in childhood, but their artificial recreation in the analytic situation takes away from their credibility and furthermore produces anger that is then analyzed as if it were the unjustifiable product of the patient's neurosis. Freud called this the "transference neurosis" and thought that to induce it through the abstinence of the analytic situation was the optimal road to cure.

If an individual is uncertain about the authenticity of his or her feelings, however, the very foundation of reality testing is challenged. The uncertainty is felt not only in relation to one's own emotions, but spreads to include many aspects of reality itself. The patient loses the conviction of the validity of his or her own perception of reality and instead internalizes the analyst's belief in the truth of *his* (the analyst's) perceived reality. I would add that the loss or impairment of this important ego function is scarcely the way to cure.

Furthermore, if a patient's psychic disturbance is not primarily the result of repression but rather of deficits in the emotional nutrients in the course of development, then only the opportunity for positive mirroring and for idealization in the transference can be of help. For such patients—and today they are in the majority—the contrived experience of projection in the transference that is mandated by the technique of classical psychoanalysis, can be extremely destructive. These are the patients who used to be referred to pejoratively as unanalyzable. There was no thought of giving up or altering the sacred cow. A second pitfall of the transference is created by the analyst's inability to listen for and perceive the real nature of the patient's needs.

There are in every human interaction or relationship, in varying degrees, both types of transference reaction: the one that offers the opportunity for projection and the one that offers the opportunity for introjection. In the first instance, the premise on which cure is based is the offering of insight to the patient—insight into the ways in which the unconscious heritage of the past has influenced present-day feeling and behavior. To achieve such insight the repetition compulsion is invoked and the theory contends that the conscious knowledge and experience of repeated and undesirable patterns of behavior and feeling can inhibit their further repetition. We know from experience that this is not necessarily the case; at best, that insight can be partially helpful in altering and integrating personality. In the second type of transference reaction the premise on which the concept of cure or change is based depends on the analyst's ability to offer him- or herself for new internalizations on the part of the patient—internalizations that will correct the developmental insufficiencies and deficits of the past. The original personality disorder is thought to be the result of an arrest in growth; therefore the chance to provide an opportunity for growth is essential.

At this point I am reminded of the fact that Freud inveighed precisely against the analyst's offering himself as an object for identification on the part of the patient. This important statement is to be found in a footnote in the *Ego and the Id* within the context of Freud's (1923/1961) discussion of the treatment of masochistic patients. He was aware of the difficulty such patients have in giving up old destructive patterns of behavior, precisely because they have learned to find satisfaction in them. Knowing the extent to which personality is formed on the basis of identifications, Freud concluded that the patients' masochism was, at least in part, the product of a masochistic relationship to the internalized parental imagoes, and he saw no way of neutralizing the power of these identifications short of forming new ones based on the relationship to the analyst. To encourage such identifications, however, would, according to Freud, put the analyst in a godlike position, a situation that Freud strongly opposed.

To my mind he failed to see that the transference in the analytic situation as he conceived it inevitably created precisely that masochistic stance of the patient that he wished to cure. This is the product of the hierarchical relationship between therapist and patient in which the patient must be submissive, must accept the analyst's truth as well as his or her rejection and lack of responsiveness. The classical analytical situation thus becomes a breeding ground for the formation of masochistic character structures. This is certainly a pitfall to be avoided. But in fact the analytic situation need not be so structured.

Kohut's work in self psychology addressed a very different aspect of the transference relationship. While Freud used the transference to address unconscious *libidinal* needs, Kohut addressed *developmental* needs of the self. Let me use a very simple example. A young female patient wishes to disidentify with her mother and adopts the particular, rather unique dressing style of her female analyst, thus expressing the striving to consolidate a self according to a new, freely chosen model. This is not to say that in doing so the problem is solved. Not at all. Neither the original conflict with the mother nor the imitation of her analyst is understood in any depth. The behavior is only a symbolic expression of the striving to reintegrate and recreate a new cohesive self.

An interesting question arises. Should the analyst interpret the idealizing transference? For in the wish to be like the analyst there is certainly some idealization. While the answer cannot be an unequivocal 'yea' or 'nay,' for much depends on the particular individual in question and on the point in treatment at which the issue arises, the key to the answer lies in the fact that a *constructive process* is going on, and an interpretation would interrupt that process. The patient would become self-conscious and therefore inhibited. The answer then, in general, is 'no.' It is best not to interpret these aspects of the transference that pertain to the structuring of the self.

Sometimes an embarrassing situation can arise for the analyst. Recently I experienced this with a very sophisticated, middle-aged female patient whom I shall call Katherine, who suffered from an extreme work inhibition. In former years she had been successful as a consultant in the business world. But when she came to me she could not even mobilize herself to look for a job. She had had many years of analysis at the hands of outstanding classical analysts and had acquired considerable insight into the origins of her conflicts in relation to her family. She was a middle child of three. Not only was there considerable rivalry with an older sister, but her parents had focused all their expectations for success on this sister, expecting practically nothing in the way of achievement from my patient. She understood the connection between her childhood experience and her lack of will to work. Since there were no expectations, there were also no rewards. We established very good rapport in our work together; I shared some of my own experiences with her, especially as they referred to the way in which I worked and my enjoyment of my work. It was also clear that I liked her and enjoyed our interactions. It soon became apparent that she was beginning to idealize me. One day she asked me quite bluntly if the way for her to be helped with her inhibition was to identify with me. It was an awkward moment. One feels immodest in recommending oneself to someone as a person to be emulated. However, I stuck to what I perceived to be true. I confirmed her own statement; it might indeed be helpful to her if she could identify with my way of working and my enjoyment in my work. I never pushed her to work, but I expressed my confidence that she would overcome her inhibition; and at one point I actually put her in touch with an agency that could help her with some vocational counseling.

We have not yet reached our goal. My patient is not yet free to express herself, to make use of her abilities and talents, as well as of her experience. There have been a number of ups and downs in the course of her treatment: there are times when she is able to take action, other times when she is so severely depressed that she can barely get out of bed. While insights gained in previous therapies as well as those gained in her work with me have been helpful in orienting her within her emotional world, they have not liberated her from her profound inertia. To my mind, her "cure" will depend heavily on her ability to make new identifications. Hopefully she will introject my positive response to her as a person as well as her idealization of me as someone—at least in certain respects—to be emulated.

It is interesting and instructive to observe two aspects of the transference as they have played themselves out in the course of my work with Katherine. The transference based on projection makes its appearance at times. For example, I became the hated and envied older sister. This is especially the case when she is extremely depressed and experiences me as insufficiently helpful. But even when Katherine is feeling these emotions, is in fact quite authentically involved in them, she can spontaneously take some distance from them. She is aware of the projection and knows that what she is feeling toward me is not a reaction to the "real" me. At times she can even laugh at her own distortions of reality.

And then there are the introjective aspects of the transference, when the self of the patient makes use of the analyst in order to grow. The personality of the analyst, as well as his or her own feelings for and relationship to the patient act as nutrient, when they are ingested, for the developing self. It is extremely important that the reality and authenticity of the analyst's personality be expressed in the analytic situation so that the patient can identify with an actual reality.

One of the most important pitfalls of the transference is to confuse those transference reactions of the patient that grow out of libidinal needs, result in distortions, and are induced by the abstinence requirement of the analytic situation with those that strive to nourish and consolidate the self through identification with the analyst and to which the analyst should respond in terms of the reality of one of the profoundest human relationships.

## REFERENCES

Breuer, J., & Freud, S. (1955). Fraulein Anna O. In *Studies on hysteria* (A. A. Brill, Trans.) (pp. 21–47). New York: Basic Books. (Original work published 1895)

Freud, S. (1953). The dynamics of the transference. In *Collected papers, vol. 2* (J. Riviere, Trans.) (pp. 99–108). London: Hogarth Press. (Original work published 1915)

Freud, S. (1961). *The ego and the id* (Joan Riviere, Trans.). New York: Norton. (Original work published 1923)

Kohut, H. (1977). *Restoration of the self.* New York: International Universities Press.

CHAPTER 3

# THE ROLE OF "ACCOMPLICES" IN PREVENTING AND FACILITATING CHANGE

## PAUL L. WACHTEL

A neurosis is a powerful and wondrous thing. In the face of plentiful guidelines from reality and from the rough edges of daily experience, the neurotic individual somehow persists in the same self-defeating pattern day after day and year after year. The sheer staying power of neurotic patterns is little short of miraculous, but we are prone to give the neurosis—and the neurotic—too much credit for this prodigious, if unfortunate, tenacity. My contention is that maintaining a neurosis is hard, dirty work, that cannot be successfully achieved alone. To keep a neurosis going, one needs help. Every neurosis requires accomplices.*

*The term neurosis has gone out of favor lately. Partly as a result of its seeming lack of precision, and very largely as a result of the politics that produced that camel of a document, *DSM-III*, the term has rapidly taken on a measure of quaintness. I use it here, however, not only because astute investors know that charming antiques have a tendency to escalate rapidly in value, but for the very generality that so annoyed those psychiatrists who hoped to be writing a manual about particular medicines for particular diseases. My focus here is on certain psychological processes that I believe are central in maintaining maladaptive behavior regardless of the particular simulation of medical diagnosis one writes on the patient's insurance form. In the same spirit I wish to suggest that the processes described in this chapter are relevant as well for those difficulties that clinicians alert to current fashion have learned to call borderline.

PAUL L. WACHTEL • Department of Psychology, City College of New York, New York, New York 10031.

We are all aware of how difficult it is to bring about change in neurotic patterns of living. Psychotherapists of various stripes have found that once one moves away from the treatment of isolated symptoms and takes on the task of dealing with broader and more pervasive complaints—the personal and interpersonal troubles that most often characterize the real agenda of therapy patients—the clinical enterprise becomes a daunting challenge. Improved methodologies in psychotherapy research in recent years (see, for example, Garfield & Bergin, 1985) have simultaneously made clear both that psychotherapy does help people and that its impact all in all is less than earthshaking.

In attempting to get some further leverage in this difficult endeavor, it can be useful to consider that, hard as it is to change neurotic patterns, it also takes work to keep them going. By understanding just how they are maintained, we can see better where there are possibilities for change. I have suggested, only partly tongue in cheek, that maintaining a neurosis is so difficult we can only do it with help. Why then does the maintenance *appear* to be so effortless and the change in fact prove so arduous? The answer, I believe, lies in our ability to recruit—indeed, in our considerable *inability* not to recruit—the very help that is needed to keep the neurotic patterns going. As I will illustrate shortly, we are often unfortunately and unwittingly experts in turning other people into accomplices in our neuroses.

Understanding how people change first requires understanding how neurosis is a joint activity, a cooperative enterprise of a most peculiar sort. Without the participation of the cast of characters in a person's life—or, to put it differently (since nothing in human behavior occurs in a vacuum), with *different* participation of significant others in the patient's life—the neurosis would not continue. Indeed, one might even argue that the process whereby others are continually recruited into a persisting maladaptive pattern *is* the neurosis.

Let me illustrate with an example. Consider the individual who is extremely cautious and distant in interpersonal relationships, who is perhaps excessively self-sufficient and self-contained, who (consciously or unconsciously) makes a very high priority of preventing himself from being hurt and as a consequence also prevents himself from being touched or reached. Such a person may seem rather sad but he may equally well appear to the world like a successful, independent, highly competent person. If one looks closely, however, one sees a tinge of bitterness and a feeling of loneliness, emptiness, desperation.

Many readers will have a favorite diagnostic term for such people. I prefer a simple description of the pattern for two reasons. First, these people have enough troubles already. They are vulnerable enough without therapists calling them names. But more importantly, the diagnostic labels usually imply a one-person system; what is being described is something "in" the patient since childhood. That is precisely the perspective I want to question here.

This is not to say that the pattern may not well have started early in life, most likely in relation to the parents. I assume that the kind of person I am discussing had good reason for being cautious, for expecting the worst of opening himself up to needing another person. The question, though, is why that fear, mistrust, and consequent deprivation persists. Why, now that he is an adult and no longer subject to the inordinate neediness of early childhood or the unreliable parenting that first produced his caution, does he continue to live as if the circumstances, needs, and limited capacities of his early years were still the reigning reality?

To many in our field, the answer lies in an internal structure or internal world that is largely impervious to the potential lessons of new realities. Such explanations, however, seem to me to border on the tautological: Old patterns persist because they persist; internal worlds do not change because that is their nature.

It is not that the careful delineation of the person's subjective experience, of his fantasies and wishes and of the images to which they are tied, is irrelevant. Far from it. Rather, the problem lies in an excessively dichotomous view of human beings and their relation to the world, in a split vision that distinguishes far too sharply and artificially between, on the one hand, an inner world, a subjective world, internal dynamics, what have you, and on the other hand, the so-called outer world, the social world, the world of overt interactions. These are not two separate realms. They are part and parcel of each other. Efforts to understand the one without the other are basically nonsensical and incoherent. The phenomena to which "internal world" theorists point are ignored at our peril. But the peril is equally great if they are discussed without an appreciation of their continued rooting in a social and interpersonal context.

To illustrate this further, let us look more closely at the daily experience of an individual of the sort just described. Let us see how the pattern of his life—indeed how his "inner world"—is maintained by the way in which he induces others, even if unwittingly and unwillingly, to become accomplices in his unfortunate life patterns.

Consider what happens when this individual, who we will call Jim, goes out on a date with a woman, Judy, he has recently begun to see. He has initially been lively and engaged as there is not yet a threat of his becoming vulnerable to her charms, and she in response has been inter-

ested in him and eager both to hear him and to talk to him. A relationship has begun to form, and it is at a crucial stage.

Today he begins to be aware that he feels something for her, and,
sensing her interest and her good sense, he is tempted to ask her for
help in sorting out some difficult things that have been happening at
work. He starts to, but as he does he begins to feel uneasy. Some dim
recollection emerges of the last time he opened up to a woman. He felt
then that he stuck his neck out and the woman was unresponsive, alternately complaining he was not open enough or simply ignoring his
needs by making light of what to him was serious or by going on to
another subject. This woman was the last accomplice in a long chain,
and Judy is about to become the next.

Neither Jim nor Judy quite know what is going on. The elaborate
and all too familiar dance they are about to begin goes on largely outside
of awareness, though they are both aware of many of the steps; for
example, of the painful feelings of awkwardness and vulnerability, of
being let down, unappreciated, perhaps even betrayed.

Jim thinks he is reaching out to Judy, that he is baring his soul, and
he feels hurt and disappointed at her response. She seems not to be very
sensitive, not to quite get what he is saying, sometimes even to be
annoyed at him for reasons he cannot quite comprehend. Rather than
the warm glow with which the evening began, the experience is increasingly one of frustration, anxiety, and futility.

What Jim does not appreciate is how hedged is his reaching out,
how tentative and cautious. He does not see how excessively self-
sufficient he appears to be because he does not realize how threatened
he feels by the feelings of neediness that Judy's previous responsiveness
to him drew forth. Because the feelings of neediness are largely unacknowledged, he cannot let himself see that he is reacting defensively
to that neediness by an exaggerated demonstration (more for his own
benefit than for Judy's) of how little he really needs any help, of how on
top of things he really is.

Jim thinks he is asking for help and not getting it, indeed not even
getting the respect, caring, and attention that is the necessary precondi-
tion for getting help. In fact, what he is doing is telling Judy about an
"interesting" problem that—so far as one could make out without very
perceptively reading between the lines—he neither wants nor needs
much help with. If one hears primarily what he is actually saying, he is
basically on top of things, he is not really very upset about what happened, and indeed, he thinks little of people who do get upset about
such things or who cannot handle things on their own.

What Judy experiences is being with someone who does not seem to need her very much, who does not seem to really *want* much response from her, except for a casual, relatively uninvolved response. Taking her cue from him, she acts as if—and perhaps feels as if—he does not need very much, and the result is that *he,* notwithstanding the message that his behavior seemed to convey, goes home feeling not attended to or understood, with a not quite articulated sad and hurt feeling that translates, in its consequences for his life, into a strengthening of his conviction that you cannot expect very much of women. And of course you *cannot*—not if you are going so out of your way to keep strong needs under wraps.

So the next time he sees Judy, or sees some other woman, neither of them may have much desire to get together again; he begins the encounter still more convinced that women will not come through for him, and thus becomes still more resolved (whether conscious of the resolve or not) not to be hurt by opening himself up. And given his skewed history, there is a certain inevitable logic to his actions and point of view.

Thus in his next encounter he will once again, acting on the basis of past experience, be hesitant, play it close to the vest, and get one more confirmation of the view with which he started: a view that to most of us seems a distortion, but which squares quite well with what he has experienced over and over.

But what if Judy were not to go along with Jim's signals so readily, what if her own history and her own inclinations led her instead to try hard to connect with him? Could she avoid becoming an accomplice in his neurosis? Perhaps. As I will indicate shortly, the therapeutic impact of people other than therapists is seriously underestimated in most of our discussions of the therapeutic process. But the odds are against it. Consider what is likely to happen:

Judy tries hard to connect. She responds to Jim's cues, subtle and hedged as they are. And what he does is back off, knowing—on the basis of experience after experience—that no good can come of this.

And indeed, no good does. After a while Judy becomes frustrated with his tease, with his lack of follow-through, with what she experiences as his withholding, and she starts to complain. She tells him perhaps—as each week thousands of women tell thousands of men (who tell thousands of therapists)—that he is "cut off" from his feelings. And so he leaves the encounter still more convinced that it is like entering a meat grinder to begin to bare your feelings. Here, too, Judy has become an accomplice—an unwilling and perhaps unwitting one—but an accomplice nonetheless.

Now, to be sure, the outcomes I have described thus far are not the only ones possible. It is likely that had Judy been able to just keep listening and being there, neither backing off nor complaining about *his* backing off, and could she do this over and over, and (another big if) had Jim stayed in the relationship through instance after instance of this, the pattern would begin to shift and Judy would become not an accomplice in Jim's neurosis but an accomplice in change.

Perhaps this is too much to ask. It's hard enough, after all, to do this even in the protected role of psychotherapist. But in understanding how change occurs in entrenched patterns of living it is important to recognize that sometimes, against all odds, accomplices—or potential accomplices—do manage not to play the old game. And when that happens, when significant figures in the person's daily life become instead accomplices in change, they are the most potent therapeutic force a person can encounter.

Indeed, I think it likely that such unscheduled change, for which no fee is paid and no license is required, remains the source of more change than is brought about by the explicit efforts of mental health professionals. Daily life is the power source to which our neuroses are plugged in, but it is also potentially the most powerful source of cure.

This is by no means to say that it is easy for this to happen. Most neuroses are perpetual motion machines, generating their own justification over and over again, making a kind of depressing, self-defeating sense that is exceedingly hard to overcome (compare Horney, 1939, 1945; Shapiro, 1989; Wachtel & Wachtel, 1986; Wachtel, 1977, 1987). Outside of Hollywood, happy endings do not come easy.

We mental health professionals do earn our keep. The people who come to see us tend to be the people for whom the unplanned therapeutic events of daily life have been insufficient or simply not forthcoming. But the accomplice perspective highlights two aspects of our influence that tend to be insufficiently appreciated. First, a great deal of our effect as therapists derives from our own role as potential accomplices—*potential* accomplices who, because of our training and because of the protective structure of the therapeutic situation, manage fairly successfully not to get drawn into the role but rather to respond to the patient in a new and health-promoting way. Second, when we are effective, a good deal of our effect is due not to our direct influence, even our direct influence in being disconfirming figures, but rather in our being *catalysts* for change, in our interactions with the patient promoting changed behavior vis-à-vis others.

It is in the more than 100 hours a week the patient spends with others, not in the 1, 2, 3, or even 5 hours a week he or she spends with the therapist, that the most powerful possibilities for change reside. Conceptions of the therapeutic process that place too primary an emphasis on what transpires in the sessions and insufficient attention to how the influence of the sessions is played out in daily life are likely to lead to prolonged, if not altogether unsuccessful, therapy. When changes in daily life are expected to *follow* therapeutic success, to be a sign that the time for termination is at hand, a crucial source of change is foregone. Change in daily life is not just an outcome of successful therapy; it is an essential part of the *process*.

In effective psychotherapy, change in the sessions and change in daily life work hand in hand, mutually enhancing and promoting each other. When insufficient attention is paid by the therapist to how the insights achieved in the sessions are carried forth into the patient's daily interactions, and to how they can lead to changes in the transactions that keep other people accomplices in the neurosis, then the result is likely to be that good work in the sessions is undermined by the interactions that occur outside (compare Wachtel, 1977).

If the reader detects in the last few paragraphs echoes of Alexander's emphasis on the corrective emotional experience and on the therapeutic impact of daily life (e.g., Alexander, 1948, 1961; Alexander and French, 1946), that is no accident. It is my strong belief that one of the greatest setbacks to progress in the field of psychotherapy was the rather dismissive treatment received by Alexander and his work by what was then the therapeutic establishment.*

Versions of the corrective emotional experience as an alternative to the predominant emphasis on insight in traditional accounts continue to appear in the most vital and influential of contemporary approaches to psychoanalytically influenced psychotherapy; for example, in the object relations approach (e.g., Greenberg & Mitchell, 1983; Guntrip, 1968; Winnicott, 1965), in Kohut's self psychology (e.g., Kohut, 1977, 1984) and in the work of the Mt. Zion group in San Francisco (e.g., Weiss & Sampson, 1987). But, almost always, explicit acknowledgment of Alexander or of the concept of corrective emotional experience is absent.

The emotional forces that maintain neurotic patterns, and the power of the participation of multiple other people in those patterns, make insight alone usually insufficient to produce meaningful and lasting change. Insight remains one important piece of the process, especially

---

*At the time Alexander introduced his innovations, the clearly predominant influence in the field of psychotherapy was psychoanalytic; and in psychoanalytic circles, Alexander's work, when it was not attacked directly for daring to suggest that a mere "psychotherapy" might be a more powerful application of psychoanalytic principles than classical analysis, was paid dismissive lip service as an approach that might be a useful or necessary compromise for those patients who are not capable of participating in psychoanalysis proper.

important in extending and consolidating changes that have begun to occur and in clarifying just what sorts of changes the patient actually seeks; but without an appreciation of the participation of accomplices either in maintaining neurotic patterns or in making change possible, significant and lasting change is unlikely to occur.

## REFERENCES

Alexander, F. (1948). *Fundamentals of psychoanalysis.* New York: Norton.

Alexander, F. (1961). *The scope of psychoanalysis.* New York: Basic Books.

Alexander, F., & French, T. (1946). *Psychanalytic therapy.* New York: Ronald Press. (Paperback edition: University of Nebraska Press)

Garfield, S., & Bergin, A. (1985). *Handbook of psychotherapy and behavior change* (3rd Ed.). New York: Wiley.

Greenberg, J., & Mitchell, S. (1983). *Object relations in psychoanalytic theory.* Cambridge: Harvard University Press.

Guntrip, H. (1968). *Schizoid phenomena, object relations, and the self.* New York: International Universities Press.

Horney, K. (1939). *New ways in psychoanalysis.* New York: Norton.

Horney, K. (1945). *Our inner conflicts.* New York: Norton.

Kohut, H. (1977). *The restoration of the self.* New York: International Universities Press.

Kohut, H. (1984). *How does analysis cure?* New York: Norton.

Shapiro, D. (1989). *Psychotherapy of neurotic character.* New York: Basic Books.

Wachtel, E. F., & Wachtel, P. L. (1986). *Family dynamics in individual psychotherapy: A guide to clinical strategies.* New York: Guilford.

Wachtel, P. L. (1977). *Psychoanalysis and behavior therapy.* New York: Basic Books.

Wachtel, P. L. (1987). *Action and insight.* New York: Guilford.

Weiss, J., & Sampson, H. (1987). *The psychoanalytic process.* New York: Guilford.

Winnicott, D. W. (1965). *The maturational process and the facilitating environment.* New York: International Universities Press.

# CHAPTER 4

# TRANSTHEORETICAL INGREDIENTS IN THERAPEUTIC CHANGE

## MARVIN R. GOLDFRIED

As part of my interest in understanding more about how people change and the specific psychotherapeutic processes involved in such change, I have become increasingly involved in building bridges. Not, obviously, architecturally, but more in an ecumenical sense. The assumption that I have operated under in trying to find common themes associated with therapeutic change across the different orientations is as follows: To the extent that there exist commonalities across different approaches to therapy, then what we are likely to find in such commonalities are probably robust phenomena, in that they have managed to emerge despite the theoretical biases inherent in each specific orientation (Goldfried, 1980).

I was particularly intrigued by Aronson's (Chapter 8) and Klineberg's (Chapter 9) chapters on stereotyping, as that issue is clearly related to the social behavior of psychotherapists, who to a very great extent tend to stereotype each other. Thus, we have the behavior therapist as the cold, calculating manipulative individual; we have the psychodynamic therapist as the woolly-headed, fussy-minded speculator; and we have the experiential psychotherapist as something else alto-

MARVIN R. GOLDFRIED • Department of Psychology, State University of New York, Stony Brook, New York 11794

gether quite different. For those of us interested in psychotherapy integration, the question then becomes how to break down the stereotypes. According to the advice that we get from Aronson (Chapter 8), two factors are required. First, we need direct contact between the individuals who stereotype each other, and second we need a cooperative rather than a competitive set in the way we approach the entire task.

In his chapter on the jigsaw classroom, Aronson has described the impact of direct experience plus cooperation as a way of changing the system. A question may be raised as to whether or not this general strategy may be applied in getting therapists to change, so that they are likely to be more open to what other orientations may have to offer. Perhaps what is needed is something akin to a therapeutic jigsaw group. The situation might involve a team of therapists that specialize in a certain aspect of the patient's/client's functioning. Thus, we may have the behavior therapist who focuses on how to alter the behavior of the patient/client, so as to increase competence. We can also have the psychodynamic therapist, who is an expert on how to detect and alter misperceptions that patients/clients may have about the world around them. Finally, we can have experiential therapists, who can bring their expertise to bear on how to get patients/clients to get in better touch with their emotions. In this hypothetical situation, these separate orientations may be able to work in collaboration on a given case, with the goal of bringing about as much therapeutic benefit as possible.

The variables of direct experience and collaboration have indeed served as the cornerstone of efforts made by an increasing number of professionals dedicated to the integration of the psychotherapies, including many of the individuals who have contributed to this volume (Sam and Diana Kirschner, George Stricker, Hans Strupp, Paul Wachtel, and myself). Specifically, the Society for the Exploration of Psychotherapy Integration (SEPI) has been formed to allow for such ongoing communication and is dedicated to fostering the kind of meaningful dialogue among the different orientations that hopefully will undercut the stereotypes that have so unfortunately characterized the field up until now.

The primary issue that I would like to address in this chapter is the therapy change process, particularly what would appear to be similar across different orientations. Having been immersed in behavioral terminology for a number of years, however, I realize that a special effort needs to be made to avoid jargon. Not having totally lost contact with my mother tongue—ordinary English—I will try to be as theoretically neutral as possible.

## THE PSYCHOTHERAPY CHANGE PROCESS

During our early social learning experiences, we develop certain cognitive, emotional, and behavioral patterns that help us to adjust to the realities of our life at the time. With the process of maturation from childhood to adulthood, with the development of varying and more complex social roles in our lives, and with the changing nature of the environment in which we function, our patterns of living—or "scripts"—become outmoded. Within the supportive context of a therapeutic relationship involving a trustworthy and credible therapist, we become more willing to step back and reevaluate some of the scripts, the cognitive–affective–behavioral patterns, and become more keenly aware of the negative impact that they may have in our current life situation. Moreover, we become encouraged, both within and outside of therapy, to take risks, whereby we try our new ways of interacting that hopefully are more adaptive in our current lives.

Having said that, it is possible to become a bit more specific as to what seem to be common themes that cut across the different orientations. A review of various descriptions of the change process (Goldfried & Padawer, 1982) suggests the following common principles: (1) The facilitation of expectations that psychotherapy will be helpful; (2) the existence of an optimal therapeutic relationship; (3) the offering of feedback for purposes of increasing the patient's/client's awareness; (4) the encouragement of corrective experiences; and (5) the emphasis on continued reality testing.

### EXPECTATIONS THAT THERAPY WILL HELP

To some extent, patients/clients, particularly if they are self-referred, will enter therapy with some degree of expectation that they can be helped. This may result from the positive reputation of the therapist or clinic, or may be due to the view of therapy they have obtained through the media. To a much greater extent, however, positive expectations are facilitated by the caring, understanding, and optimistic stance conveyed by the therapist.

Jerome Frank (1961) has argued that the therapeutic ingredient associated with the facilitation of such positive expectations is in offering a sense of *hope* to an otherwise demoralized individual. In many ways, however, this is really providing the client/patient with a promissory note that the treatment is going to be helpful, and probably little more than that. It is an essential first step, but there has to be something to back it up. What it does is perhaps take the intransigent skepticism that certain individuals bring to the therapeutic situation and transforms it into one that is more benevolent.

## THE EXISTENCE OF AN OPTIMAL THERAPEUTIC RELATIONSHIP

Carl Rogers wrote extensively about the role of the therapeutic relationship in the change process, indicating that it comprises the very essence of the change process (Rogers, 1957). Although I am convinced that it is a necessary condition for therapeutic change, I am less optimistic that it is sufficient. Nonetheless, the research on the therapeutic relationship indicates that the existence of a positive alliance early in therapy will predict therapeutic success, regardless of one's orientation (Orlinksy & Howard, 1986).

As a behavior therapist, I must give credit to my psychodynamic colleagues for helping me to take the notion of the therapeutic relationship and become more specific in thinking about it. In the early days of behavior therapy, we called these the "nonspecific aspects of change." It was nonspecific, however, only in the sense that it was not specified within our theoretical framework at the time. From the vantage point of other orientations, it was quite specific. In this regard, the writings of Bordin (1979) on this topic are particularly invaluable. Bordin maintains that the therapeutic alliance is comprised of three factors, each of which can be observed, measured, and hopefully altered when necessary. To begin with, there is the therapeutic *bond* between therapist and client/patient. The bond is what we usually think of when we think of a positive relationship, namely the so-called "chemistry" between therapist and patient or client. The patient/client perceives the therapist as caring, understanding, and knowledgeable. In addition to the bond, the therapeutic alliance is also characterized by an agreement on the *goals or aims* of therapy. Thus, both client/patient and therapist concur that the goal(s) of therapy should be of a certain sort. The third element in the therapeutic alliance also consists of an agreement between therapist and patient/client, an agreement on the *means* by which these aims may be accomplished.

Metaphorically speaking, the therapeutic alliance is much like the anesthesia necessary for conducting surgery. The primary goal when one enters an operating room is clearly not to receive anesthesia, but to have certain surgical procedures accomplished. Without the anesthesia, however, successful surgery cannot take place. Moreover, if there are any problems with the anesthesia during the course of an operation, the surgery becomes less important and the anesthesia becomes central. During the course of psychotherapy, if the therapeutic alliance is breached, it similarly must receive the highest priority. We either know this under the guise of negative transference or we see it in the client/ patient who forgets to do homework, misses sessions, or in other ways leads us to conclude that something may be wrong with the therapeutic alliance. Without an optimal alliance, therapeutic change is unlikely.

## HELPING THE PATIENT/CLIENT TO BECOME MORE AWARE

Taking an information-processing view, we can say that an important role of the therapist is to help patients/clients to redeploy their attention to certain aspects of functioning about which they may be not aware, such as certain thoughts, feelings, motives, or actions. Clients/ patients may not be aware of certain connections between thoughts or feelings, between feelings and actions, the impact that clients'/patients' actions have on others, or the impact that others make on them. Moreover, they may not be aware of the way that their perception of someone may impact on the way they deal with this other person which, in turn, has implications for how the person reacts to them. To facilitate such awareness, the therapist becomes an "attention redeployer."

This is certainly not a notion that is new to psychodynamic or experiential approaches to therapy, nor is it terribly new to cognitive– behavior therapy. Of particular interest is that this is an idea that is even completely consistent with radical behaviorism. In an *American Psychologist* article, Skinner (1987) made the point that "all behavior, human and nonhuman, is unconscious," and it becomes conscious when someone or something prompts an individual to engage in self-observation. What he is referring to here is that people have been trained under a certain set of contingencies earlier in life that may no longer be relevant, and that a step toward the change process is to verbally label these contingencies. Once people become aware that these environmental forces may now be different, they are more likely to test out this possibility in real life.

As an interesting footnote to this, not too long ago I conducted a mock interview with a radical behaviorist at Stony Brook, Howard Rachlin. The interview focused on how a radical behaviorist would conceptualize and treat agoraphobia. We translated the jargon reflected in his comments into the vernacular and sent out a transcript of the interview to a group of clinical psychologists belonging to Division 12 (clinical psychology) of the American Psychological Association. The essential finding was that most people thought he was psychodynamic, essentially because he spoke of forces outside of the patients'/clients' awareness that may be causing them to behave the way they do.

Like the therapeutic relationship, however, I would maintain that awareness remains a necessary, but not sufficient, condition for change. What is also needed is the facilitation of corrective experiences.

## ENCOURAGING CORRECTIVE EXPERIENCES

This component of the change process, which has its origins in the writing of Alexander and French (1946), involves patients/clients taking certain risks. In doing what they previously had been reluctant or afraid to do and then realizing that the consequences were not nearly as bad as they anticipated—and, indeed, might even be quite favorable—this novel experience can be used to update their thinking, feeling, and behavior. Their view of themselves may begin to change, as may their perception of others. This aspect of the change process is a particularly robust one, in that it occupies a salient place in most forms of therapy. It can also be found in the ancient Chinese proverb that states: "Go to the heart of danger, for there you will find safety."

This risk-taking factor, the corrective experience, may very well represent the core of the therapeutic change process. Where there may be differences between therapeutic schools is the setting where the corrective experience takes place. In psychodynamically oriented therapy, the corrective experience is likely to take place within the session itself; in behavior therapy, the corrective experience is more likely to occur between sessions. It is here where a fair amount of miscommunication between behavior therapists and psychodynamic therapists has occurred, particularly in emphasizing the key aspect of change. If we can construe the essence of the change process as involving corrective experiences, then both are correct; the disagreement lies in where the experience occurs, not necessarily in its therapeutic value.

A source of miscommunication among different schools of thought can be attributed to the fact that we use different language systems in talking about the corrective experience. From a more experiential or psychodynamic point of view, we are likely to refer to it as an "experience." Behavior therapists, having a long tradition of objectively observing phenomena, are more likely to talk about the client's/patient's new "behavior." In reality, however, we are all talking about the same phenomenon, but from a different vantage point. As seen from the point of view of the patient/client, it is a subjective experience. When seen externally from the point of view of the therapist, it is behavior. Nonetheless, the mechanisms of change, whatever vantage point we choose to take, and whatever we prefer to call it, remains the same.

From time to time, I have attempted to speak with some of my behavioral colleagues about the relevance of in-session change and have at times chided them with the "T-word." Because terms such as "trans-

ference" are x-rated in behavioral circles, where indeed behavior therapists have developed "conditional emotional reactions" on hearing
them, we have tended to give little credence to its significance in the
therapeutic change process. Some years ago, Hans Strupp and I partici-
pated in a panel discussion at the Association for the Advancement of
Behavior Therapy meetings, in which therapists from different orientations all discussed the same case. In the process of commenting on the
case at hand, Strupp made use of various relevant psychodynamic concepts, which seemed to result in a fair amount of seat-squirming behavior on the part of the audience. From their subjective point of view, they
were apparently experiencing a sense of emotional discomfort.

Interestingly enough, the concept of "in-vivo interventions" occupies a very salient role in the behavior therapy literature, as it is believed
to be a more powerful aspect of the change process than discussions
*about* behavior. Thus, if we construe transference as representing an in-
vivo intervention, in which the client's/patient's behavior within the session represents a sample of what needs to be changed, this particular
aspect of the therapeutic focus can fit quite nicely within a behavioral
orientation.

## CONTINUED REALITY TESTING

This principle essentially involves a combination of the previous
two, where clients/patients are becoming more aware, redeploying their
attention to things that are relevant in their lives, and as a result become
more willing to engage in corrective experiences. These corrective experiences in turn allow them to further increase their awareness about
what does and does not work in their lives. In essence, they are taking
those corrective experiences and using them to update the scripts by
which they have been living their lives prior to therapy. This process
recurs repeatedly and, akin to working through, a synergistic interaction between action and insight takes place, both of which are necessary
in providing patients/clients with the kinds of information that will correct their false beliefs, emotional distress, and problematic patterns of
behavior. During the insight phase, our task as therapists is to provide
clients/patients with hypotheses that the world may be different from
the way they think it is. Following this, we need to encourage them to
ultimately test out these hypotheses in real life.

There is another aspect associated with this continued reality testing that I have become more appreciative of in my own clinical work and
which cognitive–behavior therapists are paying increasingly more attention to, namely, the notion of the patients'/clients' image of themselves. Bandura's (1982) work on self-efficacy has been particularly

influential in this regard, in that it has demonstrated that individuals' belief in their ability to make an impact on the world is a better predictor of future behavior than is their past behavior.

How does this concept fit into the change process? The concept of self-efficacy—as well as other related conceptions, such as "self-esteem" and "self-confidence"—may usefully be viewed as the endpoint in the larger change process. Clients/patients obtain certain awarenesses during the course of therapy, engage in corrective experiences, and repeat this synergistic, reality-testing process. After having obtained a critical mass of new therapeutic experiences, this information becomes incorporated into the new script that they use in interacting with the world. Part of the change in the script also involves a change in the view that they have of themselves, providing an index that the therapeutic learning experiences are likely to have a lasting impact.

The parameters associated with enabling clients/patients to update the view that they have of themselves is an essential, but still poorly understood process. Some individuals experience considerable difficulty in making use of therapeutic experiences, whereas others benefit more readily. Hopefully, psychotherapy process research will one day shed light on how this change occurs.

## CONCLUSIONS

When individuals enter therapy, they often do so because the cognitive, emotional, and behavioral patterns that may have originally helped them to adjust to the reality of their life are no longer working for them. In order to develop a new mode of functioning, the individual needs to be supported by an understanding, insightful, and helpful therapist with whom he or she will be working collaboratively in achieving the agreed-upon therapeutic goals. An important function of the therapist is to help clients become aware of their outmoded scripts, and the ways that they inadvertently may be undermining their own needs and wants. It is within the context of a good therapeutic relationship that patients/clients become more willing to acknowledge that they, indeed, rather than other people, may be the cause of their own misery. Having gained such an awareness, they then become better able to think through and take certain risks, trying out new ways of thinking, feeling, and behaving. These corrective experiences may then be used to update their original expectations about themselves and others, which can further help to reinforce other changes that they might attempt in the future. The overall goal of therapy may be seen as the place where the patient/client can build up a new set of learning experiences, hopefully until a critical mass has allowed them to change their view of themselves. Once such change in self-perception has been achieved, there is greater room for optimism that they have indeed learned a new way of more effectively dealing with their world.

ACKNOWLEDGMENT

Work on this chapter was supported in part from grant MH40196 from the National Institute of Mental Health.

# REFERENCES

Alexander, F., & French, T. M. (1946). *Psychoanalytic therapy: Principles and applications.* New York: Ronald Press.

Bandura, A. (1982). Self-efficacy mechanism in human agency. *American Psychologist, 37,* 122–147.

Bordin, E. S. (1979). The generalizability of the psychoanalytic concept of the working alliance. *Psychotherapy: Theory, Research and Practice, 16,* 252–260.

Frank, J. D. (1961). *Persuasion and healing.* Baltimore: John Hopkins.

Goldfried, M. R. (1980). Toward the delineation of therapeutic change principles. *American Psychologist, 35,* 991–999.

Goldfried, M. R., & Padawer, W. (1982). Current status and future directions in psychotherapy. In M. R. Goldfried (Ed.), *Converging themes in psychotherapy: Trends in psychodynamic, humanistic, and behavioral practice* (pp. 3–49). New York: Springer.

Orlinsky, D. E., & Howard, K. I. (1986). Process and outcome in psychotherapy. In S. L. Garfield & A. E. Bergin (Eds.), *Handbook of psychotherapy and behavior change* (pp. 331–381). New York: Wiley.

Rogers, C. R. (1957). The necessary and sufficient conditions of therapeutic personality change. *Journal of Consulting Psychology, 21,* 95–103.

Skinner, B. F. (1987). Whatever happened to psychology as the science of behavior? *American Psychologist, 42,* 780–786.

# CHAPTER 5

# EMOTION IN THE CHANGE PROCESS

## LESLIE S. GREENBERG AND RENÉ H. RHODES

## EMOTION IN THE CHANGE PROCESS

Emotion is involved in change in a variety of ways. Greenberg and Safran (1989) have delineated a number of ways in which emotions are involved in the therapeutic change process. These are:

1. Acknowledging previously unacknowledged emotion provides information that enhances orientation and problem solving.
2. Evoking emotion to motivate action. Thus anger organizes us for fight, fear, or flight.
3. Emotional restructuring. This involves accessing and changing affective–cognitive schematic structures that are involved in the construction of the emotional meaning in our lives.
4. Evoking emotion in order to access state-dependent core beliefs or "hot cognitions."
5. The modification of expressive–motor and physiological aspects of maladaptive emotional responses as in phobias.

LESLIE S. GREENBERG • Department of Psychology, York University, North York, Ontario M3J 1P3, Canada.    RENÉ H. RHODES • Program in Clinical Psychology, Teachers College, New York, New York 10022.

These different categories of change processes suggest that emotion plays a variety of different roles in change, roles that extend from providing information to motivating behavior to accessing cognitions to emotion being the target of change itself.

In addition to noting that emotions play a variety of roles in change, it is important to stress that emotions are discrete and that each emotion functions differently in the change process. We need ultimately to deal with each emotion in the change process as a unique phenomenon with its own characteristics. Each emotion possesses unique motivational properties and a distinct phenomenology. The nature and function of anger, for example, is quite different from that of distress, which again is different from that of fear and joy. Thus, certain universal statements may be made about emotion, such as, emotion is information that guides action and emotion is basically adaptive. If we are to truly understand the role of emotion in the change process, however, we need to study each emotion separately.

In this chapter we will first address some general issues about the nature of change in the self and the role of emotion in this change. We will then discuss some of the features of working with emotion in therapy. Following this we will focus on a specific discussion of the role of distress in therapeutic change.

## A PROCESS PERSPECTIVE ON HUMAN EXPERIENCE AND CHANGE

In understanding human change our first assumption is that "process" is primary in human functioning. This principle of the primacy of process leads to a view in which one sees human beings as always in the process of becoming. Activity is thus primary and people are in a continual process of becoming, constantly creating or constructing themselves and their world afresh. People by nature cannot be captured by an idea of an enduring, impervious, substantial existence with essential qualities. Thus a process perspective puts us in opposition to modes of thought that induce us to think of people or the world as static or substantial. From a process perspective, being is always a process of becoming and is itself constituted by becoming (Whitehead, 1929).

From this process perspective the self is not static enduring "stuff" but is describable only as an organic process of organization. Any stasis or regularity in the self is best understood as a process of the recurring construction of the same experience or as the self-organization of regularity. Structural integrity or enduring traits in the personality need to be seen in terms of the dynamic processes of self-organization that maintain this structural integrity, rather than as things in themsevles that may need changing. Thus when a person wishes to change some aspect of him- or herself or therapists try to help people change, it is the rigidity or "stuckness" of an intrinsically dynamic process, which is repeatedly organizing itself maladaptively in a rigid manner, that needs to be addressed, rather than changing the self itself.

In therapy it is the process by which the self-system maintains a particular set of experiences that becomes the focus of the change process. Thus therapy is not like repairing a structural crack in a foundation of a building or healing a damaged "child within" or making up for an internal deficit, but is rather like changing an organization (Bohart, 1988), dealing with a set of dynamic processes that produce a given structure, such as organizing the person to experience the self as a damaged child. If the process of organization can be influenced, the resultant self-organization will change.

Our second assumption about the self concerns its relational nature. We view the person from a process–relational perspective as a system constantly interacting with an environment. This "ecological" view thus sees "being" as constituted by interconnectedness. A person is a complex pattern of interactive activity over time and any experience or event is highly context dependent. A particular experiential event or human experience in any moment is an occasion that is a creative integration of internal and external stimuli into a momentary construction of the person's relation to the world. The possible relations are rich and varied and there is much ongoing originality in humans' constructions of their experience in relation to their world. Momentary self-organization grows out of an interactive field (Greenberg & Johnson, 1988). Flux and change in organization is normative; stasis and regularity in the self are the phenomena to be explained.

In order to understand change we need to understand how stability is created, as change will involve destabilization of the stability–maintaining operations that produce system organization. Stability is an aspect and an aim of all self-organizing processes (Maturana, 1975; Varela, 1979; Prigogine & Stengers, 1981). The unity of any organism, as we have said, is defined not by the substantiality of the organism, which is in a constant interchange and exchange with the environment, but by the organization of processes that continually regenerates itself (Varela, 1979). Through this constant regeneration, identity is possible. We thus make ourselves afresh each moment in much the same way as we did a moment ago. The result of this dynamic self-organizing process is that we have both the ability to change constantly in response to circumstance—a type of plasticity—and the ability to maintain the basic organization of our process—a type of structural stability.

In the biological domain, in organism–environment interactions, the environment can affect the structure of the organism but does not affect the basic organization of processes which themselves remain invariant. The organism, then, in its normal course of existence, is in a sense closed to information that could change its basic organization but open to adaptation by changing its form to mesh with the environment. This view of self-organizing systems has strong implications for a view of change. One cannot easily instruct the self to change or modify its organization because one cannot get information in to affect the processes that maintain the organization. As one cannot teach the child to speak or walk (in fact too much instruction can damage its natural development), so one cannot teach a person to change his or her self-organization. The self-organizing process is highly self-determined. Content learning does not produce developmental change. Living systems change by organisms reorganizing themselves as a function of self-feedback about their own functioning. Development involves a change in the organizing processes that promote the formation of a more complex, more differentiated, more highly organized system than existed before. This more highly organized system will be more adaptive and have more creative alternatives available to it. For example, remaining a child in relation to a peer and being rigidly stuck in that self-organization regardless of the context is maladaptive. Being flexibly organized is the best adaptive solution. Thus a self that is able to be organized as a child in response to a caretaker, a peer in response to a peer, and a superior in response to a subordinate is a more complex adaptive system. This flexibility, of course, is a complex constructive process of self-organization, one that has often gone wrong in people who have begun to cling too tenaciously to familiar patterns of self-organization. Change, then, involves regaining the flexibility and ability to respond to the demands of the situation in an adaptive fashion in terms of one's repertoire.

In our view the self is a flexible process with an aim of self-coherence but a capacity to organize in response to the demands of the situation. The apparent paradox of our assertion that the self is always in process but, as a living system, possesses an aim of self-coherence is resolved when we realize that the aim is a process aim, that is, of maintaining coherence rather than of maintaining a particular type of coherence or specific form. The self in its essence, as Stern (1985) has suggested, is constituted by the development of a sense of such qualities as continuity, agency, and coherence. It is these qualities that are the only real constants. A stable sense of self is not dependent on stable content but rather on a sense of the self as an agent with continuity over time and as possessing coherence as an autonomous existence. Thus a person can be organized as vulnerable at this moment, as assertive at the next, and as nurturing at the next. A person is not dependent on a stable form for a sense of identity but rather on a sense of self as the agent of experience with continuity over time. It is the knowledge that it is *me* who is vulnerable, assertive, and so on that provides identity.

Pathology emerges when the self-organizing process becomes stuck in organizing the experience of self in a rigid fashion and is organized as always vulnerable or always assertive. The self also then loses its sense of agency "that it is me who is doing or feeling something," and loses its sense of continuity as process. The self then becomes the form it has organized and becomes a rigidly organized vulnerable self, angry self, and so forth. Thus when people repeatedly organize themselves as "damaged children" or even as "special favorites," they have lost their natural capacity for responsive and adaptive organization. The aim of self-coherence and stability has become misdirected toward holding a particular form of self-experience stable. This complex rigidification often occurs because of certain overlearned responses to recurring threatening environmental conditions in which the person, as a function of anxiety, repeatedly organizes himself or herself in a particular manner. In threatening circumstances in which the self is being damaged, the trauma of the situation appears to produce such anxiety that the person hangs onto the familiar sense of self as a source of security and self-protection and forms a sense of coherence around a sense of being damaged. In so doing the person loses the capacity for flexible and spontaneous organization. It is as though the risk of being the process that one is and entering varied forms of organization is too high because the consequences are unpredictable. A sense of control of one's world can only be maintained by being a particular familiar way. The advantages of being this self are that the experiences, even if negative, are at least known. It is possible that when the sense of agency, continuity, and coherence of the self, that is, its survival, is sufficiently threatened, the aim of self-maintenance appropriates a particular content to its aim and hangs on to it as an attempt to maintain self-coherence in a threatening environment. The person then becomes stuck in organizing himself or herself in response to a situation that no longer exists.

What we are suggesting, therefore, is that in the ongoing process of self-organization, a person who repeatedly organizes him- or herself as damaged, is not actually structurally damaged and requiring a therapy to modify some aspect of functioning or to repair the damage, but rather that a change in self-experience in therapy will in effect be a change in the system's manner of organizing itself. The self-system will then create new future possibilities for organizing in this way and ultimately of becoming more flexibly and spontaneously organized again.

Psychotherapy thus offers people an opportunity to experience themselves in a new way, to discover that they can survive what is dreaded or feared, that they can once again experience themselves as agents of their experience, rather than as victims, and that they can trust in their own continuity regardless of the content of their experience. A sense of one's own continuity is important because it frees up the person to again trust in the self as a process and trust that the self continues and survives regardless of what is admitted to awareness and experienced. What is regained in therapy is the self as organizing process. Therapy, rather than attempting to repair the self, reengages the self in the process of self-organizing. New experience in therapy is a change in the manner in which the person is organizing him- or herself. A system that has grown overly conservative or rigid is opened once again to its own flexibililty.

## EMOTION AND EXPERIENCE

In addition to the above process–relational view of change experience and self-organization, we view human experience as being characterized by emotion more fundamentally than by anything else. We view humans as primarily emotional beings. The self is affectively, not rationally, based. The basis of experience is fundamentally emotional and people are essentially feelers as opposed to thinkers. My being at any moment (Descartes, "I am") is my process of organizing a welter of internal feelings, of hopes, regrets, fears, evaluations, and enjoyments into a consistent pattern of feelings. Any actual occasion of conscious experience is a synthesis of much that is going on inside me and of my relation to the world.

Human experience, in addition to being fundamentally emotional, is also purposeful. The integration into conscious experience of emotion includes an aspect of purpose or intention. In fact it is final causation, "the end," for the sake of which we do things, which helps integrate the disparate emotional ingredients, the sensation, the internal feelings, hopes, regrets and so, into a unified whole. Our self-organization is thus directed by a definite goal orientation, the most fundamental goals being survival and growth. In human experience there is, however, always a mingling of determination with purpose. Human emotional experience, the hopes, fears, regrets, evaluation, and enjoyments, is thus always a consequence of both determination and purpose, a consequence of what has occurred and what is intended. Occasions of the past that bring on certain reactions are the efficient causes, but the present reactions would not be what they are but for some end in mind, some ideal entertained, some aim pursued, or a possibility imagined—a final cause. Thus all experience as well as being emotionally based is to different degrees and blends purposeful and determined. Experience always involves final aims as well as prior occasions coloring and giving rise to the present experience. All this determination and aim is part of the present construction that emerges into consciousness as feeling. Felt experience as we will suggest is the result of a complex integrative informations processing system that constantly integrates a variety of constituents in an ongoing process of self-organization.

## EMOTION AS SYNTHESIS

Central to our theoretical argument about emotion is the idea that the experience of emotion is the end product of a set of parallel, automatic, or unconscious information-processing activities. We argue (Greenberg & Safran, 1987b), based on a constructive theory of emotional processing (Leventhal, 1979, 1982) that emotion comes into consciousness by a tacit synthesis of subsidiary information. As Leventhal (1979, 1982) and Lang (1983, 1984) have suggested, emotion is constituted by a number of different types or levels of information processing that are all integrated preattentively to emerge into awareness as the holistic emotional experience. Emotion supplies a synthesis of expressive motor responses, autonomic responses, images, and memories of important events—the efficient causes—and conceptual processing including aims and intentions—the final causes. Emotion provides a constant readout of the synthesis of much of the automatic parallel processing in which we are continually engaged.

## EMOTION IN CHANGE

Our thesis is that emotion is an action tendency that serves to maintain the organism and is a biological signal of the state of the organism's equilibrium. Certain emotions such as fear, distress, anger, and disgust are responses to a sense of threat to this equilibrium or to threats to maintenance of self-coherence. Emotions involve the evaluation or appraisal of the relevance of environmental stimuli to our deeper concerns, to our needs and goals. Thus emotion organizes us for action and provides us with information about our system's response to situations that affect our survival and coherence. Some emotional reactions arise in direct response to the environment, others, however, arise reflexively in response to self-reorganizing processes or internal threats to coherence. An interesting by-product of the automatic appraisal process involved in emotion is that when a person is undergoing a change in the basic self-organizing process, the current organism responds to this with anxiety, terror, and dread because change is experienced as destruction of the self. Reciprocally, the formation of a new integration (a new self-organized coherence) often brings experience of relief, joy, and excitement.

Anger in response to violation, sadness to loss, and fear to threat are all survival-oriented responses to the environment. These are emotions functioning in the service of maintaining self-coherence in relation to environmental impingements. These are predominantly adaptive and produce action tendencies to guide adaptive behavior. Another set of circumstances gives rise to emotion as an aspect of the reorganizing process itself. Change in the self-organizing process thus produces fear of loss of organization and distress and pain of the destruction of the self. In these instances, pain, distress, and sadness thus signal that change is taking place and that support is needed. The lack of distinction between these two processes, emotional responses to reflexive threats to self-organization and emotional responses to direct environmental threats, can lead to theoretical confusion. On the one hand, emotions are information about our response to the environment and they inform us, both by increasing the salience of certain meanings that draw our attention and by organizing us to act in certain ways to maintain self-coherence. On the other hand, and at a more complex level, emotions can be responses to the change process itself in which the organizing process is changing. This type of change can be terrifying as we sense the demise of all we know to be our selves and experience the dread of not knowing what, if anything at all, will replace our previous structure which is all we currently know. Thus the moment of change contains the fear of destruction, dread of the unknown, and the agony of loss of our only known stability.

Tolerance of fear of change is thus important in a change process. Ultimately learning that the self is a *process* makes people less afraid of and more able to change. Health is thus the ability to allow one's process to unfold without fear that one will lose one's sense of self-coherence. This ability is experienced as faith in oneself, the ability to take risks, and openness to experience. Disease is rigidity and blockage, prevention of the fluidic process of adaptation to circumstance, by the maintenance of forms of self-coherence that are no longer adaptive in the present context.

The emotions of terror, fear, and agony at change can then be positive signals that change is occurring. These feelings need to be endured to allow change to take place. Much support is needed, however, to help endure these experiences and the person involved in the change process must not be pushed beyond his or her limit of endurance. Disintegration of the old and reintegration into a new form needs to take place at a pace that is natural to the organism and must not be imposed by outside forces. For therapeutic results this process of reformation must be supported and facilitated but not engineered or forced by the therapist.

In general terms emotion plays two broad roles in change. First, emotion is biologically adaptive information to us about our responses to situations and as such orients us in the world and aids problem solving. Change in therapy often involves helping people access this previously avoided or unattended to information and use it to function more adaptively. Second, emotional distress often signifies an internal reorganization process that is inherently frightening to the conscious, image maintenance, non-process-oriented Western mind.

## PRIMARY EMOTION IN THERAPEUTIC CHANGE

Primary biologically adaptive emotions inform us of our needs and basic concerns and facilitate problem solving (Greenberg & Safran, 1987). Anger facilitates aggressively protective solutions to threat; fear facilitates avoidance or "flight" solutions to threat; and sadness facilitates reparative solutions to loss.

People have, however, learned to avoid their primary emotions and often need permission to feel. Certain socialization processes, insensitive to distinctions between biologically adaptive primary emotions and defensive secondary and instrumental emotions (Greenberg & Safran, 1987a; 1989), have taught us to control all our emotions and have labeled certain adaptive emotional experiences and expressions as weak and out of control. In addition to this socialized restriction of emotion, the organism has learned to cope with certain painful experiences by developing intricate psychological strategies to avoid the pain. People in therapy thus need to learn that fear is not weak, that pain will not kill, and that anger is not necessarily bad. They need to learn that rather than being signs of weakness, of losing control, or of being unable to cope, these emotions inform them of their deeper concerns and can facilitate problem resolution. Therapy seen in terms of this framework involves a certain amount of affective reeducation.

Clients often come into therapy unable to discriminate what they are feeling. Not only lacking a data base against which to check what they are feeling but also being out of touch, they are vulnerable to being led by a more knowing therapist into believing anything that might explain their problem. Incorrect labeling of emotion by the therapist then simply compounds their own confusion. The therapist must therefore be careful not to impose a label on the client's emotional experience. Instead, he or she must support emerging experience in the client until it is felt vividly as a subjective experience.

Therapeutic change thus often involves helping people access their own emotional responses that have not been available to awareness for a variety of reasons. Access to this information makes for a more unified and congruent system. A person who is thinking, feeling and doing the same thing will act more efficiently and be adaptively oriented.

## DISTRESS AND SADNESS IN THE PROCESS OF CHANGE

In the preceding sections we have presented our fundamental approach to change in the process–relational self, a self in which emotions define experience, provide synthesis, and produce adaptational change.

The process–relational perspective conceives of the self as an ongoing, fluid, and dynamic process of organization. When this fluidity is obstructed, pathological processes that interfere with growth and adjustment result. One central question that is raised by this perspective is how the self maintains a sense of continuity and coherence while in the process of change and reorganization. As we stated, the aim of the self is to remain stable, but paradoxically, it is through the process of destabilization that change and newness occurs. We would suggest that an important dimension of the self that bridges stabilized and destabilized moments in the change process is the dimension of self-agency: "It is me who chooses to feel this new emotion which represents the unknown to me." The experience of self-continuity does not come from the enduring content of experience but rather from the continued sense of agency in the organizing process. We will explore how anxiety over the expected loss of agency can obstruct the potentially helpful and adaptive function of emotions in change processes.

In this section we will apply the process–relational view of change to therapeutic episodes involving the expression of sadness. We were especially interested in the actual steps clients moved through after being confronted with an emerging painful feeling in psychotherapy. Greenberg and Safran (1987a,b), from the intensive analysis of a number of in-therapy episodes of allowing of painful experience, hypothesized that given a sufficiently safe environment, the client overcomes avoidance of the painful feeling, attends to the internal state, allows the emotion to emerge, and through the acceptance of this emotion is both able to access an adaptive action tendency and access and reevaluate a dysfunctional appraisal. In order to begin to investigate this sequence, we decided to focus on the allowing and acceptance of one emotion, sadness, hypothesizing that each emotion might present its own unique sequences of expression.

Avoidance of emotional experiences, the first step in the above-hypothesized sequence, occurs because of the perceived threat of destabilization and produces reactive secondary emotions in defense against this threat. For therapeutic change to occur, it is important to be able to distinguish primary adaptive affective experiences from reactive, instrumental, and learned maladaptive emotions. Each primary emotion has its own adaptational aim and therapy must seek to help the person experience this aim. We will discuss the adaptational purposes of distress and suggest ways in which reactive secondary and learned maladaptive emotional responses can interfere with the productive uses of distress in the change process. We will then discuss how attending to the moment-by-moment sequence of the experience and expression of distress in psychotherapy is diagnostic and can help uncover what is feared in the allowing of the primary distress.

## ADAPTATIONAL DIMENSION OF THE EXPRESSION OF SADNESS

One of the most common causes of sadness is separation from a loved person. In the young infant the cry of distress will elicit empathy, care, and attention from the caretaker. As human beings are extremely vulnerable for the first five years of life, attachment to the caretaker is essential to survival and the distress cry functions as a prime connector (Bowlby, 1969). The coming to terms with aloneness and various forms of psychological separation is one of the basic existential tasks we must face. In the fundamental experience of loss of a loved one, distress mobilizes us to combat the loss of the actual loved one. As humans develop, distress emerges in addition in response to other losses such as the loss of self-esteem. Feelings of sadness frequently follow experiences of failure. Here the loss is not defined in terms of the other but in terms of a failed self-goal. In this instance the sadness is often a message to the self to mobilize strategies to reduce the unpleasant feeling. Thus distress has a strong motivational component in it to act to reduce the distress. A study by Bartlett and Izard (1972) demonstrates that people report feeling less tension in distress than in any other negative emotion and therefore find it the least noxious of the negative primary emotions. They are therefore able to tolerate feeling sadness for longer periods of time and attempts during this to repair the loss are therefore sustained for longer periods. Sadness closes us down in order to help deal with the loss. We withdraw to engage in a period of grieving. When overwhelmed by loss, the individual turns in and closes down to protect the self and interrupt further stimulus input. This period of withdrawal allows for a rejuvenation and mobilization of internal resources to face the world again.

The way in which an adult copes with the experience of loss and sadness, however, can be more complex than simply being motivated to adaptive action by this universal, adaptive emotional response. Each individual's emotional behavior is also the product of the history of the interaction between that particular individual and their interpersonal environment over life. To understand the process of expressing sadness it is therefore necessary to have an understanding of how expectations of certain interpersonal responses to it can constrict or warp an individual's affective experience.

## IN-THERAPY SEQUENCES OF THE EXPERIENCE AND EXPRESSION OF DISTRESS

In psychotherapy, we are more often than not dealing with the negative range of emotions including fear, anger, disgust, shame, and sadness. We rarely encounter these emotions in a pure form, however, but rather observe combinations or sequences such as fear of anger or a blend of sadness and shame. The nature of the combinations of emotions is complex, as all emotions have, to varying degrees, components of other emotions within them. From our observations of sad moments in therapy, fear and shame commonly occur during sad episodes and can be considered as components of the process of the allowing of sadness. Each basic emotion has different adaptational aims and is best studied keeping its unique motivational and phenomenonological properties in mind. Thus, as stated earlier, primary sadness is over loss and, when experienced, provides motivation to regain or come to terms with that which has been lost. In addition, the expression of sadness has a universal impact on others, different to the expression of fear or anger, for example, and this component of sadness is best understood as interpersonal communication aimed at bringing aid to the self from others.

Determination of a person's primary emotion is of prime importance in psychotherapy, but attention to the sequence in which related secondary or reactive emotions occurs is also important. For example, a person might experience a wave of sadness in therapy when recalling an incident but might immediately become so anxious at the expression of this sadness in front of the therapist that the person reacts with a shame response in an attempt to show submission and thus avoid criticism. Focusing first on the shame response will help the person approach the issues of dangers in expressing sadness. Therefore, attentiveness to the sequence of emotional expression can provide the therapist with an understanding of clients' histories around the expected consequences of the expression of certain emotions.

## THREE ASPECTS OF EMOTIONAL PROCESSING IN PSYCHOTHERAPY

In order to understand and describe the underlying adaptational components of distress and the sequence of emotions associated, we have divided the emotional experience of distress into three different aspects of emotional processing. These aspects are descriptive categories that suggest how the threat of rejection by others, the dread of loss of coherence, and the fear of the action implications of the emotion interfere with the experience and expression of emotion. The following three experiential aspects of emotion processing occur simultaneously within the therapeutic relationship:

1. The historical–interpersonal aspect. How a person responds to expressing an emotion in the present, in front of and to the therapist, as a function of the consequences of having expressed these emotions to others in the past;
2. The phenomenonological aspect. How this experience feels in terms of a person's ability to tolerate it, focus on, and stay with it;
3. The motivational aspect. To what degree is the person able to apprehend, tolerate, and therefore further explore the feeling in terms of the action implications that emerge from accessing the feeling.

These three aspects of emotional expression in therapy became more evident when we started investigating how clients allow and accept painful feelings. The following discussion will focus on the allowing and accepting of sadness in psychotherapy using the three experiential aspects of emotional processing outlined above—historical–interpersonal, phenomenonological, and motivational—as a conceptual guideline in understanding the process as it unfolds.

In order to better understand the steps of emotional expression we targeted our investigation to actual episodes in psychotherapy that included the process before, during, and after the expression of sadness. We chose sadness because we believe it is a particularly salient emotion in the process of change in psychotherapy as it typically involves issues of separation and loss, failure, and identity.

As we began to collect and analyze sadness episodes we were struck with some similarities in that interruptive or preventive processes surfaced time and time again when clients, however briefly, got in touch with sad feelings. Two patterns began to emerge that helped clarify our understanding of the role of avoidance in the process of allowing and accepting. We recognized the first pattern by noticing how often the expression of sadness was aborted due to feelings of shame. Clients were embarrassed to express their sadness in the presence of others. Explanations of the origin of this shame, when the client was questioned by the therapist, ranged from anxiety about overwhelming the other to fear of feeling threatened at revealing their vulnerability in the presence of a potential rejecting or withholding other. What distinguished this sadness/shame combination is that it could usually be traced to interpersonal anxieties.

The second pattern we noticed was the expression of fear (often deep terror) that if the client allowed themselves to feel their sadness and pain they would fall apart, lose control, go out of their mind. As stated above, these two patterns suggested that there is both an interpersonal component that prevents the expression of sadness because of the expected reaction of the other and a phenomenonological component of dread where the actual experience of the emotion is feared. Moreover, we suggest that what is feared is not only the actual feeling of sadness but the third component, which is the call to action that facing the sadness (over a particular loss for example) will trigger. Since distress or sadness is potentially an adaptive emotion, we tried to understand why the underlying motivational properties of sadness were experienced as so toxic to many of the clients we observed. So we went back and looked at the hypothesized adaptive purposes of sadness to see how these inwired universal signals when combined with unique relational histories could result in the inability to use this emotion adaptively.

## THE INTERPERSONAL ASPECT OF AVOIDANCE: SOCIALIZATION OF DISTRESS

Parents' reactions to the infant and the young child's cry of distress mold the child's self-concept in relation to this emotional experience. Tomkins (1963) described the two main types of socialization of distress as punitive and rewarding. Punitive responses, that is, punishing a child instead of helping him or her cope with the source of the distress, will create even more distress and thus bring the expectation of pain and not relief. In the rewarding of distress, parents comfort the child as well as attend to the actual source of the distress. By providing comfort along with coping strategies to alleviate the source of distress, the child learns that allowing pain is the first step to alleviating it. When there has been a pattern of incomplete rewarding of distress by providing the comfort without the coping strategies, children can come to feel vulnerable, dependent, and lack courage and agency in facing their sadness. These children can later develop into adults who are overwhelmed in their sadness.

Stern (1985) goes farther in describing how parents influence the infant's self-concepts in terms of their emotional expression. He uses the term "interaffectivity" to describe the realm where the parents' reactions combine with the child's experiences to create the meaning of the emotion to the child. Stern explains that the infant perceives distress as having a certain status for parents through the way in which the parent attunes to the infant's distress. Stern outlines four maladaptive ways parents attune to their children's emotions. These are nonattunement, selective attunement, misattunement, and inauthentic attunement, all of which interfere with the healthy development of the infant's sense of self.

In summary, the ways in which interpersonal factors come to isolate and alienate people from their feelings of sadness because of repeated experiences of punishment, vulnerability, helplessness, and aloneness thwart the productive motivational properties of sadness. In psychotherapy the goal of the therapist is to explore these maladaptive expectations and help the client connect with the feeling without fear of reprisal or alienation and rejection. Both the therapist and the client need to monitor their reactions to the client's expression and experience of emotion. The therapist needs to be sure that he or she is not indirectly sending unsupportive signals, even ones that might be experienced as caring, such as trying to clam the client up or offering advice or analysis of the emotions. All of these behaviors by the therapist send the signal that the therapist has difficulty with intense emotion. The therapist also needs to help clients verbalize what their experience of the therapist's reactions are. Clients often check in with the therapist immediately after revealing an emotion. The way in which they check in usually tells about what they expect. For example, after expressing loneliness, a client we observed immediately remarked, "I guess this is kind of useless of me to say to you...it's not as if you can do anything about it." Another client, after revealing how painful the loss of her mother's attention had been when her younger sister was born said, "But telling you this is so painful and makes me feel all these feelings all over again and I am afraid that you or anybody else won't be able to make up for it." In both these cases, the secondary emotions of hopelessness that interrupted the sad experience were reactions to the feeling of vulnerability evoked by allowing the sadness. The client must learn to recognize these secondary feelings as reactive and focus on these before more primary experience of sadness can emerge. This is a process of training clients to be aware of the different levels of their emotions. Also, the reaction of the other to emotional expression plays a critical role in creating a safe and hopeful environment and the client needs to learn how his or her fear of the other can hinder emotional expression.

## PHENOMENONOLOGICAL ASPECT OF AVOIDANCE: FEAR OF DISINTEGRATION

In this section we will discuss the actual experience of feeling sad. When people speak of their fear of sadness they often speak of feeling like they will go out of control, become overwhelmed, fall apart, or be humiliated and embarrassed. They are implying that the sadness itself will be too painful to face. If we take a close look at the phenomenon surrounding sadness, these ominous feelings are spoken about immediately following accessing the sad feeling but before the sadness has truly emerged. The process proceeds something like "If I let myself be sad I will fall apart" or "I have been sad before and feeling the yearnings and pain openly made me vulnerable and I will avoid this state at all costs."

The fear of falling apart, losing control, or going to pieces has its origin in a person's sense of coherency and agency. Both of these issues are problems in how to maintain a core sense of self. Winnicott (1965) speaks of six basic terrors that the infant experiences when the environment fails to provide adequate comfort, nurturance, and containment necessary for the infant to have a secure sense of self. He describes these as: going to pieces, having no relation to body, having no orientation, falling forever, not going on being, and complete isolation. Stern (1985) speaks of the following dimensions when describing the core self: agency, coherence, affectivity, and continuity. When people say they will lose control, fall apart, and go to pieces, they are referring to their fear of losing their sense of coherence and continuity of themselves. That somehow this new emotion will take them over and change them. We believe that what is at risk of being shattered is a static and rigid sense of the self. This is a self that has grown tolerant of and familiar with needs not being met but is too frightened to risk further disappointment.

People ward off feelings because the anxiety about the unknown that comes with fresh emotions is powerful. Feeling the emotion is therefore a reorganizing moment where people often experience a feeling of disequilibrium. The act of allowing loneliness can threaten a sense of self-coherence because now there is some awareness of yearning and incompleteness. Attaining that for which one yearns becomes a threat to the me-as-I-know-myself-now. In a sense there is a cycle of disintegration and reintegration as the self-system lets down barriers, allows new experiences and feelings, and then reorganizes around these new feelings.

## MOTIVATIONAL ASPECT OF AVOIDANCE: AGENCY—THE CHALLENGE TO ACTION

If a child's expression of sadness was constantly ignored, minimized, or rejected by caretakers, the child would possibly still consciously experience the feeling but would then feel forced to suppress it quickly to maintain contact with the caretaker. Thus the child would never learn that the needs aroused by the feelings can be met and would not benefit from experiencing the satisfaction of needs that can occur when feelings are contacted. If, on the other hand, people have had the experience of using feelings to guide the self in the awareness of their needs and have been productively able to use this information to facilitate having these needs met, the feeling of sadness will not be uniformly dreaded.

It is thus critical to recognize, and to help the client recognize, that what is dreaded is not only the actual experience of the sadness itself but also the expected consequences that will result by letting this new feeling into awareness. The fear is of the action potential, the need evoked by the feeling, and the courage it will take to face the action tendency associated with the feeling. For example, will the process of accessing one's deep sadness and loneliness and the associated desire for contact/comfort turn into an overwhelming experience because of an underlying belief that one is damaged and is not capable of intimacy or that one is unlovable? Part of the task of the therapist is to help identify the irrational beliefs that interrupt experience and stand beneath clients with a net as they go out on a limb with their emotions. This net is composed of the therapist's empathy and validation. The therapist is, in effect, affirming the person by saying "Given your experience, how could you have helped but be who you are and feel what you do." The therapist validates what the client experiences rather than explains or attempts to alter it. The therapist also focuses on clients' potentials for growth selectively attending to their available resources for attaining what they need or for letting go of what they cannot obtain.

The very act of apprehending one's sadness is a change experience. When the buried yearnings associated with the sadness enter into awareness, a person can either act to change or suffer from the inaction. The awareness of unmet needs suggests a decision point. The decision is whether to act on the need and the possibilities that are revealed when one allows oneself to recognize what one lacks. For clients to let themselves feel their loss is also to acknowledge the need to repair. This is a very risky process. In this process of allowing and accepting a painful feeling it is as if the client is letting the feelers go out to see exactly where all is not right, like examining oneself after a fall. It is a check by the organism of what is malfunctioning. The act of checking implies that one has some intention of repairing. The act of repair implies that there is some fundamental hope that what is wrong is repairable. The act of acknowledging what one feels prefigures a set of inevitable consequences. Therefore, besides the sadness associated with acknowledging the experiences of loss or rejection, there is also the fear of being damaged, of deserving the pain, of being incapable of closeness, of being doomed to failure, and fated to be lonely that needs to be faced. The client is not likely to allow the feeling of sadness if there is a basic belief that the loss being experienced is irreparable. The struggle becomes the tension between the desire to change and the anticipated dread of not being able to make the pain go away once the sadness has been accessed.

When there is no hope about repairing or surviving the loss that underlies the sadness, the experience of vulnerability alongside a sense of helplessness can result in despair. Although therapists cannot directly repair the loss, they can provide the sense of someone else offering their presence, validation, and support when the client is facing feelings that are expected to overwhelm or cause despair. This type of interpersonal support engages the client in a process of relearning how to approach feelings with the help of the presence of the other. Just as Winnicott (1965) spoke of the developmental advance that the infant achieves when he or she is able to be alone in the presence of another, a similar development is occurring when a client learns to use the comfort of the accepting other to face feelings, alone and within themselves, of being damaged and irreparable. Deep sadness is then not experienced as annihilation because the concurrent acceptance and regard of the therapist act as a stabilizing reality to counteract possible feelings of being out of control, as new self-organizations are coming into being.

## SUMMARY

In the beginning of the section on distress and sadness in the process of change we suggested that the notion of self-agency and self-coherence are central to understanding the process of the avoidance of painful emotions. Part of the goal of psychotherapy is to free people to have emotional experiences in the presence of others that feel safe and are the product of self-agency rather than an assault on it.

We described how past negative experiences with expressing emotions in front of others acts as a powerful inhibitor and suggest how this interpersonal aspect of avoidance of emotion thwarts the adaptational purposes of its experience and expression. We then focused on how people described their experience of the expression of sadness. We found that past experiences of showing sadness combined with a current sense of vulnerability can result in the prohibitory fears of going to pieces and losing control if the sadness were to be allowed. These fears, in turn, create further secondary emotions and maladaptive reactions to the experience of sadness and take on a life of their own in the process of avoidance.

Lastly we suggested that one key aspect of the avoidance of the expression of sadness is fear of the motivational implications of the acknowledgment of the emotion. The faith that the self can survive the loss once it has been recognized and experienced is essential to having the courage to allow the feeling. Once accessed, the feeling will be a guide in how to take steps toward adaptive action.

## REFERENCES

Bartlett, E. S., & Izard, C. E. (1972). A dimensional and discrete emotions investigation of the subjective experience of emotion. In C. E. Izard (Ed.), *Patterns of emotions: A new analysis of anxiety and depression* (pp. 87–108). New York: Academic Press.

Bohart, A. (1988). A cognitive client-centered perspective on borderline personality development. Paper presented at the Internal meeting of Client Centered and Experiential Psychotherapy, September 1980. Leuven, Belgium.

Bowlby, J. (1969). *Attachment and loss:* Vol. 1. *Attachment.* New York: Basic Books.

Greenberg, L. S., & Johnson, S. (1988). *Emotionally focused therapy for couples.* New York: Guilford.

Greenberg, L. S., & Safran, J. (1987a). *Emotion in psychotherapy.* New York: Guilford.

Greenberg, L. S., & Safran, J. (1987b). Emotion, cognition and action. In H. Eysenck & I. Martin (Eds.), *Foundations of behavior therapy* (pp. 295–314). New York: Plenum.

Greenberg, L. S., & Safran, J. (1989). Emotion in psychotherapy. *American Psychologist, 44,* 19–29.

Lang, P. (1983). Cognition in emotion. Concept and action. In C. E. Izard, J. Kagen, & R. B. Zajonc (Eds.), *Emotion, cognition and behavior* (pp. 192–226). New York: Cambridge University Press.

Lang, P. (1984). The cognitive psychophysiology of emotion: Fear and anxiety. In H. Tuma & J. D. Maser (Eds.), *Anxiety and anxiety disorders* (pp. 130–170). Hillsdale, NJ: Erlbaum.

Leventhal, H. (1979). A perceptual–motor processing model of emotion. In P. Pliner, K. Blankstein, & I. Spigel (Eds.), *Perception of emotion in self and others* (vol. 5, pp. 1–46). New York: Plenum.

Leventhal, H. (1982). The integration of emotion and cognition. A view from the perceptual–motor theory of emotion. In M. S. Clarke & S. T. Fiske (Eds.), *Affect and cognition: The 17th annual Carnegie symposium on cognition* (pp. 121–156). Hillsdale, NJ: Erlbaum.

Maturana, H. R. (1975). The organization of the living: A theory of the living organization. *International Journal of Man–Machine Studies, 7*, 313–332.

Maturana, H. R., & Varela, F. J. (1987). *The tree of knowledge.* Boston: Shambala.

Prigogine, I., & Stengers, I. (1981). *Order out of chaos: Man's new dialogue with nature.* New York: Bantam.

Stern, D. N. (1985). *The interpersonal world of the infant.* New York: Basic Books.

Tomkins, S. (1963). *Affect, imagery, consciousness: Vol. II. The negative affects.* New York: Springer.

Varela, F. J. (1979). *Principles of biological autonomy.* New York: North Holland.

Whitehead, A. N. (1929). *Process and reality.* Cambridge: Cambridge University Press.

Winnicott, D. W. (1965). Primitive emotional development. *The maturational process and facilitating environment.* New York: International Universities Press.

# CHAPTER 6

# DAVANLOO'S SHORT-TERM DYNAMIC PSYCHOTHERAPY
## A CROSS-THEORETICAL ANALYSIS OF CHANGE MECHANISMS

### LEIGH MCCULLOUGH

## INTRODUCTION

Short-term dynamic psychotherapy, or STDP (Davanloo, 1978, 1980), is an intensive form of psychoanalytically based therapy that appears to provide a powerful treatment package for effecting change in severe, long-standing maladaptive behavior. The innovative quality of Davanloo's approach, however, seems to warrant careful study from a broader and more integrative theoretical perspective than psychodynamic theory alone, for STDP appears to incorporate cognitive behavioral maneuvers and principles of learning woven into the fabric of the treatment. Of course, this was not Davanloo's intent, but in his quest for effective techniques (examining his own videotapes over a 20-year period) he appears to have isolated certain mechanisms that bear resemblance to operant, respondent, and cognitive techniques.

A learning theory basis as an alternative explanation for psychodynamic change has been suggested for many years (Dollard & Miller,

LEIGH MCCULLOUGH • Department of Psychology in Psychiatry, University of Pennsylvania, Philadelphia, Pennsylvania 19104.

1950; Fenichel, 1945; Pavlov, 1927). More recently, Wachtel (1978) has provided an indepth exploration of areas of convergence and divergence between psychoanalysis and behavior therapy. A growing number of integrationist theorists are referring to such mechanisms as conditioning, stimulus control, reinforcement, and extinction as agents influencing therapeutic change in general (e.g., Prochaska & DiClemente, 1982) and specifically in STDP (Western, 1986). Relevant to this discussion is a set of procedures called "covert conditioning," which uses principles of learning to alter the frequency, intensity, and duration of internal responses; that is, thoughts, feelings, and images (Cautela, 1977; Cautela & McCullough, 1978). Although Cautela does not apply his covert conditioning principles to psychodynamic issues, these mechanisms appear to occur in STDP; that is, the influence of reward, punishment, and extinction on psychodynamic issues as presented in thoughts, feelings, and images. By examining this psychodynamic treatment in the light of other theoretical perspectives, it is hoped that comparisons may become evident that would not be deduced from psychodynamic theory alone.

The main elements of STDP involve two steps; first, a form of cognitive restructuring and second, a desensitization through exposure to conflictual inner experience. This chapter will discuss these elements in terms of common change mechanisms (e.g., Goldfried, 1980; Rice and Greenberg, 1984) and how they may be operative in behavior change. A case illustration and clinical examples will be provided to begin to operationalize the theoretical constructs. Following the discussion of the STDP techniques, hypotheses and research questions will be suggested for testing the relative effects of these different theoretical components, for specific patients under specific conditions.

## CASE ILLUSTRATION

Picture a therapy session in progress. The therapist and the patient are sitting facing each other with a videotape camera recording the process. The patient has come for STDP treatment for help with anxiety following being fired. He has not been able to seek another job and instead has been working in a position far beneath his capacity for several months. Following a thorough assessment of the anxiety to rule out the need for medication, the therapist asks for a specific description of the incident which elicited the anxiety.

PT: Well, Jim called me into his office and told me I wasn't needed anymore. It didn't make any sense. I had just been given a raise and a promotion the month before. They always liked my work. I didn't know what to say. I just walked out. I've been in bad shape ever since. The anxiety has been terrible.

TH: How do you experience the anxiety?

PT: It's awful. My heart races, my palms get sweaty, and I just get confused. I can't concentrate on anything...

(The patient is able to vividly describe the experience of anxiety. The therapist then questions the frequency, intensity, and duration of these symptoms before continuing with the analysis of the anxiety-provoking event.)

TH: So we can see that in response to the firing, you became loaded with anxiety and unable to function as well as you use to. (Here the therapist provides the patient with feedback on patterns of behavior and then moves to examination of feelings.) Can we look at your feeling toward Jim?

PT: I was just shocked. I couldn't believe he'd do something like that. We were friends.

TH: Do you notice that you described thoughts, not feelings. (The therapist begins with a gentle reflection of the defensive behavior.)

PT: Well, what's the use. What's done is done. I can't change anything.

TH: Can you see that you give me a helpless response when you say it is useless to look closely at these feelings? Do you see what I'm saying? (The therapist invites the patient to examine a maladaptive behavior pattern.)

PT: Yeah, I can. I don't like to get angry...and I was real angry at Jim. I wanted to let him have it! But I'd never do anything like that. I don't even like to think those things. So I just shut up and withdrew.

TH: So you seem to have tremendous difficulty with angry feelings, and instead become crippled with anxiety, so that you are taken advantage of. Do you think it would be helpful to look at these angry feelings that have caused you so much conflict? (The therapist sums up the work thus far to assess the patient's degree of alliance with her.)

PT: Yeah, I've got to. (Tears in eyes.) I can't stand living like this anymore. (The patient indicates a willingness to face the difficult feelings that have been avoided.)

At this point the therapist may proceed to the deeper and more affectively focused work in the second step of the treatment. If the patient had not been able to see or feel their maladaptive behavior as problematic, however, then the therapist would have needed to stay with the more gentle and cognitive process of pointing out destructive behavior and consequences until the patient and therapist came to an agreement.

TH: O.K. Can we go back to the incident of the firing. Can you tell me how you experienced the anger toward Jim? (This patient, unlike many others, is able to give a vivid description of anger; a buildup of energy in his body, tension felt in his arms and fists, and a desire to lash out at Jim physically. The therapist assesses impulse control to rule out the possibility of the patient acting out the impulses that now will be fantasized so vividly. The length of time spent on this procedure is a function of the patient's capacity to experience anxiety-laden emotion.)

TH: You say you want to lash out. Can you describe how this lashing out would take form in your thoughts and fantasies?

PT: Oh, I'd never do anything to harm him!

TH: Of course. We're not talking about acting out these feelings. I am asking you to describe the experience of these feelings in your fantasies.

PT: Well, I don't know what I'd do.

TH: So you're helpless to describe this! (Pressure begins!)

PT: But, I don't know!

TH: More helplessness! (The therapist now will intensify the process by simply pointing out the defensive behavior, which is done to intensify the patient's affective experience.)

PT: What good will it do?

TH: Now you rationalize.

PT: (Laughs sarcastically and looks away.)

TH: And now you laugh and avoid my eyes. Are there feelings toward me?

PT: Sure. You're pressuring me!

TH: So you make yourself my victim.

PT: What do you want me to say...that I'd shake you?

TH: It's not what I want, it's what you're experiencing right now here with me that's important to look at. (The STDP therapist is vigilant in regard to emotional responses directly between the patient and therapist because it is this factor, according to Davanloo, that leads to the most rapid change.)

PT: Well, I do feel like shaking you...to shut you up!

TH: So lets look at this...

PT: I hate what I see...I can see me knocking you on the floor (cringing). I hate these feelings.

TH: Do you see the anxiety and discomfort that comes up when you face strong angry impulses toward me, just as it did when we began to look at the anger toward Jim.

PT: Yeah, I see it. I want to get away from it. (The patient has always avoided facing such negative feelings.)

The session continues in like manner with the therapist confronting the patient's avoidance of anger toward herself as well as toward Jim. This particular patient, though reluctant to face these feelings, was not highly resistant so the work could proceed fairly rapidly. The patient goes on to recall that he felt like killing Jim a few days after the incident, and could not bear to face that "killer instinct" in himself, even though he knew he would never act on such feelings. At the height of the anger at Jim, the patient started to sob because Jim was "like a father" to him. His own father had died the year before and the patient had not been able to cry. The emotion in both events is elicited, experienced intensely, and described in detail.

The therapist sums up the session with feedback in the form of an interpretation: "So now we have seen that you have used a number of mechanisms (defenses) to avoid looking at your angry feelings (warded off impulses) because you feel a lot of discomfort (anxiety and guilt) about expression of negative feelings. And this happened here with me, just as it did with your boss, Jim, and earlier with your father. Avoidance of these angry feelings has led to your anxiety as well as your inability to mourn your fathers death."

The patient responded, "I feel the first sense of relief in a long time. I knew I was bottled up, but I didn't know what it was about."

Subsequent therapy sessions will focus on mourning the loss of the father, as well as avoidance of appropriate expression of anger to expose the patient to these internal responses.

After reading the above case illustration, a psychodynamic theorist might say that the agent of change is bringing the unconscious into consciousness. The cognitive behaviorist might see a process of desensitization occurring, or the revision of irrational beliefs. Interpersonal theorists might credit the relationship factors between the patient and the therapist as maintaining or shifting maladaptive patterns. A learning theorist might see the therapist exposing the patient to conditioned aversive feelings to extinguish avoidance responses. This chapter will examine how each of the above mechanisms can be seen to contribute to the process of behavior change in STDP.

## OVERVIEW OF STDP PROCEDURES
## AND CHANGE MECHANISMS

This discussion will use common factors noted across many forms of treatment to illustrate the change mechanisms that may be operative in STDP. As outlined in Table 1, STDP involves two major steps. Within each of these steps there are both cognitive and affective "patient tasks" (Rice & Greenberg, 1984) that must be mastered in sequence in order for the patient to be prepared for the subsequent task. The predominant components of STDP in the case illustration (i.e., cognitive identification of defenses and experiencing of previously avoided affect) also show much similarity to two mechanisms identified by Goldfried (1980) that may be common to all theoretical orientations: offering the client/patient "direct feedback" and providing the client/patient with "new corrective experiences" (p. 994).

## STEP ONE

Step one is predominantly (though not exclusively) a cognitive task for the patient, that is, a recognition of the operation of defensive behaviors, anxiety, and impulses.

> In the early 1960s I decided to break away from the traditional approach...I began to reverse the tendency towards passivity, becoming more and more active in my technique...working on and interpreting resistance or defenses. What emerged to my amazement was that the hidden conflict became conscious in an unmistakable way. (Davanloo, 1980, p. 45)

In step one the therapist gives direct feedback in the form of specific discriminations about defensive thoughts, behaviors, and feelings. This is much like a behavioral analysis but focusing on hypothesized conflictual unconscious feelings. Although sorrow, anger, or tenderness may emerge here to a greater or lesser degree, the *primary* goal is a cognitive recognition of defenses used to avoid such feeling. Thus, this step is used as a gentle, educational phase of treatment before the pressure toward exposure begins, providing an opportunity for the alliance to build, for trust to develop (when necessary), and for maladaptive patterns to become clear so that the patient and the therapist can later work collaboratively in the confrontation of and exposure to the difficult issues.

Step one can be seen as a restructuring of the patient's irrational cognitions similar to Beck (1967), but concerning *inner* experience. Thoughts, behaviors, and feelings are brought into awareness, given verbal labels, reframed as defensive or avoidant, and analyzed in terms of antecedents and consequences. Though not utilizing the concept of the "unconscious," the cognitive behaviorist also attempts to make the patient "aware."* In cognitive behaviorism, cognitions that the patient

*Christine Cooke (personal communication, July 21, 1989).

TABLE 1. Cross-Theoretical Comparison of STDP Treatment Components

| | Step one | | Step two | |
|---|---|---|---|---|
| | Defense analysis | Identification of consequences | Preinterpretive phase: confrontation | Interpretive phase |
| Patient task (Rice & Greenberg, 1984) | Cognitive | Affective | Affective | Cognitive with affective and interpersonal awareness |
| Change mechanism (Goldfried, 1980) | Direct feedback | New corrective experience | New corrective experience | Direct feedback |
| Learning principles | Discrimination learning about avoidance of internal responses | Identification of negative consequences of avoidance | Exposure, extinction, desensitization —to internal responses | Positive consequences —expression —acceptance —mastery |
| Similarities to other treatments | Behavior analysis Cognitive restructuring | Operant methods with affective consequences | Response prevention, implosion, flooding | Analytic treatment |

had not previously attended to are pointed out, reframed as irrational, and revised in terms of their antecedents and consequences. (Th: "Each time you think about a problem, you seem to catastrophize, and dwell on the worst possible outcome.") Thus, direct feedback may function as a mechanism of change in STDP and cognitive behaviorism by discriminating patterns of behavior that were not previously evident. (If you are not aware that you're doing something, you do not have the option of assessing its value or choosing an alternative.)

In Rice and Greenberg's terms, the "marker" that indicates that the patient has mastered the cognitive task is an affective response of grief that results from *seeing and feeling* the destructive consequences of their defensive behavior as well as a stated desire to change the behavior. Step one represents the preparatory work for the even more affectively intense work to follow.*

## STEP TWO

This is the more widely known and controversial component of the Davanloo technique. It begins with a "preinterpretive phase" involving confrontation, pressure, and challenge to the patient's defensive behavior. Both direct feedback and corrective experiencing are involved here, but the primary patient task is an affective one.

Many aspects of this phase show similarity to behavioral treatments for conditioned phobic avoidance reactions. A behavioral therapist might use "response prevention" to stop a patient from phobic avoidance, and then expose the patient to the phobic stimulus until anxiety subsides. In an analogous fashion, but focusing on inner experience, Davanloo uses confrontation in a manner similar to response prevention to abruptly prevent a defensive response (the phobic avoidant reaction) (e.g., "Do you see how you become withdrawn now?"). The patient is then encouraged to experience the previously avoided affect until avoidance subsides and appropriate expression is possible (e.g., "What are you feeling now, here with me?"). Furthermore, this rapid experiencing of feeling, which is similar to desensitization, or flooding, occurs through a process of *imaginal* exposure (imagery concerning feelings

---

*Step one may be brief, lengthy, or under certain conditions may be omitted entirely, for each patient requires a different admixture of cognitive insight and emotional awareness. Patients who can readily acknowledge their defenses and who see them as destructive can move rapidly through this phase. But other patients with more "ego syntonic" defenses will proceed more slowly. (See Fosha, 1988, for an excellent discussion of some specific applications of step one with depressed patients.)

toward significant others) as well as in vivo exposure to feelings in the real ongoing relationship to the therapist. Davanloo writes:

> What I have observed is that actively and relentlessly confronting the patient with his defenses, one forces him to experience his true feelings at any given moment with the result that the core neurosis is derepressed and experienced fully, and...the neurosis is dissolved. (1980, p. 70)

Davanloo's emphasis on experiencing of warded-off affect can also be seen as analogous to Alexander and French's (1946) "corrective emotional experience," described by Goldfried as "encouraging patients to engage in previously avoided actions in order to recognize that their fears and misconceptions about such activities were groundless" (1980, p. 994). In the STDP case illustration above, the therapist used confrontation to expose the patient to the experience of the intense feeling of anger ("the killer instincts") so that the patient could become more aware and *more in control* of such feelings, and could be freer to choose more appropriate ways of expressing angry feelings.*

After the affective task has been experienced and mastered, the therapist moves into the "interpretive phase." Feedback is given about the defensive (and destructive) avoidance of certain feelings in relation to the significant others as well as to the therapist. Therefore treatment can be seen as similar to a conditioned avoidance paradigm in that maladaptive patterns, anxiety, and self-punishment may be decreased by exposure to the conditioned aversive ("inner") stimulus with benign consequences. New corrective experiences may be "new" because the consequences are different; that which appeared to result in punishment (e.g., expression of anger, tenderness, grief, etc.) is no longer punishing; that which appeared to result in reinforcement (e.g., passivity, withdrawal, avoidance) is no longer reinforcing. This may free the individual to attempt alternative and more constructive responses.

In summary, step one is primarily a cognitive task for the patient with direct feedback from the therapist about defensive behavior. Davanloo has identified as a sign of mastery an affective response to signal that the cognitive task has been deeply integrated by the patient or "restructuring" has taken place. Step two is primarily an affective task for the patient eliciting the second corrective experience (which occurs through exposure to impulses and extinction of avoidance). The goal is the patient's cognitive awareness and acceptance of the deeply

---

*Although there is a focus on warded-off impulses, it is important to note that it is not the impulse itself that is extinguished, but the anxiety-laden defensive maneuvers used to avoid the impulse. The goal of treatment is to encourage appropriate expression in the place of destructive avoidance.

experienced interpersonal feeling. Both of these steps are incorporated into the "initial evaluation" to determine the treatment focus, as well as intermixed as needed in the subsequent treatment.*†

# HYPOTHESES AND RESEARCH QUESTIONS

In this section, hypotheses will be suggested where relationships have been made explicit. In cases where relationships are less clear, or where certain patterns are stable only under certain conditions, research questions will be posed. This list is not intended to be exhaustive, but will begin by identifying a few of the most obvious comparisons. All of the hypotheses and questions presented here may be tested by use of a standard outcome battery and specific process instruments applied to videotaped therapy sessions; for example, patient–therapist interaction patterns (McCullough, 1990), or patient-affective experiencing (Klein, Mathieu-Coughlin, & Kiesler, 1986).‡

## COMPONENTS OF CHANGE MECHANISMS IN STEP ONE

This discussion will address three components of the step one procedure that are suggested as mechanisms of change: (1) extensiveness of behavioral description, (2) degree of focus on consequences of irrational beliefs and behavior, and (3) affective response to consequences.

---

*Michael Laikin brought to my attention that in clinical practice these steps are not as rigidly delineated and separated as presented here. In a sensitively conducted clinical session, the therapist might vary from the order of these basic components and interweave steps one and two as needed. For the purpose of research study, however, these mechanisms do approximate both the order presented and the basic tasks required of the patient in the process of change. It is beyond the scope of this chapter to go into the extensive technical requirements of the STDP procedure. For detailed discussion and case illustrations of the therapy process, the reader is referred to *The International Journal of Short-Term Dynamic Psychotherapy.*

†A very important component of treatment efficacy is the identification and maintenance of the correct focus on the patient's core disturbance (e.g., Oedipal conflicts, grief or loss, etc.). Even masterfully executed treatment procedures will not be as effective if applied to the wrong focus. Although there is a growing awareness of what is the best form of treatment for major problem areas (e.g., alcoholism, manic–depressive illness, etc.), it is much less clear how to determine precise foci within an individual treatment that will rapidly lead to cure. Davanloo's "trial therapy" offers a promising method of isolating core disturbances, but there remains much work to be done to verify its efficacy empirically.

‡Many such studies are underway at The Beth Israel Psychotherapy Research Program in New York City (see Winston et al., 1989).

Multilevel Description of Behavior

The STDP feedback procedure, though similar to a behavioral analysis, carefully identifies many aspects of inner experience and environmental events preceding and following behavior. While a cognitive behaviorist may focus primarily on irrational beliefs and problem solving, STDP also encompasses affective and interpersonal experience, both in the past and present. Furthermore, a detailed description of the physiological experience of the affect is examined so that the individual will be able to immediately recognize when anger is building, when sadness is coming to the surface, when sorrow is coming in waves, when tenderness and warmth are gently emerging. Distinctions are made to teach the patient how these feelings are blocked by anxiety and defensive maneuvers, as well as how these responses occur with specific people in the patients life. Patients demonstrate awareness by noting their defensive behavior in their daily life. ("Now I can see how I constantly avoid even the slightest conflict at home. I never knew how much I was doing this.") Therefore, hypotheses could be generated to examine the efficacy across treatments of the extensiveness of verbal description of behaviors, as well as the number of experiential levels addressed in the description (e.g., physiological, cognitive, behavioral, environmental).

*Hypothesis 1.* The greater the extensiveness of the therapist's description of the maladaptive cognitions, feelings, or behaviors (both number of statements and levels of experience addressed), the greater the patient's recognition of these patterns both inside and outside the session and the greater ability to see the consequences. Different therapies could be compared for degree of patient self-reported insight across various levels of extensiveness of feedback.

Focus on Consequences

Another component of the extensiveness of description emphasized in STDP is the therapist's focus on consequences. According to Davanloo, when the patient sees the punishing consequences of behavior, there should be a concomitant "grief-laden" response. Typical patient comments are, "I've wasted 20 years of my life" or "So much love has been lost to me because of the barriers I have put up toward people."

This particular attention to grief-laden affect is a unique contribution of Davanloo's. He refers to this as a procedure for building motivation in a patient. In other words, if consequences are seen by the patient as *so* punishing that grief is felt in response, then the motivation to change will be high, and the confrontive work will be able to proceed more smoothly. The cognitive behaviorist places much less emphasis on affective experiencing of consequences than STDP. Hypotheses could thus be generated to examine the effects of "potency" or "intensity" of response to feedback about negative consequences of maladaptive behaviors across different treatments.

*Hypothesis 2.* The greater the attention to consequences of behavior (as measured by the number of therapist statements regarding negative consequences of the patient's maladaptive behavior), the more frequent and intense the occurrence of grief-laden responding (as measured by coding of patient affective experiencing from videotaped segments).

In the operant literature (e.g., Reynolds, 1975), the construct "motivation" is seen as caused by environmental contingencies (e.g., the consequences of an action) rather than resulting from inner experience. Davanloo may unintentionally incorporate operant technology through his in-depth focusing on observable negative consequences both in the environment and in the patient's affective response. Learning theory predicts that negative consequences following a response decreases the likelihood of that response occurring. Cautela's theory of "covert conditioning" suggests that learning principles apply to thoughts and feelings as well as overt behavior. Therefore, the identification of negative consequences of defensive behavior should decrease the *desire* to perform the maladaptive behavior.

*Hypothesis 2a.* The greater the intensity and duration of the grief-laden response, the greater the patient's motivation to revise the irrational beliefs or to change the defensive behavior, and the greater the cooperativeness of the patient in facing the exposure procedures to follow. The dependent variables could be: (1) the patients' self-report that their problematic beliefs or behaviors are less desirable (i.e., more "ego-dystonic"), (2) the number of defensive behaviors occurring in step two, or (3) the intensity of affect elicited during subsequent exposure. The independent variables might be treatment conditions (STDP and cognitive behaviorist, for example) that share some similarities in behavioral analysis but some differences in specific application that allow for contrast and comparison.

In summary, the agents of change in step one seems to be: (1) the more extensive the therapist's description of experience, the better the recognition of behavior patterns and consequences; (2) the better the identification of consequences, the greater the sense of grief and loss; and (3) the greater the grief response, the greater the motivation to change the maladaptive behavior. These propositions seem to be either implicitly or explicitly accepted by various theoretical positions, but making these relationships explicit permits empirical examination.

## COMPONENTS OF CHANGE MECHANISMS IN STEP TWO

There are four main components of the step two procedure that this discussion will address: (1) style of confrontation of the defenses, (2) the focus of the exposure, (3) use of the patient–therapist relationship, and (4) interpretation. In order to generate hypotheses and research questions, these components will be compared and contrasted to other treatment approaches.

### Style of Confrontation of Defenses

The technique of confronting defenses is attempted in many treatments, but there are a wide range of methods utilized to do so. For example, those who use flooding or implosion therapy (Boudewyns & Shipley, 1983) describe "going over" the defensive barrier by "flooding" the patient with conflict-laden images that the patient wants to avoid until extinction or "desensitization" occurs. Those who do hypnosis describe "sneaking under" the defensive barrier through metaphor or simile, and are able to effect deep structural changes in the patient. Those who do experiential therapy will disarm the patient or "get around" the defenses by using a procedure like the two-chair technique (i.e., asking the patient to speak openly to an imaginary person in an empty chair to enhance the intensity of the experience). Therapists who perform long-term treatment may "wear down" the defenses over time, or bring the defenses to the forefront through the development of the transference neurosis. Havens (1986) has presented powerful examples of the use of empathy in his book entitled *Making Contact* (which, indeed, exemplifies the task that therapists are aspiring to do). It may be that accurate and profound empathic statements might be the best way to reach the depth of a patient's feeling (at least in some cases). But it might also prove correct that Davanloo's relentless confrontation, though at times difficult for the patient, is the only "accurate empathy" to reach certain individuals. This is an empirical question. We all have our special ways of trying to reach our patients, and Davanloo offers some important innovations to consider.

*Research Question 1.* Which of the therapies noted above could elicit the greatest degree of affective experiencing from what type of patient under what circumstances?

Focus of the Exposure

"Therapeutic exposure" is defined as "repeated or extended exposure either in reality or fantasy to objectively harmless, but feared stimuli for the purpose of reducing negative affects" (Boudewyns & Shipley, 1983, p. 3). This discussion will address two main components of the exposure process: (1) *what* the patient is exposed to (i.e., the focus of either anxiety or impulse), and (2) *how* exposure is presented, either by the therapist or by the patient.

The issue of what the patient should be exposed to can be examined by looking at the treatment models that use therapeutic exposure. Learning theory-based therapies that appear most similar in form to STDP* view phobic symptoms in particular and neurotic symptoms in general as conditioned avoidance responses acquired in accord with Mowrer's (1960) two-factor theory of avoidance behavior. Two-factor theory suggests that aversive stimuli (i.e., warded-off feelings) come to elicit negative emotion, which in turn leads to defensive or avoidant responses. Responses that successfully reduce or terminate the conditioned aversive stimuli are reinforced by the resulting decrease in negative affect, so that avoidance continues and extinction does not occur.

A treatment model surprisingly similar to STDP is implosion therapy (Stampfl and Levis, 1967)†, which was derived from Mowrer's two-factor theory as well as the learning theory applications of Dollard and Miller (1950), but which uses psychodynamic formulations as the focus of treatment.‡ Implosion therapy is an exposure form of treatment in which the therapist presents to a patient psychodynamically based images (e.g., scenes of humiliation over rejection, violent behavior toward others, etc.) in an extremely intense format with the goal of extinguishing avoidant responses to these fearful images.

---

*The most often used terms are "flooding," "implosive therapy," "deconditioning," or "extinction therapy." See Boudewyns and Shipley (1983) for a discussion of these treatment models.

†The similarity between STDP and implosive therapy was first pointed out to me in 1983 by Nora Noel.

‡Mowrer's model has been called into question in regard to its applicability to complex human behavior. While Stampfl and Levis (1967) report that certain features related to the basic two-factor model required modifications and extension in their clinical application to human behavior, they nevertheless demonstrate *substantial improvement* in patients as a result of 15 to 30 sessions of implosive therapy. Thus, the use of Mowrer's model as a heuristic tool has demonstrated utility in the development of an effective clinical intervention. It is also noteworthy that STDP, using a somewhat similar method of exposure to intense affect, makes similar claims in terms of strong results occurring in a similarly short time of 10 to 40 sessions (Davanloo, 1980).

Flooding (Boudewyns & Shipley, 1983) is another behavioral method based on a conditioning paradigm. The patient is prevented from avoiding the phobic stimulus and forced to remain in contact with the stimulus until the phobic reaction extinguishes. This is essentially the same paradigm as used by Davanloo except that the exposure in flooding is to only *consciously* reported anxiety while the exposure in STDP is to unconscious feelings.

Cognitive behavior therapy provides yet another distinct contrast with procedures such as systematic desensitization (Wolpe, 1969). The phobic stimulus can be a memory, a feeling, or a thought which sets off a phobic reaction. This then leads to avoidance of or escape from the phobic stimulus. Treatment proceeds by "graduated exposure" in amounts that increase as the patient is able to tolerate the phobic stimulus. This continues until the phobic reaction subsides. Thus, systematic desensitization is less confrontive than STDP and less intense than flooding, but follows the same conditioned avoidance paradigm. Like flooding, the focus is on conscious anxiety, or maladaptive cognitions, not on unconscious impulses.

In the treatments above it could be argued that the psychodynamic theorists tend to focus on the conditions that *originated* the avoidance problem (e.g., unconscious impulses), while the behavioral approaches tend to focus on conditions *maintaining* the avoidance, that is, the conscious anxiety. It is interesting that ample research has demonstrated successful outcomes for all these treatments. However, it is often overlooked that the conditions that give rise to a problem are not necessarily those that maintain it. Therefore, therapy might need to intervene in *both* areas.

*Research Question 2.* Using comparisons as noted above, clinical trials could assess which patients with which problems respond better to a focus on unconscious feeling, conscious anxiety, or an admixture of both. Use of carefully controlled flooding and desensitization conditions could assess the relative impact of a focus on conscious anxiety, in comparison to STDP and implosion which would assess the relative impact of two treatments focusing on *unconscious* feeling. The dependent variable could be the frequency of avoidance behavior during exposure or the time taken for the cessation of avoidance behavior.

How Exposure Is Presented

A main difference among exposure treatments discussed above is the *origin of the presentation of the images.* STDP challenges the *patient* to initiate the emotional scenes while implosion therapy, flooding, and cognitive behavioral approaches have the *therapist* assist or generate part or all of the experience for the patient.

Although exposure to feeling is theorized to reduce avoidance, many patients demonstrate great difficulty responding effectively. Unlike STDP, implosion therapists intentionally stay the "helper" and "side-step" the patient's hostility at being subjected to the aversive scenes (Stampfl & Levis, 1967). Cognitive behavior therapists and therapists using flooding also employ the therapist's assistance in the generation of images. This distinction provides a worthwhile contrast to examine the method of presentation of the aversive images. For certain fragile patients the negative feeling generated toward the therapist in STDP might be too aversive to bear, but might instead be possible to face if desensitized or flooded through therapist-assisted procedures. Other patients might be able to more spontaneously generate affective imagery. Therefore, the therapist-assisted imagery might be less accurate than the patient's own depiction and lessen the intensity of the experience.

*Research Question 3.* Therapist-generated, therapist-assisted, or patient-generated exposure could be compared to identify which approaches were the most helpful in reducing avoidance for which patients.

### The Patient–Therapist Relationship as a Change Agent

Learning theorists have long maintained that environmental variables are the agents that increase, decrease, or maintain behavior (e.g., Ferster & Skinner, 1957). It is noteworthy that progressive psychodynamic theorists are now beginning to emphasize the crucial role of the environment in maintaining and changing behavior; however, it is the *interpersonal* environment they are addressing—and specifically the interactive relationship of the patient and therapist (Mitchell, 1988; Thoma & Kachele, 1988; Wachtel, 1978). The most unique treatment component in STDP is the use of the therapist–patient relationship as the focus for exposure of impulses.

If the goal of treatment in step two is to provide feedback on and exposure to conflictual impulses, nowhere will this be more vividly depicted than in the relationship between the patient and the therapist. If the patient can look the therapist in the eyes and express (and fully feel) deepest anger, or feeling of tenderness, or heartfelt sorrow over termination, this is when "exposure" is at its most intense. Also, when a patient is avoiding these very feelings, and the therapist can point out the specific behaviors being used in the avoidance, this is when the "direct feedback" is the most profound (e.g., gently stated, "Do you see how you avoid your tender feelings toward me by using sarcasm, right now? And now do you notice that you changed the subject when I asked about feelings of closeness? Do you see how you push me away?").

Thus face-to-face human interaction, occurring in the here and now, rather than imaginal interaction, might more closely approximate real-life situations in which interpersonal problems originated. Because of the demonstrated efficacy of *in vivo* desensitization, the real-life procedures should be even more effective than in imagery work concerning current significant others or past persons. This may be the single most powerful intervention in the Davanloo technique and it may carry the weight of the variance in prediction of outcome in comparison to other treatment components.

*Hypothesis 3.* If the exposure to the feeling is experienced *"in vivo"* in the patient–therapist relationship, then a greater degree of extinction (i.e., decrease in avoidance behavior) will occur than when the exposure to the feeling is experienced in imaginal exposure to a third person. (I feel like lashing out at you right now, versus "I feel like lashing out at my boss.") Another interesting facet of Davanloo's exposure procedure is its similarity to operant principles. It is a widely recognized phenomenon in the operant methodology that "extinction bursts" or (i.e., a rapid increase in responding) will occur when reinforcement is withdrawn (e.g., Ferster & Skinner, 1957). In a conditioned avoidance paradigm, the avoidant behavior is reinforcing (negatively reinforcing because the feared stimulus is removed by the avoidance). If a fearful stimulus is presented and avoidance is prevented, an increased attempt to avoid will occur. In a similar fashion, Davanloo speaks of an increase in defensive behavior initially following confrontation but a subsequent decrease in responding until "the defense is exhausted." Thus, the patient initially attempts to avoid the unpleasant feeling or thought but subsequently becomes desensitized to it and thus less avoidant. These similarities in responding across very different theoretical applications might serve as a heuristic device for the study of patient responding to exposure conditions.

*Corollary 1.* Patient response to confrontation of defense shows a similar curve (i.e., graph of responding over time) to the extinction burst in operant technology.*

*A dissertation presently underway by Anu Makynen at Columbia University Teacher's College is examining this phenomenon in the Beth Israel data set. Preliminary analyses demonstrate as predicted a sharp rise and then drop in defensive responding.

INTERPRETATION AND CROSS-THEORETICAL COMPARISONS

There are two components of interpretation that will be addressed here: (1) When should interpretation occur? and (2) What are the change factors?

Timing of Interpretation

Short-term dynamic psychotherapy is most similar to traditional psychoanalytic therapy in its interpretive phase, and correct application of interpretation is supposed to be done only after experiencing of affect. Greenson (1967) has warned about the futility of the "inexact interpretation," which is given only on an intellectual basis, without affective awareness. Others have suggested that with certain patients under certain circumstances, it can be more effective to "strike while the iron is cold," or interpret when affect is not present (e.g., Winston, Pinsker, & McCullough, 1986). This variation in patient response to interpretation needs to be empirically delineated.

*Research Question 4.* What are the relative effects of interpretations with and without prior affective experiencing across patients? The dependent variable could be the patient response immediately following the interpretation.

*Change Mechanisms in Interpretation.* Research at the Beth Israel Psychotherapy Research Program (McCullough, Winston, Farber, Porter, Pollack, Laikin, Vingiano, & Trujillo, 1989) has demonstrated that patient affective responding to interpretation is significantly correlated with improvement at outcome. It is unclear, however, what components of interpretation contribute most to the positive patient response and change. Wachtel (1978) has suggested that the interpretation may be experienced as reinforcing on several levels: (1) acceptance by the therapist, (2) the affect is generally experienced with a sense of relief by the patient, and (3) the patient can see new and more adaptive (i.e., more rewarding) alternatives of action (pp. 239–268). Another possibility is that interpretation aids in stimulus generalization by noting similar patterns throughout experience. It seems likely, however, that patients might respond differently to these various components of change. Interpretations might be made more effective if tailored to specific patient needs.

*Research Question 5.* Which factors (e.g., acceptance, relief, alternative action, generalization) contribute to an interpretation being helpful or reinforcing to a patient? Interpretations could be isolated and assessed for affective or defensive responding and then evaluated for components that tend to reliably distinguish the positive or negative patient response. In terms of generalization, interpretations could be assessed for the number of linkages made and the relationship to outcome (e.g., McCullough, Winston, & Vitolo, 1989). Another approach, in the spirit of discovery-oriented research, would be to interview patients in regard to what was seen as helpful in specific interpretations.

In summary, step two shows much similarity to treatments of conditioned avoidance where exposure to a feared or unpleasant stimulus is maintained until anxiety or avoidance subsides except that the focus is on inner experience. Interpretation follows and provides a cognitive rationale which may be reinforcing, relieving, or organizing.

## CONCLUSION

This analysis of STDP has suggested that a blend of cross-theoretical treatment components contribute to behavior change. The specification of components of change has permitted the generation of testable hypotheses and research questions. In step one, the components that were identified as contributing most to therapeutic change are: (1) extensiveness of the behavioral description, (2) degree of focus on consequences, and (3) affective experiencing of consequences. In step two, the components that contribute most to therapeutic change are: (1) type of confrontation, (2) exposure, (3) role of therapist, and (4) interpretation.

Additional hypotheses could be generated to compare the efficacy of step one to step two. If we perform only step one and do not go one to step two, then the patient is left with awareness of the problems, defenses, and maladaptive patterns, but still retains the emotional avoidance that elicits these patterns. Treatment conditions could be established where patients were given step one alone, step two alone, and step one and two in combination to assess which type of patient responded better to which admixture. It seems possible that the more severely disordered patients would demonstrate better response to the more cognitive approach in step one (at least initially), while the more highly functioning patients could benefit the greatest from a predominance of step two "exposure."

These hypotheses and research questions are intended, at best, to only approximate clinical reality. There is no doubt that empirical scrutiny will result in a continual regeneration of more specific and more sophisticated predictions applied to more specific patient groups. This discussion of some common clinical strategies and responses, and the functional relationships among them, has attempted to move toward the operations of basic science. As Hall and Lindzey told us over 30 years ago:

> The student of human behavior should immerse oneself in one theory...wallow in it, revel in it...and think that it is the best possible way to conceive of behavior. Only reserve in one small corner of the mind the reservation that the final crucible for any theory is the world of reality studied under controlled conditions. After the romance is over...then can one set about the cold hard business of investigation...to find out whether the theoretical marriage will withstand the ravages of reality. (1957, p. 602)

### ACKNOWLEDGMENT

I would like to thank George Valliant and Michael Alpert for helpful comments on this chapter and special thanks to Herbert Fensterheim for thought-provoking discussions that greatly helped in the development and refinement of the hypotheses and research questions.

# REFERENCES

Alexander, F., & French, T. M. (1946). *Psychoanalytic therapy, principles and applications.* New York: Ronald Press.

Beck, A. T. (1967). *Depression: Clinical, experimental and theoretical aspects.* New York: Harper & Row.

Boudewyns, P. A., & Shipley, R. H. (1983). Flooding and implosive therapy. In *Direct Therapeutic Exposure in Clinical Practice.* New York: Plenum.

Cautela, J. R. (1977). Covert conditioning: Assumptions and procedures. *Journal of Mental Imagery, 1,* 53–64.

Cautela, J. R., & McCullough, L. (1978). Covert conditioning: A learning theory perspective on imagery. In J. L. Singer & K. S. Pope (Eds.), *The power of the human imagination* (pp. 227–254). New York: Plenum.

Davanloo, H. (1978). *Basic principles and techniques in short-term dynamic psychotherapy.* New York: Spectrum.

Davanloo, H. (1980). *Short-term dynamic psychotherapy.* New York: Jason Aronson Press.

Dollard, J., & Miller, N. E. (1950). *Personality and psychotherapy.* New York: McGraw-Hill.

Fenichel, O. (1945). *The psychoanalytic theory of neurosis.* New York: Norton.

Ferster, C. B., & Skinner, B. F. (1957). *Schedules of reinforcement.* New York: Appleton-Century-Crofts.

Fosha, D. (1988). Restructuring in the treatment of depressive disorders with Davanloo's intensive short-term dynamic psychotherapy. *International Journal of Short-Term Psychotherapy, 3,* 189–212.

Goldfried, M. R. (1980). Toward the delineation of therapeutic change principles. *American Psychologist, 35*(11), 991–99.

Greenson, R. (1967). *The technique and practice of psychoanalysis.* New York: International Universities Press.

Hall, C. S., & Lindzey, G. (1957, 1970). *Theories of personality.* New York: John Wiley.

Havens, L. (1986). *Making contact: Uses of language in psychotherapy.* Cambridge, MA: Harvard University Press.

Klein, M. H., Mathieu-Coughlan, P., & Kiesler, D. (1986). The experiencing scales. In L. Greenberg & W. M. Pinsof (Eds.), *The psychotherapeutic process: A research handbook* (pp. 21–72). New York: Guilford.

McCullough, L. (1990). Psychotherapy interaction coding system. Unpublished manual, Department of Psychiatry, Hospital of the University of Pennsylvania, Philadelphia, PA 19104.

McCullough, L., Winston, A., Farber, B. A., Porter, F., Pollack, J., Laikin, M., Vingiano, W., & Trujillo, M. (1989). The relation of patient–therapist interaction to outcome in brief psychotherapy. Manuscript submitted for publication.

McCullough, L., Winston, A., & Vitolo, A. (1989, June). Effects of content of interpretation on outcome in brief psychotherapy. Society for Psychotherapy Research Annual Conference, Toronto, Canada, June, 1989.

Mitchell, S. A. (1988). *Relational concepts in psychoanalysis: An integration.* Cambridge, MA: Harvard University Press.

Mowrer, O. (1960). *Learning theory and behavior.* New York: Wiley.

Pavlov, I. (1927). *Conditioned reflexes.* London: Oxford University Press.

Prochaska, J. O., & DiClemente, C. C. (1982). Transtheoretical therapy: Toward a more integrative model of change. *Psychotherapy: Theory, Research and Practice, 9*(3), 276–288.

Reynolds, G. S. (1975). *A primer of operant conditioning.* Glenview, IL: Scott, Foresman and Company.

Rice, L. N., & Greenberg, L. S. (1984). *Patterns of change; Intensive analysis of psychotherapy process.* New York: Guilford.

Stampfl, T., & Levis, D. (1967). The essentials of implosive therapy; a learning-theory-based psychodynamic behavioral therapy. *Journal of Abnormal Psychology, 72,* 496–503.

Thoma, H., & Kachele, H. (1988). *Psychoanalytic practice: Principles.* Berlin: Springer-Verlag.

Wachtel, P. (1978). *Psychoanalysis and behavior therapy; Toward an integration.* New York: Basic Books.

Westen, D. (1986). What changes in short-term psychodynamic psychotherapy? *Psychotherapy, 23*(4), 501–512.

Winston, A., McCullough, L., Pollack, J., Laikin, M., Pinsker, H., Nezu, A. M., Flegenheimer, W., & Sadow, J. (1989). The Beth Israel Psychotherapy Research Program: Toward an integration of theory and discovery. *Journal of Eclectic and Integrative Psychotherapy, 8,* 344–356.

Winston, A., Pinsker, H., & McCullough, L. (1986). A review of supportive psychotherapy. *Hospital and Community Psychiatry, 37*(11), 1105–1114.

Wolpe, J. (1969). *The practice of behavior therapy.* New York: Pergamon Press.

# CHAPTER 7

# CHANGE IN
# THE CHANGE AGENTS
## GROWTH IN THE CAPACITY TO HEAL

### SHEILA M. COONERTY

As we focus on the process of change in people, it may be of interest to turn our attention to those whose job it is to be agents of that change. Within the world of psychotherapy, mental health professionals assume this role. The role of therapeutic change agent can be a difficult and demanding one, involving extensive schooling and supervised training in working with patients or clients. The focus of the training is generally on developing the natural interests and beginning skills of would-be therapists into the professional knowledge and expertise necessary to understand human functioning and to help those who suffer as they struggle to change. The training, like the work itself, is arduous and demanding, and the development of the clinician is a complex process.

Early in training, the anxiety produced in those new to the role of change agent leads to a fascination with, and retreat to, the rules of the trade: what is forbidden and what is allowed. This is often accompanied by a subduing of personal beliefs and doubts as well as some shutting off of the therapist's deepest, most vulnerable reactions to this new role. To doubt too much or feel too deeply may endanger the stability of

SHEILA M. COONERTY • Department of Psychology, Long Island University, Forest Hills, New York 11375.

the fledgling clinician within, as well as the development of a sense of professional identity.

Of course, a complete sense of comfort with, and knowledge about, one's identity as a therapist may be years in coming. Personal experience and a review of the literature, however, reveal strong indications that students are ready to move beyond the simple acquisition of technique after passing through an initial phase of training. The following incident in a graduate seminar for Ph.D. psychology students which was held in the summer of 1989 may serve as an example of the process of growth. The seminar focused principally on the works of Sigmund Freud. In this particular class, the students (many were just finishing their first year of training) were stymied by his comment about an interaction with a patient referred to as "Rat Man." The comment, found in Freud's process notes on the case, described the opening of a session and stated simply: "He was hungry and was fed" (Freud, 1908/1989a, p. 341).

Having been trained in a program with a psychoanalytic orientation, the students had been taught that any direct gratification of a patient's needs was to be avoided. Puzzled and expressing both surprise and dismay about this seeming "mistake" by the father of psychoanalysis, students protested that feeding was not to be done. When asked to explain why this action would be so forbidden, the explanation was a simple one: It's the rule. When urged to go further in thinking this rule through, the beginning students were taken aback. Uncomfortable with the implied challenge to their newly acquired beliefs and technical skills, they resisted further involvement, not ready to explore and question what they had just learned.

It was left to the advanced students in the course to go further in sorting out the rationale for such "rules" and to offer possible explanations for Freud's digression. Slowly, as the more experienced students accepted the challenge to explore their assumptions about therapy, they moved away from the rules of the work to a thoughtful discussion of the complexities of the therapeutic relationship. Some were able to relate the experience to personal struggles of their own to sort out what was "right" for a particular patient. The difference in reaction at various levels of experience highlighted a change in students' relationship to their work from their earliest days to later points in their training. It is this implied growth of clinical skill and awareness that will be explored later.

The development of clinicians, like the development of all professionals, begins with intensive training in a particular theoretical approach and with associated skill building. Within several years, most trainees from established graduate schools become at least adequate beginning technicians. But, as the above incident suggests, the next task is more difficult: movement from technician to more fully developed clinician. What helps these change agents change and grow in depth as well as skillfulness? What changes are important to that growth and how might such changes be encouraged?

It could be said that simply becoming an effective technician is enough. After all, in most fields of work, to master the skills of one's trade is the hallmark of success. The ability to attain even higher levels of understanding and involvement in one's performance could be considered the sign only of a gifted master technician. Therefore, a question could be posed as to why any further change is assumed to be necessary in the training of a clinician.

If it is to be successful, however, clinical work involves much more than good technical skills. As Jerome Frank (1961) stated in his book, *Persuasion and Healing,* the ingredients of successful therapeutic experiences extend well beyond technique. In fact, Frank goes further. In summarizing research on the crucial aspects of such success, he identifies other major components of that change. Two essential components are the therapeutic relationship itself and the therapist's belief in the theory and methods involved in his or her type of healing process. Of course, the importance of skillfulness cannot be diminished by this shifting focus. As Orlinsky and Howard (1986) have pointed out in their recent review of psychotherapy research, the measure of skill is more consistently related than any other measure to therapeutic outcome. They found, however, that the quality of the therapeutic alliance and the general contribution of the therapeutic relationship were equally as important to outcome. In turning our attention to these aspects, a continual emphasis on skill development throughout training is assumed. However, it is apparent that the education of the fledgling clinician reaches past mere technique to other aspects of clinical development.

In this chapter, an attempt will be made to focus on the aspects of clinical development separate from skill building itself. In order to do so, we will begin by exploring what areas of growth are crucial to the role of psychotherapist. The literature on development in training will be reviewed with an eye to the process of change. Finally, our attention will turn to the learning process in the middle phase of training, which appears to be a crucial turning point in the development of a clinician.

## THE THERAPEUTIC RELATIONSHIP
## AND THERAPIST CHANGE

If good treatment depends on a well-functioning therapeutic relationship, it would seem that clinicians would necessarily have to extend beyond technique to a deeper personal understanding of how they function in their relationships. To do so would aid in avoiding the misuse of personal power or the playing out of conflicts of which they may be unaware. In addition, it would be expected that one of the tasks involved in developing as a clinician would be that of becoming knowledgeable about, and comfortable with, the peculiarities and demands of one's role in the therapeutic relationship. Farber (1983), in his study of the effects of psychotherapy practice on therapists, asserts that the change brought about is enormous, changing the therapist's view of the world outside of his or her work as well as in it. He states that most changes are positive, involving increased psychological mindedness and self-awareness, as well as the use of one's theory of growth to structure one's view of the self and others. Such increased awareness of one's own personality and the development of the self as a therapeutic tool is challenging, yet essential, and comprises a major element in the beginning therapist's growth and change.

This aspect of therapist change is similar to an important area of concern for the person seeking help in treatment. The patient or client is also expected to develop a greater understanding of his or her own personality and assumptions about roles in relationships. A therapist's capacity to understand and come to terms with his or her own assumptions in relationships may serve as a model for such self-knowledge and growth. In addition, the therapist's own struggle to become aware of previously unknown aspects of the self may also aid in the development of the ability to empathize with this difficult process in patients. As Farber (1983) notes, changes in the therapist parallel changes hoped for in patients: self-awareness, assertiveness, self-disclosure, introspection, reflectivity, and self-reliance.

There are varying opinions as to the role of the therapist in the therapeutic relationship. Within the cognitive and behavioral schools of thought, the therapist's role is generally seen as a straightforward one of expert and collaborator. The therapist has certain skills that the patient needs, and in his or her professional role collaborates with the patient in acquiring those skills. Less emphasis is placed on the role of the therapist's personality or emotional involvement in such interactions, although success is seen as being, at least in part, a function of the therapist's capacity to engender enthusiasm and confidence in those seeking help. Thus, indirectly, the therapeutic relationship and personality of the therapist become important tools in the work.

Within the realm of psychoanalytic theory, the original concern with the person of the analyst was introduced in Freud's (1912/1989b) description of the role of transference in psychoanalysis. Freud's original conception was one of a "neutral" analyst, serving as a blank screen on which patients could transfer intense reactions and feelings that were originally aroused by important early figures. This process was crucial to the development of a transference neurosis and an eventual cure. In his efforts to describe the importance of the transference elements in the therapeutic relationship, Freud assumed a neutral, objective figure in the analyst, who played no role in the patient's perceptions. Thus, all material that the patient presented was intrapsychic, and not interpersonal in origin. The real person of the analyst was seen to be of negligible influence. Efforts to engage the analyst in discussions as to the part reality played in the patient's perceptions were to be the subject of further analysis.

Freud (1924/1958) did introduce the role of the therapist's reactions and feelings in his concept of countertransference. He saw countertransference as a primary impediment to progress in therapy, which Freud asserted could only be removed through a training analysis. More recently, countertransference is seen as "reflecting the totality of the therapist's personal attitudes and reactions to the patient" (Strupp, Butler, & Rosser, 1988, p. 689). There is still disagreement, however, whether countertransference must be "banned" from the therapeutic relationship or understood and used as part of the process of therapy.

Although many analysts practicing today still work from Freud's assumption of the analyst as a blank screen, the influence of interpersonal factors has been a major concern of the interpersonal and relational schools of psychoanalytic thinking. Sullivan (1954) stressed that the clinician functioned as a participant–observer, this term underscoring the inevitability of interpersonal influences on the therapist and patient in the therapeutic encounter. To Sullivan and his followers, the analysis of that interpersonal process was of paramount importance in helping the patient to change. By implication, the therapist must now come to terms with the role that his or her needs, desires, worries, and general personality characteristics play in the process of therapy. Wachtel (1987), in his integrative approach to psychoanalytic and behavior orientations to treatment, agrees. He states that "the therapist's reactions cannot be really eliminated or hidden. They can only be removed as a topic to address explicitly" (p. 186). This leads, Wachtel feels, to an experience of confusion for the patient and an unnecessary mystification of the therapeutic relationship.

To the extent that the clinician accepts the importance of the interpersonal aspects of the therapeutic relationship, a greater awareness of both one's own emotional reactions in relationships and one's stance as therapist is demanded. Accepting the interpersonal aspects of the therapeutic relationship does not free the clinician to react simply without consideration of his or her duties to the process of therapy. Mitchell (1988), in his recent description of relational concepts in psychoanalytic thought, summed up the therapist's challenge in this way:

> The analyst discovers himself a coactor in a passionate drama involving love and hate, sexuality and murder, intrusion and abandonment, victims and executioners...The struggle (for the analyst) is toward a new way of experiencing both himself and the patient...The struggle is to find an authentic voice in which to speak...a voice more fully one's own.... (p. 295)

It is this struggle, the effort to find one's own voice in the therapeutic experience, that brings the clinician past mere technique to the deeper reaches of clinical work. The different views described here lead to a range of uses of the therapeutic relationship in working with the patient. To varying degrees, all imply a knowledge of one's own reactions and a capacity to make use of the self in the treatment relationship.

## THE THERAPIST'S BELIEF SYSTEM AND THERAPIST CHANGE

As to the second of Frank's (1961) major contributions to successful therapy, the therapist's belief system, he argues that the indoctrination process into one theoretical system and a strict belief in that system may be crucial to the therapist's sense of self as healer. If this is so, it could be argued that the students in the Freud seminar described earlier who were unwilling to explore and question the rules should not be encouraged to do so. Accordingly, to encourage an open mind in regard to the therapist's belief system could be considered detrimental to the therapist's experience as healer.

I would argue, however, that such a view would simplify the reality of a therapist's work. The complexity of human existence and of emotional disturbance constantly challenges the clinician's personal and professional belief system. As research into the science and art of therapy proceeds, new concepts and new information must be assimilated into present beliefs. To the extent that a clinician is capable of absorbing and exploring challenges to present beliefs, he or she will be better able to accommodate to the complexities of patients' needs and the growing body of information in the mental health field. A strong and integrated sense of one's own theoretical beliefs is one of a therapist's strongest tools. As Norcross and Prochaska (1982) discovered in their national survey of clinical psychologists, 95% felt that their theoretical orientation strongly influenced how they practiced and was essential to their therapeutic work.

Beginning clinicians are thought to be in need of strict belief systems and standard techniques that aid in adjustment to the demands of their new role as therapist. Yet many, having long mastered the basic skills of the therapeutic process, may receive little encouragement to develop more thoughtful and critical understanding of their work. It may be that the great sense of responsibility in those charged with the training of beginners makes them somewhat fearful of allowing trainees to question and experiment, in the process certainly making some mistakes. Alternatively, the questioning and growth of a newly developing clinician may occasionally be threatening to the teachers or supervisors, challenging closely held beliefs of their own.

Such problems were illustrated in a recent meeting of experienced supervisors discussing their supervision of middle-level trainees. The clinicians found themselves struggling with the awareness that they tend to encourage students to be much more restricted in the use of their own ideas and selves in clinical work than the clinicians were in their own. It is my position that growth in the students' capacity to extend, challenge, and even learn to "play" with their belief system and its attendant rules is an important and often neglected aspect of clinical training. Later in this chapter, some elements of this process will be explored.

## CLINICIAN DEVELOPMENT: CONCEPTS AND RESEARCH

The clinical literature on the training process is extensive, but often characterized by theoretical generalities or anecdotal descriptions (Caligor, 1984; Ekstein & Wallerstein, 1958/1972; Freud, 1971; Rogers, 1957; Stone, 1961). Empirical studies and efforts at describing the specific needs of training development are less frequent. Nevertheless, this decade has shown an increase in such works. A brief review of some of the major articles on training may aid us in our efforts to understand the process of change.

The majority of works exploring the process of therapist training use various theoretical conceptions of the process of human development as a model for clinician development to delineate a framework for training. In addition, nearly all such literature focuses on the supervisory relationship as the major area for therapist or counselor development. This reflects a bias in the field that it is in supervision that the clinician develops his professional identity and skills. As Davis (1987) noted, as far back as 1963, a conference on ideal training programs showed "unanimous agreement that supervised experience was of utmost importance" (p. 71). Few would dispute the importance of such supervised experience in the training process. The training of a mental health professional, however, includes much more than supervision, and it is interesting that the training literature maintains such a narrow focus. Possible extensions of this focus will be explored later in this chapter.

One seminal theoretical article using a developmental focus to understand the training process is that of Hogan (1964). Hogan was among the first to suggest that counselors pass through stages of training, their developmental needs changing as they progress. Hogan postulated four stages of development that accounted for a trainee's progression from an anxious, method-bound, naive stance through a painful process of acquisition of skills and self-discovery to the final stage of independence and creativity in their work. He saw these stages as discrete and progressive and suggested that supervisors must tailor their teaching to the stage at which the trainee is presently functioning. Thus, he focused on a process that was seen to be unfolding from within the trainee as a result of a natural progression in the development of a clinician rather than on a model in which training is dispensed uniformly from the experts. The basic foundations of Hogan's formulation have been widely accepted as a starting point for exploring the process of clinical growth, and initial efforts at establishing construct validity have met with some success (Reising & Daniels, 1983).

Attempts to extend Hogan's concepts further could be organized around two major developmental aspects. Some authors (Lutwak & Hennessy, 1982; Stoltenberg, 1981) chose to focus on the trainee's conceptual development while others (Friedman & Kaslow, 1986; Loganbill, Hardy, & Delworth, 1982) chose to draw an analogy between the development of the trainee and the theories of emotional development in children as outlined by Erikson and Mahler. With the exception of Lutwak and Hennessy, all of these have in common the tendency to view the training process as a series of discrete stages that follow along the lines familiar to us from our present concepts of early human development.

Stoltenberg (1981), in his efforts to extend and explore Hogan's model, stressed the individual's movement through increasingly complex conceptual levels. This implies that the trainee begins at a lower level of conceptual thinking when entering graduate school than he or she is using to function in the rest of life. As the task of clinical work is gradually mastered, conceptual ability increases. Holloway (1987), in a critical analysis of developmental models, questions whether it is in fact reasonable to assume that trainees truly regress in their normal level of conceptual functioning when training begins. She suggests that in fact the trainees may be responding to expectations and demands of their new role, and to the assumption that those who enter training cannot possibly know until they have been trained.

Stoltenberg and Delworth (1988) and Stoltenberg, Pierce, and McNeil (1987) claim that the use of "conceptual level" is simply a metaphorical way of viewing the complex training process, insisting that their major findings involve the reaffirmation of the progressive stage model as well as provide evidence for considerable individual variation in that process. The Stoltenberg *et al.* model, with its belief in progressive growth, is in contrast to Lutwak and Hennessy's (1982) research into the abilities of trainees at different levels of conceptual functioning to grasp the complex demands of empathic participation in the change process. Their research suggests that students who are functioning at a lower cognitive conceptual level do not, in fact, have the capacity to work beyond the level of technician. Such assumptions, of course, lead to the conclusion that a developmental model has its limits. Therefore, more focus on the selection process for training is seen as crucial, an issue of importance that reaches beyond the scope of this chapter.

In contrast to these works are the identity development models, best represented in the literature by Loganbill *et al.* (1982) and, within the psychoanalytic point of view, by Friedman and Kaslow (1986). These authors, while still assuming a developmental model of training, focus not on conceptual level but on the process of developing a sense of identity as a clinician. Both use as a foundation the psychodynamic theories of Mahler and Erikson, and both again see the process as one of distinct hierarchical stages leading to maturation. Loganbill *et al.* emphasize that the developmental process does not stop at training, but continues through the professional life of the clinician. Although they postulate several stages of development, they also suggest that an individual may "cycle and recycle through these various stages at increasingly deeper levels" (1982, p. 17). Many theorists and researchers in the field tend to agree with this concept of increasing depth and complexity in the formation of a clinician.

Friedman and Kaslow (1986), while beginning from the same developmental assumptions, also draw from Winnicott's (1965) work on the development of the infant in stressing the need for "good-enough mothering," or nurturing, of the fledgling clinician. They postulate discrete, hierarchical stages of growth of professional identity, ranging from anxiety and dependency through independence to a capacity for calm and collegiality. Again, the assumption that the supervisor must match the trainee's inherent and changing developmental needs is essential to this model. It should also be noted that both developmental models imply a regressive state in the trainee's identity development. The trainee is assumed to be functioning below normal levels of identity development while in training. In addition, Friedman and Kaslow run the risk of seriously infantalizing trainees in the establishment of a model so heavily focused on the need for an empathically in-tune holding environment and the supervisor as mother and nurturer of an "infant" therapist.

Heppner and Roehlke (1984), acknowledging that evidence of a developmental process in clinical training still remains fragmented, decided to approach the problem from the point of view of the trainees themselves. These authors studied the trainees perceptions of supervisor's helpful behaviors, the influence of the interpersonal process in supervision, and, finally, the trainee's perceptions of important "critical incidents" throughout the supervisory training process. They studied each of these areas at three different stages of training: beginning practicum, advanced practicum, and doctoral internship, finding different perceptions of these at each level. Broadly, the results showed that different skills were seen as highly regarded at different levels of training, an initial interest in skill acquisition being replaced by a search for alternative conceptualizations as students advanced, and an additional interest in personal issues at the most advanced level. In addition, issues viewed by trainees as critical differed at each level of training. The findings were viewed by the authors as giving broad support to the concept of developmental progression in training. Their effort to look at the training process through the eyes of the trainees themselves also allows for a view of the process not laden with preconceptions. As Holloway (1988) cautions, however, it must be remembered that trainees' perceptions of their needs do not necessarily lead to the conclusion that fulfilling those needs will lead to effective clinicians.

Several assumptions of most of these models are of interest in our exploration of the process of change. The concept of discrete and hierarchical stages is in its simplicity appealing and shows some validity in the apparent progression of development shown in the students who were subjects of research. The notion that change happens in such a lockstep fashion, however, is being challenged within the larger field of human development. Holloway's (1987) provocative challenge of an assumption of emotional or cognitive regression in training also remains to be answered. Is there another, reasonable explanation for the observation in these and similar pieces of research that students begin with a dependent, technique-oriented focus and eventually grow into independent clinicians capable of greater complexity and depth? Finally, is the assumption that this progression is inherent in the trainee's development and that it is incumbent on the supervisor to empathically match that development to optimize growth, the best way to conceive of the role of those in charge of training in this supervisory process?

While most research in clinical training tends to lend general validation to the concept of a developmental progression (Heppner & Roehlke, 1984; Reising & Daniels, 1983; Robbins & Jolkovski, 1987; Stoltenberg *et al.*, 1987; Worthington, 1984), there is much doubt and disagreement as to the actual content of stages. Only two stages, the dependency and skill orientation of the beginners and the capacity for complexity and deepened personal involvement of those in the final stage, are generally agreed upon. The middle stages of training appear to be enshrouded in a foggy confusion. If, in fact, we can think of training along the lines of a continuum, it would seem that this middle stage would be the richest with possibilities and offer the most information as to the making of a clinician. It may be that the path of change at this point must respond to the idiosyncratic needs, strengths, and weaknesses of each trainee; therefore, when studied together the results may become clouded.

It is in the afterthoughts, the side comments of these authors and researchers, that one finds the most compelling evidence for the growth of an increasingly complex sense of self, beliefs, and attitudes toward the therapeutic relationship in the later stages of clinical development. Robbins and Jolkovski (1987) note that the most successful clinicians must develop a solid, comprehensive theoretical understanding of their work. Worthington (1984) notes that his evidence supports the notion of "spirals and progressively integrated attempts" (p. 74) at understanding theory and practice. Stoltenberg (1981) finds such individual attempts at integration essential to the process of growth.

The importance of increased self-awareness and involvement and an increasingly complex integration of theory is also seen as being an integral aspect of developing an increasingly complex understanding of the work. Thus, Strupp *et al.* (1988), in their review of training in psychodynamic therapy, conclude from their findings that "routine or mechanical application (of skills) fails to yield competent treatment.... The therapist's contribution to this interpersonal context is an essential component of his or her overall competence" (p. 691). Reising and Daniels (1983) also observed that the doctoral interns, the most advanced group studied, showed a capacity to tolerate doubts while working effectively because of a "deepened self-awareness" (p. 241). The indications are numerous that, as Frank (1961) originally stated, becoming a clinician involves learning more than technique. Rather, becoming a clinician seems to involve a deep and personal involvement in both the concepts of human development and the interpersonal process of psychotherapy.

## TRAINING AND LEARNING
## IN THE INTEGRATIVE PHASE OF DEVELOPMENT

The growth of a clinician, then, is a complex and highly personal process. The majority of those who study this process assume that it unfolds through clinical experience and supervision. The role of academic instruction is rarely mentioned, except as the correct forum for acquiring knowledge of theory and attendant techniques. Yet, both Holloway (1987) and Blocher (1983) make strong cases for considering the instructional model as a tool for aiding students in developing conceptual complexity.

Certainly those in the middle level of training are deeply involved in both the instructional and the experiential aspects of training. It is most likely that they are being deluged with considerable theoretical material while simultaneously struggling with their first clinical work and the attendant supervisory relationship. Future growth of the clinician depends on the degree of success in the struggle to integrate information from these two spheres. If so, those who train these clinicians may need to turn their attention to what can be done to encourage the process. In order to do so, a shift in thinking may be necessary, away from an "unfolding" developmental model in which both student and supervisor passively experience growth to an active, constructive model in which both trainee and expert become emotionally and intellectually involved in the effort of development and integration of clinical capacity.

In a beginning effort to explore the integrative phase of development and its relevance to academic instruction, I have studied the growth process of students in an advanced course in psychotherapy over several years. The resulting impressions must at present be viewed skeptically, due to the limited and informal nature of the data on which they are based. While teaching a course that focused academically on advanced technique and theory in the therapy of children and adolescents, I also attempted to encourage an active curiosity and questioning on the part of the students. They were rarely allowed to use jargon or to take a theoretical stance without encouragement to explore their suppositions. The students found this process both exciting and difficult. Due to their initial anxiety and the accompanying worry about "right and wrong," a system of individual journals was developed. In these weekly journals, students were asked to explore the areas of the class that posed particular difficulty or involved strong personal relevance to them. In addition, students quickly added a third subject matter: they often used the journals to try to integrate what happened in supervision and with patients with what they were learning in graduate school. Although invited to ask any questions of the instructor that they felt necessary, most students preferred to focus on their own thoughts, emotions, and reactions. I read the journals and returned them with comments calculated to encourage personal knowledge and integration as well as to occasionally challenge a student's preconceptions. I will share a few of my observations here, pointing out their relevance to our present knowledge of trainee development.

As noted earlier, of major interest was the students' quick adjustment to the orientation of the course, once given an avenue through which they could process change at their own pace. Most students spontaneously acknowledged the two aspects of the course of prime importance to them: the encouragement to think through their assumptions and integrate theory with practice and the opportunity to get to know their own reactions through the journals. Students also commented that the lack of a place to explore their reactions and gain their own sense of a theoretical stance had left them hesitant in, and critical of, their own ideas and work. It would seem then, that students in this middle phase are concerned with the process of integraton; however, it is also clear that they welcomed a structure that was, in effect, a half-step ahead of them, encouraging and developing their conceptual and integrative capacities.

Not all of the students developed a more complex orientation to therapy and theory during the year-long course. Some remained at the level of skill and information gathering, happily using the journals to ask questions, sort out "right" answers, and explore in more detail the skills they had learned. Whether they were not yet ready to develop a sense of greater complexity or whether they would not be *able* to do so is an unanswered question. It is also possible that the changes seen in most students were simply a natural progression in the students' sense of professional and personal identity, rather than due to the course or experience.

Among the students, several avenues of change stood out. Those students who came to the course with a strong personal orientation to clinical work began the course feeling extremely uncomfortable with theorizing and thinking of themselves as "not intellectual." As they progressed, these students used the journals to tackle their fear of theory first, then found themselves able to apply their new grasp on theory to the comfortable arena of clinical work. The students who were comfortable with intellectual tasks very gradually moved toward personal experience and the work of a clinician. Journals that were filled with hypotheses and conjectures became concrete and increasingly personal as students found themselves reacting to the challenge to make their theorizing useful to their personal development. Some students found themselves engrossed in trying to bring their new career into line with old values, such as political or religious values. Finally, a few students who seemed to be just beginning to move out of the skill-building stage, appeared to move in the spirals noted in the literature, for a while focusing on skills, then theory, then their clinical work, and back again.

It would seem then, that the hypothesis that students move toward increased personal involvement and increased complexity in the integrative stage has some basis. In addition, it would seem that this movement is markedly individual in character and therefore demands some attention to the individual trainee's needs. To the extent that supervisors and professors can recognize and respond to the student's capacity for increased complexity, the confusing picture of the middle stage may be clarified as one in which integration of theory, personal beliefs, and knowledge of oneself as therapist is a task of paramount importance.

While students' needs seem clearer, to us and to them, in the earlier and later phases of training, the integrative needs of this middle stage may be most crucial in their development as clinicians and healers. It appears that the most personal kinds of changes are demanded of students as they move beyond skill acquisition. Through such changes they become healers, clinicians who begin to develop a therapeutic self and who come to see a theory as their own. In addition, the process that will lead to continued growth and development throughout clinical life is being established. Although the middle-level training is only one of several necessary phases of growth and development of clinicians, it appears to be the one in which students first learn to make their profession a part of them. The demands of the profession necessitate much growth and change in the would-be healers also, in ways crucial to their future identity as clinicians.

## SUMMARY

In this chapter, an attempt was made to explore the process of change in the change agents themselves. Although skills are seen as an essential part of the therapeutic process, it is clear that much more than technique is demanded of a clinician. An understanding of the roles of theory and of understanding oneself in the therapeutic relationship are crucial to one's capacity to function effectively as a clinician. The need to develop one's own personal and theoretical stance demands much personal growth and change.

The literature on the process of training primarily focuses on growth in the supervisory process, but has much to offer to our understanding of how beginning clinicians grow and change. That there is gradual growth and development throughout training that leads to different trainee needs at different stages seems to be agreed upon. However, much remains to be explored as to the exact nature of that process as well as to the implications for those in charge of the training process itself.

Although growth and change is evident throughout training, it is the middle phase of training, around the third and fourth year, that appears to have the most potential for allowing the student to engage in the task of personal change and the development of an identity as a clinician. The need to integrate seems to be an essential task and one which begins in the middle phase. It may be that we can look at this phase as a microcosm for professional growth as a whole. In so doing, it may be possible to turn our attentions to developing ways to help promote such growth and change.

The development of a clinician is a complex but important process. To the extent that a clinician develops a strong personal and professional identity, learning to integrate oneself with the work, one becomes increasingly able to function as a healer to another. Beyond technique itself, a clinician must have his or her own personal world, a sense of self as therapist, and a set of theoretical beliefs available. It is during training that the changes happen that allow one to know these aspects of him- or herself. It is also of no small importance that this demanding, sometimes confusing process of growth may help clinicians to better empathize with similar processes with those who come to them for help and healing.

## REFERENCES

Blocher, D. H. (1983). Toward a cognitive developmental approach to counseling supervision. *The Counseling Psychologist, 11*(1), 27–34.

Caligor, L. (1984). Parallel and reciprocal processes in psychoanalytic supervision. *Contemporary Psychoanalysis, 17*, 1–27.

Davis, W. (1987). The learning problem of the student in psychotherapy supervision. *Journal of College Student Psychotherapy, 1*(3), 69–89.

Ekstein, R., & Wallerstein, R. S. (1972). *The teaching and learning of psychotherapy.* New York: International Universities Press. (Original work published in 1958)

Farber, B. (1983). The effects of psychotherapeutic practice on psychotherapists. *Psychotherapy, 20*, 174–181.

Frank, J. (1961). *Persuasion and healing.* New York: Schocker Books.

Freud, A. (1971). (Ed.). The ideal psychoanalytic institute: A utopia. In *The writings of Anna Freud* vol. 7 (pp. 73–93). New York: International Universities Press.

Freud, S. (1958). Future prospects of psychoanalytic psychotherapy. In J. Strachey (Ed.), *The standard edition of the complete works of Sigmund Freud* (vol. 11, pp. 139–151). London: Hogarth. (Original work published in 1924)

Freud, S. (1989a). Notes upon a case of obsessional neurosis ("Rat Man") and process notes for the case history. In P. Gay (Ed.), *The Freud reader* (pp. 309–350). New York: Norton. (Original work published in 1908)

Freud, S. (1989b). Observations on transference love. In P. Gay (Ed.), *The Freud reader* (pp. 378–387). New York: Norton. (Original work published in 1912)

Friedman, D., & Kaslow, N. J. (1986). The development of professional identity in psychotherapists. In F. W. Kaslow (Ed.), *The clinical supervisor* (pp. 29–49). New York: Haworth.

Heppner, P., & Roehlke, H. (1984). Differences among supervisees at different levels of training: Implications for a developmental model of supervision. *Journal of Counseling Psychology, 31*(1), 76–90.

Hogan, R. A. (1964). Issues and approaches in supervision. *Psychotherapy: Theory, Research and Practice, 1*, 1739–1741.

Holloway, E. (1987). Developmental modes of supervision: Is it development? *Professional Psychology: Research and Practice, 18*(3), 209–216.

Holloway, E. (1988). Models of counselor development or training models for supervision? Rejoinder to Stoltenberg and Delworth. *Professional Psychology: Research and Practice, 19*(2), 138–140.

Loganbill, C., Hardy, E., & Delworth, U. (1982). Supervision: A conceptual model. *The Counseling Psychologist, 10*(1), 3–42.

Lutwak, N., & Hennessy, J. (1982). Conceptual systems functioning as a mediating factor in the development of counseling skills. *Journal of Counseling Psychology, 29*(3), 256–260.

Mitchell, S. (1988). *Relational concepts in psychoanalysis: An integration.* Cambridge, MA: Harvard University Press.

Norcross, J. C., & Prochaska, J. O. (1982). A national survey of clinical psychologists: Views on training, career choice, and APA. *The Clinical Psychologist, 35*(1), 3–6.

Orlinsky, D. E., & Howard, K. I. (1986). Process and outcome in psychotherapy. In S. Garfield & A. Bergen (Eds.), *Handbook of psychotherapy and behavior change* (3rd ed., pp. 311–381). New York: Wiley.

Reising, G., & Daniels, M. H. (1983). A study of Hogan's model of counselor development and supervision. *Journal of Counseling Psychology, 3*(2), 235–244.

Robbins, S., & Jolkovski, M. (1987). Managing countertransference feelings: An interactional model using awareness of feeling and theoretical framework. *Journal of Counseling Psychology, 34*(3), 276–282.

Rogers, C. (1957). The necessary and sufficient condition of therapeutic personal change. *Journal of Consulting Psychology, 21*, 95–103.

Stoltenberg, C. (1981). Approaching supervision from a developmental perspective: The counselor complexity model. *Journal of Counseling Psychology, 31*, 63–75.

Stoltenberg, C., & Delworth, U. (1988). Developmental models of supervision: It is development—Response to Holloway. *Professional Psychology: Research and Practice, 19*(2), 134–137.

Stoltenberg, C., Pierce, R., & McNeil, B. (1987). The effects of experience on counselor-trainee needs. *The Clinical Supervisor, 5*(1), 23–32.

Stone, L. (1961). *The psychoanalytic situation: An examination of its development and essential nature.* New York: International Universities Press.

Strupp, H., Butler, S., & Rosser, C. (1988). Training in psychodynamic therapy. *Journal of Consulting and Clinical Psychology, 56*(5), 689–695.

Sullivan, H. S. (1954). *The psychiatric interview.* New York: Norton.

Wachtel, P. L. (1987). *Action and insight.* New York: Guilford.

Winnicott, D. W. (1965). *The maturational processes and the facilitating environment.* New York: International Universities Press.

Worthington, E. (1984). Empirical investigation of supervision of counselors as they gain experience. *Journal of Counseling Psychology, 31*(1), 63–75.

# PART II

# PERSPECTIVES FROM SOCIAL, FAMILY, AND ORGANIZATIONAL PSYCHOLOGY

# CHAPTER 8

# HOW TO CHANGE BEHAVIOR

## ELLIOT ARONSON

### THE IMPORTANCE OF DETAILS

I have been doing experiments in social psychology for about 30 years—
basic research, mostly in the laboratory, trying to figure out how to
influence people, what motivates people to change under controlled
laboratory conditions. My early experience convinced me that, in doing
laboratory experiments, the most important difference between a successful experiment and an unsuccessful experiment is the attention to
detail. The details of the experiment are extremely important. The way
one creates an independent variable, the way one measures the dependent variable, the construction of a sensible scenario that engages the
subject—the details are extraordinarily important.

I spent the second half of my career trying to apply things that I
learned in the laboratory to social problems in the real world. Not simply
to speculate about these problems, but to intervene into problems, to
create, in effect, an independent variable and see if I could produce
changes that were valuable and useful to society. I now consider myself
not simply an experimentalist, but an *interventionist*. Whether I am doing it in the laboratory or in the field, I intervene in someone's life
experience in order to affect a change in his or her behavior.

Accordingly, as an interventionist, I would like to "change" the title
of this volume, at least as it applies to me. Instead of talking about how

ELLIOT ARONSON • Stevenson College, University of California, Santa Cruz, California
95065.

people change, I want to confront the issue a little more directly. This chapter is about how we can induce people to change when their current behavior is either dysfunctional or destructive. I would like to be able to say that there is a formula, a generalization, a statement that in effect says: "here's how you do it." But I cannot. Let me explain. I am doing research in three social problem areas. One involves an attempt to reduce racial prejudice, another involves inducing people to conserve energy, and a third involves inducing people to practice safer sex in the era of the AIDS epidemic. Having worked in those three areas, it would be really nice if I could take what I learned in those three areas and come up with a generalization that makes sense and say, "here's how you get people to change dysfunctional, destructive behavior." I do not have such a formula. The only generalization I have been able to come up with is that there are no general rules. This does not mean that we cannot succeed in inducing change. What it means is that any change agent worth his or her salt has to enter any new situation, any new realm, with very fresh eyes, and not blindly try to apply formulae that have been successful in another realm. One of the things that I have learned is that just like in the laboratory, when you are working on social problems, the details are very, very important.

If you were to ask policy makers, scholars, or the person in the street how one gets people to change, the simple answer, and often the simplistic answer, is education. If only we could inform people about the dangers of certain behavior, then people would do well, be healthy, and so forth. So, if you want people to be less prejudiced, to give up smoking, to give up drugs, all we need is Nancy Reagan on television urging us to "just say no." It is very simple and it is simplistic, and it begs the question. And it has been the single most used strategy in the Reagan administration: to change dysfunctional behavior, "just say no." Social psychologists know better.

## REDUCING PREJUDICE

Let us take prejudice, for example. Social psychologists have known for decades that deep-seated, emotion-laden attitudes are not affected much by commercials, by education, or by programs aimed at promoting tolerance. We know that people with bigoted attitudes will practice selective exposure. They simply will not expose themselves to ideas they do not want to hear. We know that if you force them to hear these messages, no matter how cute and no matter how well-constructed these messages are, most people will find a way to either deny that it applies to them or to distort the message so that they can fit it into their preexisting schema. So, where deep-seated attitudes are involved, education or propaganda alone is almost never effective. Here, direct experience is often more effective. Recall the study Morton Deutsch did many years ago with Mary Ellen Collins (Deutsch & Collins, 1951), indicating that in integrated housing projects people who had negative attitudes toward blacks became much more sympathetic toward them, simply by living in close proximity. While contact often works, more often contact in and of itself does not work. That is, it depends on the nature of the contact. This was brought home very clearly to us during the humane and exciting social experiment known as *Brown v. Board of Education.* Analyses of dozens of desegregated schools done several years afterward by Walter Stephan (1978) revealed that there was nothing like uniform success in terms of reducing prejudice as a result of desegregation. The Supreme Court decision would lead one to expect that desegregation in and of itself would raise the self-esteem of minority students and reduce prejudice. Stephan found that, in a few cases, there *was* a reduction in prejudice and there *was* an increase in self-esteem. But in many cases, there was an *increase* in prejudice and a *reduction* in self-esteem. This was a little confusing and disheartening to those social psychologists who believed that contact would be all that was necessary for a reduction in prejudice.

I became involved in this area several years ago when the schools in the city I was living in—Austin, Texas—were desegregated and riots were breaking out in the school yards. We were called in as social psychologists, as change agents, to see if there was anything we could do to improve the conditions in the schools. The first thing we did was observe the process in the classroom. What we noticed was that the atmosphere in the typical classroom was extremely competitive. We realized, as we continued to observe these classrooms, that it was the context of extreme competition that exists in most American classrooms, coupled with desegregation, that was often producing dysfunctional behavior. Moreover, because in Austin (as in many American cities) the ghetto schools were not equal to the middle-class white schools, the black children who were entering the fifth grade were approximately one year behind their white counterparts in the same class in terms of reading skills. What was happening was the white and black children were integrated and placed into a highly competitive situation in which the blacks were almost guaranteed to lose. What that did was exacerbate the problem by strengthening the stereotypes that already existed. The white children saw the black children as stupid or lazy. Meanwhile, the black children saw the white children as aggressive, standoffish, and so on.

What we did (Aronson, Stephan, Sikes, Blaney, & Snapp, 1978) as interventionists was simply to change the structure of the classroom from a basically competitive one to a cooperative one. We created a special kind of situation that we called the "jigsaw classroom." It is called jigsaw because it is like a jigsaw puzzle, where each child in a small group of say, five, holds one piece of the puzzle—an essential piece of the puzzle. For example, if the assignment is to study the life of Eleanor Roosevelt, we would divide an essay on the life of Eleanor Roosevelt into five paragraphs; one about her girlhood, one about her middle years, and so on, all the way to the end. Each child would be given one paragraph to learn and then they were supposed to share their knowledge with the other children in their group. At the end of this 40-minute sharing session, all of the children were tested on the entire life of Eleanor Roosevelt. Although each child takes his or her own exam, in order to perform well, each child has to pay attention to the other kids in the group. The difference in dynamics between this and the traditional classroom is amazing.

One case that illustrates the impact of the jigsaw classroom is Carlos, a Mexican-American child. Since English is his second language, he hesitates to speak even though he actually knows it pretty well. In the competitive classroom, if a teacher calls on Carlos, this hesitancy is magnified; the pressure is on because teachers do not tend to wait for hesitant students to get their act together. Indeed, one rather startling fact we found through our observations was that it takes, on average, about 1.8 seconds between the time a teacher calls on a student and the time the teacher starts looking for another student when the first is not forthcoming with the answer. Thus, in the competitive classroom, if you cannot come up with the answer in about two seconds, the teacher will move on to someone else who can. Your heart sinks in that situation. If you are a Mexican-American child who hesitates with English, you are finished: after a few incidents like this, the other children begin to conclude that you are stupid. Worse, you will begin to conclude that you are stupid in that context, since it is all relative.

We immediately saw as we observed these classrooms that this is exactly why the self-esteem of many minority kids decreased following desegregation—exactly the opposite of what was predicted. Contact, in and of itself, was not working. Minority children were now placed in a situation where, by social comparison processes, they looked stupid and felt stupid. The nonminority children were very good at heckling the slower kids in this competitive situation. Putting them down made them feel smarter by comparison. In the cooperative situation, however, there was little payoff for such heckling. In the jigsaw classroom, if Carlos is in my group and I am a smart, middle-class child accustomed to getting 100% on my exams, and Carlos starts hemming and hawing, I can begin to write Carlos off as stupid, but this would be terribly self-defeating. In the cooperative situation, if I do not succeed in learning what Carlos knows, I am down to 80% on the upcoming exam. If, in addition to Carlos, there is also a black child in my group who I am also inclined to write off, failing to get what he knows will bring me down to 60% — I have already flunked the exam.

What the children quickly learned was not only to listen to each other, but to give each other the time and space in which to present their material. They also learned to be very good interviewers, like pint-sized versions of Johnny Carson or Barbara Walters, often asking very probing questions designed to pull out of these children the things they knew but were having difficulty articulating. In the course of this process, instead of writing each other off and treating one another with hostility, the kids began to behave in a very encouraging way. Morever, their behavior underwent this rather dramatic change not because somebody told them it was national brotherhood week and time for us to be kind to our darker friends, but rather, because it was in their own self-interest to behave that way. In the course of behaving in their own self-interest, they produced a dynamic of listening, of attentiveness, of helpfulness, which allowed the more hesitant children to come out of their shells and come up with answers.

This produced a spiraling circle because as Carlos began to feel listened to, he was able to produce the material he had inside him, and began to feel better about himself. The other children began to realize that Carlos was not as dumb as they had thought, and began to look at him with increasing admiration, which of course made Carlos feel better and better about himself. Within a few weeks, the entire situation had changed. We found, in these initial experiments, that within six weeks, relative to a control (traditional) classroom, the children in the jigsaw classroom had undergone major reductions in prejudice. Moreover, the minority children demonstrated marked increases in both their self-esteem and letter grades. Measures of liking school revealed that all children liked school better — whites, blacks, and Mexican-Americans alike. Absenteeism, our behavioral measure of liking school, dropped significantly among students in the jigsaw classroom.

This experiment has been replicated with extensions dozens of times over the past 15 years in hundreds of classrooms across the country, as well as in Canada, Japan, and Israel. It has proved to be a highly effective technique. It is important to note, moreover, that the education received by the children is not hampered at all; white, black, and Mexican-American children all cover the amount of material covered in traditional classrooms in the same amount of time. Thus, the enormous gains in self-esteem, grades, and liking school did not come at the price of a sacrifice in curriculum.

## ENERGY CONSERVATION

The second example of changing behavior through intervention brings us out of the classroom and into the American home. In the late 1970s and early 1980s, we began to turn our attention to the energy crisis and how to get people to conserve energy. Not only is conservation important for the environment, it is the safest and most effective way of reducing our dependence on the import of oil from the volatile Middle East. A great many strategists believe that in the event of a major shortfall of Middle East oil, our government will be ready to go to war to protect those sources because our military supplies will run out within months of such a cutoff. The events of the past few months in the Persian gulf suggest that these strategists are correct. Although there has been no major shortfall as of this writing (November, 1990), our armed forces are deployed in Saudi Arabia.

The way the government first approached energy conservation was to spend hundreds of millions of dollars on media advertisement, exhorting people to conserve energy. Many people did conserve in certain ways. Most useful, people bought smaller cars. This was a major step that conserved a great deal of energy. The next step was getting people to conserve energy in their homes. Estimates suggested that although we had the technology to reduce home energy use by 50%, people were not taking advantage of such technology. The question was, and is, "How do you get people to do it?"

One of the things that people did revealed a very interesting aspect of human cognition. The first thing people tried to do to conserve energy in their homes was to run around turning off lights in rooms they were not using because this was a simple—and visible—thing to do. Because a light is such a visible use of energy, it creates the illusion that by turning it off, one is saving a good deal of energy. In fact, leaving lights on for several hours does not use much energy. But most of us were turning off lights and thinking we were saving energy because we were ignorant as to how much energy gets used by which appliances. Since the energy bill does not arrive for up to a month later, we get very poor feedback as to the utility of our energy-saving practices. Cars provide much more useful feedback because one can notice it at the gasoline pump on a day-by-day basis. Thus, people were running around shutting off lights and looking at their energy bill at the end of the month to find very little difference because generally there *was* no noticeable difference in energy consumption. Since what they believed to be effective conservation practices resulted in nothing, people became discouraged. As a result, when the government exhorted us to do something more effective—and more difficult and costly—like spending money for insulation, weather stripping, and the like, people were a little suspicious and did not undertake such measures. Half a billion dollars was spent on advertising for this sort of campaign, which in the end turned out to be a bust.

This really confounded the economists at the Department of Energy. Economists generally have a rational theory of how people behave, assuming perfect rationality in a perfect economic market. They believe that the rising cost of energy will motivate people to invest money that will save energy if we can show them that doing so would be cost-effective. All kinds of advertisements came out showing the cost-effectiveness of insulation and weather stripping. During that period, the cost of energy increased by about 300%, yet the amount of investment that people made in this kind of energy conservation device was only about 15% greater than prior to the price increase. That the increase in conservation investments did not parallel the rise in energy cost confused the economists because their models had predicted otherwise.

Some of the sociologists and social psychologists who were advising the Department of Energy came up with a very interesting notion. They proposed that in order to get people to conserve, the exhortations would have to be on a more individual level. You have to approach people in their own homes and show them how *their* home is wasting energy and what can be done—all on a face-to-face basis. This was really good advice that led Congress to pass the 1978 Energy Conservation Bill, which included a provision for home audits. The local utility company in most states will provide a free home audit if the consumer so requests. They will come to the home and explain exactly what is needed in order to be energy efficient. Actually, these "free" audits were very costly and the utility companies were empowered to raise their rates to fund them. Thus, we pay for the audits whether or not we take advantage of them. Since we are paying for them, we might well ask how effective they were. The home audit program turned out to be a dismal and costly failure. Typically, of the small fraction of the people eligible for home audits who actually requested them, fewer than 20% acted on any of the auditor's recommendations. It was a very costly failure.

At about this time, I was getting interested in energy conservation, and the Pacific Gas and Electric company asked me if I could look into why these home audits were not working. The first thing I did was to pose as a civilian home owner and schedule an audit of my own home. The most striking thing about the person who conducted the audit of my house was that he was like a walking pamphlet. He was not taking full advantage of the fact that it was a face-to-face situation. A pamphlet would say, weather-strip your doors and put a jacket around your water heater. My auditor would say, "See that door? It needs weather stripping. See that water heater? It needs a blanket." And that was it. He stayed for about half an hour and he told me what I needed, but he was literally a walking pamphlet.

Later, I revealed my true identity and got Pacific Gas and Electric to let me walk around with other auditors across the state. I found that my audit was typical—it was not just my experience. Most of the auditors were technically very sound, they were good engineers, they were very well versed, but they were not good social psychologists. After I walked around with the auditors, I came back the next week and interviewed many homeowners that we had just audited, and asked them if they were doing anything, following any of the instructions, and they said, "no." I asked, "Why? You called for the audit, why didn't you..." And they responded: "Well, you know the auditor told me to put in weather stripping, but you know, it's just a little crack under the door..." I realized that people were beginning to talk this way. I began to think about research done by people like Kahnnaman and Tversky and Nisbett and Ross about the human inference process. And it is true, the single most cost-effective thing you can do to conserve energy is weather stripping. It is very cheap, very easy to install, but people were not doing it, even following the exhortation by the auditor because cognitively a little crack under a door does not seem like very much. Insulating attics often is hard for them to conceptualize for most people say, "What good is it going to do and it seems costly and everything like that, so why bother? I've had this home for so many years and it's really not that bad." So, after asking for the audit, they would not follow the instructions.

Our next step was to ask Pacific Gas and Electric if we (Gonzales, Aronson, & Costanzo, 1988) could subject ten of their auditors to a one-day workshop, in which I tried to train them to present this material in a more vivid way. Vividness is a good cognitive ploy to overcome some of these inferential glitches that most of us are subject to. The training was very simple. We conducted a workshop and we rehearsed it several times. It consisted of training auditors to demonstrate the need for conservation devices vividly—how to not be a walking pamphlet.

Thus, we would train them to say things like, "You see that crack under your door? It doesn't look like much, but if you take that crack under your door and that crack up here and that crack up there and you look at that door and that door and if you take all those cracks and add them together and put them in a circle, it would form a circumference about the size of a basketball. Now imagine that someone cut a hole in your living room wall the size of a basketball. You would want to stick some plywood over it, wouldn't you? That's what weather stripping does." We would train the auditor to get the homeowner involved. If the auditor was going up a ladder to inspect attic insulation or crawl space insulation, we would have them get the homeowner up the ladder, too, so that they could see for themselves. We instructed them to say things like, "You see what you have there? That's a naked attic." Phrasing things in such a vivid way makes a big difference. It gives the person the image of a naked kid running around in the winter freezing.

This study had a very nice dependent variable. Pacific Gas and Electric had programs that provided zero interest loans to people to pay for conservation measures (e.g., insulation). These loans were not granted until after the contractor had already done the work. Thus, we had a behavioral dependent variable with Pacific Gas and Electric collecting the data for us. We compared our ten auditors with a matched control group of auditors and found that for our auditors, 60% of the homeowners they visited followed their recommendations—60% just by increasing the vividness and homeowner involvement in the audit. This was three and a half times greater than the national average and just over three times the average of these very same auditors before our workshop.

It turned out, however, that when we compared this experimental group with our matched control group, the results were not nearly as good. The matched control condition showed a 35% effectiveness rate, which was also significantly greater than the national average. An investigation revealed that there had been leakage between the experimental and control group. Some of the auditors who had not taken the workshop had caught the excitement of the auditors who had taken the workshop and had found out what was happening in the more vivid and involving audits. The control auditors were bootlegging it, and even without the workshop they were able to bring up their effectiveness rate to 35%, roughly double their success rate prior to our intervention.

## REDUCING THE SPREAD OF AIDS

The third and final area into which we are beginning to intervene is the AIDS epidemic. Early on, many people thought that AIDS was confined to gay men and intravenous drug users. It now appears to be spreading to the heterosexual population as well, and it is the kind of affliction that is going to rise exponentially and catch many people by surprise. In short, it is an extraordinarily dangerous situation. The Reagan administration was extremely slow to respond, but when it became apparent that the epidemic was spreading, they began to take action. Of course, the first action happened to be Nancy Reagan exhorting people to "just say no." "Just say no" to drugs had become "just say no" to sex.

Surveys of college students across the country revealed that, despite such exhortations, the AIDS epidemic had very little impact on sexual behavior of college students, who are a very vulnerable group because they tend to be sexually active. They tend to practice serial monogamy. That is, they do not sleep with several people at once, but their relationships tend to be short. They go from one partner to another. Despite their vulnerability, they have not altered their sexual behavior much. Interestingly, they are fully aware that AIDS is spreading to the heterosexual population, yet they tend to deny that it poses a threat to them. They are a little scared, but not enough to change their behavior.

We conducted a similar survey on our own campus and obtained the same results. Intensive interviews we conducted showed even less change in sexual behavior because people tended to inflate their responses. When we asked them about condom use, there was a slight inflation in the survey. However, when we interviewed them and said, "Come on, tell the truth," their responses reflected the fact that they do not use condoms as often as indicated by the survey data. This seemed to indicate that there was a good deal of denial occurring in the minds of these students. They were saying, "Okay, it is a problem, we know how serious it is, but certainly none of my friends..." This is the most dangerous way of thinking imaginable.

Since our surveys revealed that these students were unwilling to practice monogamy with a safe partner, the next approach became how to get them to use condoms. Again, there have been attempts to get people to buy and use condoms and these attempts generally fail. Even the condom manufacturers do not know quite how to do it. Condom sales are not up as much as many of us had predicted. This is interesting because the ads for condoms are really quite vivid. For example, a beautiful woman comes on the television screen and says, "I love sex, but I'm not willing to die for it."

It is hard to imagine a more vivid message than that. Vividness worked with regard to energy conservation, so why not here? Our reasoning is that denial occurs. Simply, and rather bluntly put, people do not like to think about death when they are getting ready to have sex. To the extent that condoms become associated with thinking about death, people will prefer to push them out of their thoughts as well. Here again, the details of the phenomenon are extremely important. If we want to know how we might get people to use condoms, then what we must do is ask them why they are not using condoms. Generally, people say that condoms are unromantic, too antiseptic, that they interfere with the natural sequence and flow of sexual behavior. They find using them embarrassing—like going to the bathroom. Having asked these questions and found out why people do not use condoms, we can more ably attack the problem.

Instead of trying to promote condoms by scaring people, which only drives people into denial, what we want to do is instigate them to positive action. Thus, our approach will focus on trying to eroticize the condom. Our goal is to get people to see that using a condom does not have to be unromantic, that it can actually enhance sexuality. We spent an entire summer making three videotapes. One is a straight lecture by a physician in a white coat, talking about the danger of AIDS. This is the information condition. The second tape has the same person delivering the same message, but he gradually becomes a voice-over to some rather horrifying pictures of people in the last stages of AIDS. This is the high fear condition. We think viewing this tape will arouse denial rather than problem-solving behavior. The third tape, for the erotic condition, shows a very attractive couple having sex, during which the woman puts the condom on the man. Incidentally, this is all very tastefully done—it would probably receive an R rating because most of what happens takes place under the sheets. The condom is featured in a very sensual way, in a way where it is part of the flow of sexuality. Our prediction is that by making the condom seem attractive, we will have much more impact on condom use than a simple information manipulation—and certainly more then the fear manipulation.

To summarize, there are no generalizations. The only generalization I can offer is that details are very important. When I enter a new situation, my first thought is, "Vividness worked for energy conservation, how can I do a vivid presentation?" But they have already done vivid presentations that failed, so my second thought must be toward the details. You cannot fight last year's war.

ACKNOWLEDGMENTS

I never write out my speeches; thus, this chapter had to be reconstructed from a rather casual oral presentation. I am indebted to Joshua Aronson for his help in converting these remarks into a coherent chapter.

# REFERENCES

Aronson, E., Stephan, W., Sikes, J., Blaney, N., & Snapp, M. (1978). *The jigsaw classroom*. Beverly Hills, CA: Sage.

Deutsch, M., & Collins, M. E. (1951). Interracial housing: A psychological evaluation of a social experiment. Minneapolis: University of Minnesota Press.

Gonzales, M., Aronson, E., & Costanzo, M. (1988). Using social cognition and persuasion to promote energy conservation: A quasi-experiment. *Journal of Applied Social Psychology, 18*, 1049–1066.

Stephan, W. (1978). School desegregation: An evaluation of predictions made in *Brown v. Board of Education. Psychological Bulletin, 85*(2), 217–238.

CHAPTER 9

# CHANGING ATTITUDES AND REDUCING TENSIONS BETWEEN PEOPLE

## OTTO KLINEBERG

I wonder how much we have learned since 1947 when Herbert Hyman and a colleague of his, Sheatsley, wrote an article on why information campaigns fail. Something very much like that was written about the same time by Daniel Katz (1946). How much have we learned since those days? How successful have we been in answering those questions?

I am always reminded when I talk or hear about the whole area of attitude change of the old story of a man who in every other way was perfectly normal except that he thought he was dead. Well, people tried everything to persuade him that he was not dead, but were not successful. And finally the doctor, a general practitioner, who had him under his care said, "Well, look, do dead men bleed?" And he said, "No, dead men don't bleed." And the doctor took his scalpel, made a little cut in the hand of the patient and said, "Well, look at that!" And he looked at it and he said, "By golly. By golly. Dead men do bleed."

That story left an imprint on me because I think that in a way it fits with the position taken at that time by Hyman and Sheatsley on the one hand and Katz on the other that you do find ways of protecting your

OTTO KLINEBERG • Professor Emeritus, Department of Psychology, Columbia University, New York, New York 10022.

views unless the experience is something serious and disturbing, and then you have to do some kind of reorganization, such as deciding that you are indeed dead but can bleed, or give up the view that is incompatible with other views that are widely held or becoming widely accepted. All of us who have been concerned with relations between human beings have done our best to persuade people to have healthier and happier relations with other groups but often wonder how successful we have been and can we be more successful if we take more things into consideration. What are those other things that we need to take into consideration?

I myself have worked at the task of changing attitudes, particularly in the area that has been my personal concern—the problem of race, race relations, and racial attitudes—which means, of course, that one has to get into the whole area of stereotypes and that of classification of racial groups and so on. And there are many other areas that can be pertinent, it seems to me, in changing attitudes, and yet we have not as yet succeeded very markedly in bringing about such changes. I keep on wondering what we still need to know and do, and whether we still need to do research on this task in order to be able to be a little more successful in changing attitudes in a more positive direction. There is no doubt in my mind that the material is there, but how do we get past the view that dead men do bleed and how can we affect people in the area that Morton Deutsch is expert in—the field of international contacts and relations, the relationship between the various subpopulations within a country, and how to improve the character of these contacts and their relations.

I leave that at the moment because I do not have any answers, although I do have some thoughts about it. I do feel that in the racial field there are a number of materials that if they were more widely disseminated could make a difference. Yet I do not have a great deal of evidence to prove that. I do know, for example, that if we look at what anthropologists, particularly physical anthropologists, have done with racial differences and racial classifications, we who are perhaps at a certain distance from that material can be very greatly affected by certain things that are happening, that have happened, over the years in the area of anthropological approaches to race. I mention one or two factors. One of them is that different anthropologists come out with entirely different and mutually contradictory classifications of race. That in itself should be enough to instill a certain amount of doubt about how seriously we should take race. If one person divides people according to the shape of their skull, whether they are dolichocephalic or brachycephalic or mesocephalic, or describes races according to the skin color, what happens is that if you divide people according to the color of their skin, you come out with groups of people with different head shapes but of the same skin color, whereas if you divide them according to the shape of the head, you have to include the blond Scandinavians and the much darker Africans who are predominately dolichocephalic in both cases.

Here we have, in my judgment, material that if more widely understood, and more widely accepted, should make a very real difference in the whole character of racial attitudes. And yet we have never done anything that would amount to an exploitation of that material, with the fact in mind that we have all been taking race too seriously as a means of dividing humankind. There are many other ways. For example, there was a great deal of literature at one time on dividing races according to blood groups. It turned out there, too, there was overlapping of blood groups from one area to another. There were blood groups that changed as a result of mixtures and one got results again that went counter to the classification according to skin color on the one hand or shape of the head on the other. Yet we have no way of deciding which is a correct way of dividing groups. There are no biological implications or consequences of any one of these classifications. There is just the difference in the way of looking at groups and the difficulty of deciding which way is more helpful or more accurate.

I did a little of what the French call a "stage," that is, a period of observation and reading and listening to lectures in Rome at a laboratory of a professor of anthropology, Giuseppe Sergi, a very distinguished Roman/Italian expert in race relations and race differences. He was concerned with the shape of the head. He felt sure that that was the most important and the only really sound way because skin color changes depending on how much sun exposure one has, whereas shape of the head will not change in different amounts of sunlight. Therefore, the shape of the head was for him more important and much more realistic as a means of dividing groups than basing the classification on skin color or other related factors.

Disseminating anthropological material has never been tried, as far as I know, as a means of changing people's attitudes toward race. We have much material that would be very interesting to experiment with as a means of doing some of the things Deutsch (1973) has written about; namely, changing attitudes in a fundamentally important area, the area that happens to be the one in which I have spent most of my academic life. But I am sure that you will agree that does not take away the value of working in that area, because so much still remains to be done.

That whole field has led to some very fascinating research that I have felt deserves much more widespread dissemination. I mention one study that perhaps is not well known. It is research done at McGill

University by my friend and colleague, Wallace Lambert (1968). The study that I want to describe is to me a fascinating one in the area of the judgment of people according to certain stereotypes, in this case from the sound of the voice. What Lambert did in Montreal was to have a group of people speak in both French and English over a loudspeaker. Their talks were then recorded, talking about the same subjects, with the same words used, again both in English and French. Unbeknown to the group of people chosen to make the judgments, some of the recordings were made by the same individual; in other words, the same voice, at one time speaking English and the other time French. Even though the instructions were to judge personality characteristics on the basis of the *sound* of the voice, the personality judgments varied when the person was speaking English and when that same person was speaking with the same voice in French. Lambert's study was again a very fundamental and clear demonstration of the way in which stereotypes may determine our attitudes. Therefore it could have been of greater importance, I think, in terms of, if not destroying, at least casting doubt upon stereotypic judgments. In this case people did not realize how much they were basing their judgment not on the sound of the voice but on the fact that the subjects were speaking one or the other of the two languages.

In summary, although information may be useful, we know that information alone rarely changes attitudes, people's views of the world, or their relationships with other people.

## REFERENCES

Deutsch, M. (1973). *The resolution of conflict: Construction and destructive processes.* New Haven: Yale University Press.
Hyman, H. H., & Sheatsley, P. B. (1947). Some reasons why information campaigns fail. *Public Opinion Quarterly, 11,* 412–423.
Katz, D. (1946). The interpretation of survey findings. *Journal of Social Issues, 2,* 33–34.
Lambert, W. E. (1968). The role of language and accent variations in person perception. *Psychologia Wychowawcza, 11,* 1–17.

# CHAPTER 10

# THE TWO FACES OF CHANGE
## PROGRESSION AND REGRESSION

SAM KIRSCHNER AND DIANA ADILE KIRSCHNER

## PROGRESSIVE ABREACTIVE REGRESSION

How do people change? Is it a simple linear process, an easy evolution, from beginning state A, intervening variable or stimulus B, to resulting C? Or is the process more complex and nonlinear? Clinical theory and practice, supported by empirical evidence, indicate that the latter is true and that indeed human growth and evolution follow a complex rhythmic pattern. This chapter will examine a developmental model of the growth pattern and the implications of this paradigm for psychotherapy.

In psychoanalytic thought, we find the notion of change through regression in the analytic process. The patient regresses on the analytic couch, accessing primary process thought, thereby making the repressed unconscious material conscious. The freeing of psychological energy leads to the strengthening and promoting of ego functioning. Various psychoanalytic theorists have offered variations on this theme of regression leading to progression. For example, Kris (1951) and Bellak (1958) have described regression in the service of the ego as a reduction in the cognitive and selective functions of the ego for the facilitation of the other synthetic ego functions. Kris (1951) specifically argued that in

SAM KIRSCHNER AND DIANA ADILE KIRSCHNER • Private Practice, Gwynedd Valley, Pennsylvania 19437.

the genesis of the creative arts there is a regression to primary process thought in the service of enhanced progressive functioning.

The regress to progress theme as an explanation for how people can change also appears in the literature on human development. For example, Erik Erikson (1950), in his seminal work, *Childhood and Society*, observed that young children may, at times, regress to more babyish modes of behavior. In one vivid scene, he described how Ann, a 4-year-old, became all mouth and thumb in a very "oral" display. Then, she quickly became enlivened, grabbing and kicking her doll and grasping a play car that was lying in the consulting room. In Erikson's view, children oscillate between what he called an "avenue of regression" that leads inward and a progressive avenue that leads outward toward initiative.

Margaret Mahler's (1980) description of the subphases of separation/individuation in early childhood carries the regress to progress concept out of the exclusively intrapsychic arena into the interpersonal domain. According to Mahler (1980), in the rapprochement subphase, the child ventures out to explore and master the world followed by periodic retreats into the reassuring arms of the mothering one. These retreats occur because the toddler experiences anxiety when separating from the secure base of the parent. In order for the child to venture forward again with diminished conflict, he or she needs to be emotionally anchored and held by the availability of mother's dependable nurturance and by the "go" signals he or she gets with regard to further explorations of the world. As the child separates, he or she tends to introject the loving mothering one. When all goes well, there is the development of object constancy—an omnipresent internalized image of the caring parent to whom the child can refer throughout life.

Rapprochement theory can be seen as not only expanding our view of change beyond the intrapsychic into the interpersonal arena, but also expanding our linear view of the change process, that is, regress to progress, to a more dialectical position. In the dialectical view of Mahler, an ongoing oscillation occurs between regression and progression in which progression outward is followed by a regression inward and toward a significant other (mother), which in turn is followed by further progression out to the world. While Mahler, Pine, and Bergman (1975) developed their model based on observations of young children, it is our contention that their dialectical model can be applied to human development throughout the life cycle. Specifically, we are positing that change occurs through a very active rapprochement process with different significant others throughout life.

In our view, the mother is simply the first (and most profound) figure in a series of significant others. The emotional base is first enlarged to include father. Then in later childhood and adolescence, selected extended family members and teachers who have a special affinity for the child may serve as rapprochement figures. In adulthood, mentors, therapists, paramours, and finally and most importantly a spouse (in these days several spouses) become the key people. These significant others are called on to help us evolve in the two major challenges of life: *doing* and *being*.

When we talk about change we mean growth in these two major arenas. In terms of doing, or mastery, we pursue higher and higher levels of behavioral competence as spouses or lovers, as parents, or in our own creative endeavors in work. In terms of being, we pursue the reduction of separation anxiety and internal conflict and the transformation of the internal object world in the direction of constancy and benevolence, a healthier sense of gender identification, and resolution of Oedipal or other triangulation issues.

Returning, then, to our discussion of progression and regression, we can say that the progressive trend represents our drive for mastery and self-actualization while the regressive trend represents our needs for belongingness and attachment. How are these two trends related? And how do they oscillate with each other?

Natural self-actualization drives arising out of curiosity or a desire for mastery lead to a twofold risk of loss: the actual risk of loss of the significant other and the experienced fear of loss at the intrapsychic level. For example, in marriage there is a fear of outgrowing one's mate and thereby losing the relationship. This raises the specter of abandonment. And abandonment, as Bowlby (1973) has noted, is our most basic terror—a fate that feels like impending death.

The risk of abandonment occurs because the progressively developing spouse is breaching the homeostatic contract that couples unconsciously make with each other. These contracts involve the assumption of complementary roles and personality assignments that are based on interlocking projective identificatory processes. The spouses project undesirable aspects of self on to the other, who owns and enacts these traits. For example, we have the "parent" and the "child," the "crazy" one and the "sane" one, or the "weak" spouse and the "strong, competent" one. Each spouse functions in role so as to protect the other's defensive structure. So, for example, the "crazy" wife will help to maintain her husband's sense of saneness. If she says, in the middle of a marital disagreement, "I'm not crazy—I know what's really going on," it implies that her husband *is* crazy. Thus, when a spouse attempts to move out of the assigned identity and role, via new progressive behaviors, he or she may puncture the other's defensive shell, such that the spouse's deeper fears and anxieties are closer to the surface. If the partner responds by rejecting the other, fears of "outgrowing" the partner and thus losing the relationship will flare up. Such an unsuccessful rapprochement experience may ultimately lead to the progressing spouse choosing an alternate figure such as a lover, mentor, or therapist with whom to regress and the marriage may fail.

Then there is the experienced fear of loss played out at the intrapsychic level. In the progressive trend, adults experience anxiety not only in relation to current love relationships, but also because of shifts in their own identities. As object relations theorists have noted, our identity is in ongoing dynamic exchange with internalized parental models of who, and what, we are. Fairbairn (1952) has described how sometimes these models become like internal saboteurs that interfere with our drive for growth and accomplishment. When we go beyond or attempt to go beyond what we have learned is possible for us, these saboteurs clamor for attention and loyalty. We then have conflicts between our longings to go farther and our restrictive programming for these old voices.

For example, a woman who was depressed entered therapy with the first author saying that she wanted to go back to school to finish her B.A. When Sam asked her what was stopping her, she said "I hear my father saying: You stupid girl." That woman was threatening to detach from her internal saboteur. Furthermore, she was afraid of how her husband would react to her resuming her education. When she finally registered at college, she reported feeling terrified and more clingy with her husband. In order to satisfy her need for attachment, she needed reassuring contact with a new rapprochement figure, either her husband or therapist or both.

In therapy clients can abreact the anxiety and old, stored emotions; explore the internal saboteurs' demands and detach from them. They can be psychologically soothed and comforted. The therapist, as the new, healthier rapprochement figure, can then give clients the necessary "go" signals, as well as encouragement and guidance that are needed to pursue their dreams. They can then internalize the new helpful aspects of the therapist, thereby modifying their own internal object world so that it is more supportive and validating.

This cycle of progression followed by a reexperience of old fears, doubts, separation anxiety, and a need for regressive contact with a rapprochement figure that in turn is followed by further progress in the world of mastery has been called progressive abreactive regression (PAR). The process of PAR was first described by Arthur Stein (1980) in his brief essay on Comprehensive Family Therapy. We believe along with Stein that the PAR process occurs not only in successful therapy but also in the individual and the family's development (Kirschner & Kirschner, 1986).

## PROGRESSIVE ABREACTIVE REGRESSION IN FAMILY LIFE

Throughout the family life cycle, PAR processes tug at all of the family members. In raising children, for example, parents and children experience the effects of the PAR process whenever there is growth and maturation, when a child goes to school for the first time, starts dating, works, leaves home for college, or marries, there is a countervailing regressive trend that permeates family life. Adolescence, for example, is a time in the family life cycle in which powerful PAR forces shape family process. During adolescence, the child is both moving out of the family to establish a new identity and regressing back in, to touch base and reconnect. And as we all know, the oscillations of the PAR process during this phase of the life cycle tend to be characterized at times by great volatility. During this phase, one or both of the parents will regress and reexperience aspects of their own separation from their families of origin, which may either help or hinder the separation with their children. In a normal or healthy family, the spouses can work through this material with each other and this facilitates the leaving home experience. In a dysfunctional family, one or both spouses may react to the separation process through projective identification and thereby experience and treat the child as bad, defective, crazy, and so forth. This type of family interaction, while serving to assuage the parents' abandonment fears, will also effectively cripple the child so that he or she cannot leave home successfully with a positive sense of self. The entire family then becomes stuck in the PAR cycle without the normal progressive movement forward.

Progressive abreactive regression not only affects the parenting relationships but impacts on the marriage. In couples, PAR occurs, for example, when a spouse is given greater responsibilities or challenges at work. The person will usually experience anxiety and self-doubt in connection with this progressive advance, and old fears and insecurities may erupt in consciousness. As the regression process unfolds, the spouse may become depressed, withdrawn, or argumentative. This can lead to blaming, pathologizing, or other conflictual behaviors in the couple. In a healthier marriage, the partner may be disappointed, surprised, and upset by this turn of events but nonetheless is committed to overcoming the problem and coming through for the regressed spouse. Under these circumstances, the helping partner will encourage the regressed spouse to turn to him or her for reassurance and validation. As part of successful PAR in marriage, the spouse gives loving contact in a holding environment and also supports the new movements toward separation/individuation. The regressed partner comes into contact with the reality of a benevolent spouse and can better work through the negative cognitions and debilitating anxieties that may impede successful functioning in the new situation.

In order to serve as a secure and knowledgeable rapprochement figure for the mate, the helping one must deepen his or her emotional resonance and understanding of the spouse. The helping one must also provide an atmosphere of acceptance so that conflicts and distortions including perceptions of the spouse's lack of support can be discussed and examined. Physical contact that is reassuring is often helpful for facilitating the working through process with the regressed partner. At times, this may lead to a more playful or sexual encounter.

Against the backdrop of the potential progressive change and concomitant risk of loss, attentiveness and appreciation of each other is at a height. The spouses can achieve new levels of positive symbiosis. The parental figure can then help to reprogram and enlarge the other's self-definition. And in these interchanges, he or she can also insist that the spouse meet the new level of personal challenge.

When there is success, the partners share the mastery euphoria of real teammates in a true win–win fashion. The regressed partner feels grateful and grows in self-esteem and competence while the helping spouse experiences a sense of potency and benevolence that leads to a greater feeling of deservedness. The stage is set for a role reversal. The helping spouse's increased esteem fosters the seeking of new opportunities for personal success and fulfillment, which in turn, leads to anxiety and a need for rapprochement. The tables can be successfully turned and the spouses can reverse their respective roles. We must emphasize that reciprocity is present in healthier relationships, in contrast with pathological marriages in which the spouses are locked into rigid contractual roles, with one person always being the helper and the other being the regressed one.

In healthier marriages, the cycle of positive reciprocity takes over with time and both spouses actively assist each other to achieve greater accomplishments and deeper self-understanding (Kirschner & Kirschner, 1990). They help each other deal with the stress and psychological pain that are inherent in daily life. We have come, then, to the telos, or goal, of the PAR process. The mates become increasingly more flexible and competent behaviorally as individuals and at the same time deepen their attachment to each other. At the intrapsychic level each spouse internalizes the other and develops a more positive and powerful sense of self. The positive reciprocity in their marriage enhances their win–win teamwork as spouses, parents, and in the outside world.

## CLINICAL IMPLICATIONS

In our view, psychotherapy should address both doing and being, facilitating the natural progressive and regressive trends inherent in the PAR cycle. And yet, as we survey the field, we would see that most schools of thought deal with only one or the other growth trend. For example, behavioral and cognitive therapies or structural–strategic family therapies focus almost exclusively on the progressive domain. Whether aiming at altering behavior, cognitions, or family interactions, these modalities do not usually attend to the regressive trend. Psychodynamic therapies, on the other hand, do attend to the regressive arena but generally fail to address the progressive trend. In short, then, we need to develop more integrated approaches to therapy, which address both the progressive and regressive aspects of the PAR cycle.

It also follows from our model that whenever children, married individuals, or couples present with problems, that using both family systems and psychodynamic approaches together could potentiate growth. Each modality would enhance the other in a constructive synergistic fashion. For example, when working with a family, conjoint sessions are useful at the outset of treatment for assessing and restructuring family behavioral patterns in the here and now. In these sessions the practitioner can also prescribe tasks, initiate courtship behavior in the couple, and enhance communication and listening skills of family members. While conjoint sessions tend to focus more on the progressive trend, during moments of painful abreaction, the therapist may model appropriate rapprochement behaviors for the parents vis-à-vis the children and each other.

As a result of these interventions, the couple will develop new and more functional marital and parenting behaviors and the children's problems, if any, will improve. As these positive changes occur in the family, a concomitant regressive trend will naturally come to the foreground. For example, when the spouses start collaborating more closely about the children, they each will usually experience increased anxiety and remember painful memories of their own childhoods. This state of internal conflict and tension creates the need and enhances motivation for individual psychodynamic work.

If the therapist is aware of these internal conflicts, and indicates availability for rapprochement, the spouses will turn to him or her for psychodynamic work. The spouses usually experience a positive transference toward the therapist, endowing him or her with parental authority. Through the transference the spouses can regress in relation to the therapist, who then becomes a rapprochement figure.

In the individual sessions, the therapist can provide a holding environment, with unconditional positive regard, empathy, and analytic interpretation. Over time, these sessions build basic trust and promote the introjection of an imago of the therapist as a constant, affirming, internal object. This leads to increased hope and motivation for change in work, parenting, and marital relating. Thus, there is less resistance when tasks and other prescriptions for behavioral change are made by the therapist in the family sessions. In this way, the progress of family therapy work supports and augments the psychodynamic work, and vice versa. It all works together.

In our book, *Comprehensive Family Therapy* (Kirschner & Kirschner, 1986), we describe a model in which the therapist flexibly and rhythmically utilizes both of these modalities, which are called the progressive and regressive strategies. The format of treatment combines individual, marital, and family sessions. The goal of the therapy is to remediate presenting symptoms while actualizing the latent tendency in the couple to be rapprochement figures for one another. In this way, spouses become healing and empowering for each other and their children.

## CASE EXAMPLE

A case example will illustrate how the progressive and regressive strategies work together in Comprehensive Family Therapy. A woman, whom we will call Mrs. Betty Johnson, a housewife in her mid-forties, called the second author (DAK) regarding her 15-year-old daughter, Beth. She complained that Beth was "out to all hours of the night" with a seedy young man from the wrong side of the tracks. She suspected that they were using drugs. The therapist asked to meet with the whole family, which included Al and Betty Johnson, Beth, and their son Mark, aged 12. During the family meetings the therapist observed that Mrs. Johnson maintained a distant posture with Beth, while Mr. Johnson seemed to have a close and somewhat sexually charged relationship with her. On the other hand, Mark appeared to have just the reverse pattern of the parental relating, with Mom more aligned with him. The Johnsons, who had been married for about 20 years, seemed to have a rather distant relationship. Mr. Johnson, a very successful lawyer, appeared to be highly invested in his work to the exclusion of the family.

In the opening progressive strategy, the practitioner began to restructure the family-rearing patterns by asking Betty to be more involved with Beth and Al to spend more time with Mark. She asked the parents to agree to a curfew and disciplinary measures for Beth if she missed curfew. In those first few family sessions, Diana asked Betty to express her concern and love directly to Beth, and asked her to be in charge of Beth's curfew enforcement. The therapist also asked Mr. Johnson to spend 15 minutes playing baseball every other day with Mark, who was a baseball fan. Mr. and Mrs. Johnson agreed to follow these suggestions.

After three weeks they were moderately successful; the therapist met with the spouses alone and they reported that Beth had come home on time more often than not. However, Mrs. Johnson reported that she had had two explosive fights with Beth. She seemed agitated, pained, and distressed. In the session, Mrs. Johnson burst into tears and said she felt anxious, weak, and inept in dealing with Beth. The therapist began to elicit more historical material by asking Mrs. Johnson about her relationship with her own mother. She described her mother as a depressed, weak, and ineffectual woman who had given her little attention or affection. While Mr. Johnson observed, Diana assisted Mrs. Johnson in the exploration of the memories of her own lost adolescence—a period in which she herself had acted out and was emotionally adrift while her own mother wrung her hands ineffectually. During Mrs. Johnson's emotional outpouring, the therapist acted as a rapprochement figure, by comforting her and empathizing with her pain. Afterward, she reassured Betty that she could learn to handle Beth. The therapist then contracted for individual sessions with Mrs. Johnson to work further on this psychodynamic material. During the couple's sessions, the therapist also asked Al to talk about his adolescence. He reported that he had felt neglected because his entire family was in constant emotional turmoil and conflict over problems with his older sister. Mrs. Johnson reported that he had always felt unwanted. At that point, the therapist asked Mr. Johnson if he would also like to schedule individual sessions to deal with his personal issues. He agreed. The treatment format then became one individual treatment session with each spouse each month for the regressive psychodynamic work and two sessions per month with the family or couple for the progressive family systems work.

In the individual sessions the Johnsons processed the awkward and uncomfortable feelings each of them felt with Beth. Mr. Johnson felt afraid to discipline Beth as he feared he would overdo it and she would react by running away. He was able to relate this to experiences he had growing up when his own older sister, suffering repeated clashes with their parents, wound up running off with her boyfriend. He began to look at the identification he had felt with his own father, who was alternately conflictual or seductive with his older sister. Mrs. Johnson continued to examine her feelings of impotence and weakness and to deal with the profound sense of abandonment she had felt as a child in relation to her mother. These individual psychodynamic sessions freed the parents' internal energies so that they each could be stronger in dealing with Beth.

In the family sessions, the therapist encouraged and guided the parents in their efforts with Beth and reiterated the importance of their new positions with the children. Role-playing was used to show healthier options in their child-rearing. The therapist also began to address the emptiness and distance in the marriage that had led to Beth's oedipal win with father and Mark's oedipal win with mother. To remedy this, the couple was asked to court and date each other. This progressive movement brought up a host of longings, fears, and projective distortions, all grist for the psychodynamic mill.

At the end of one year, Beth had broken up with her boyfriend and was busy taking voice lessons after school along with her mother. Mark was closer to his father. Both parents had developed in self-esteem, and Betty had decided to go back to school to complete a bachelor's degree. Al, on the other hand, was spending more time at home and emotionally supporting his wife's return to college. The psychodynamic work had augmented the family systems work and vice versa. The spouses continued in treatment to improve their sexual and romantic life together.

In this chapter we have attempted to delineate and explain two equal but opposite trends in the natural human growth process. We have explored two dialectical facets of the process: progressive expansion of mastery in the world in constructive oscillation with a deepening regression leading to intimacy in love relationships. Understanding this oscillation opens avenues for the integration of psychodynamic and family systems work. This, we hope, will further our search for treatment approaches that are coherent and maximally effective.

## REFERENCES

Bellak, L. (1958). Creativity: Some random notes to a systematic consideration. *Journal of Projective Techniques, 22*, 363–380.
Bowlby, J. (1973). *Separation.* New York: Basic Books.

Erikson, E. (1950). *Childhood and society.* New York: Norton.

Fairbairn, W. R. D. (1952). *An object relations theory of the personality.* New York: Basic Books.

Kirschner, D. A., & Kirschner, S. (1986). *Comprehensive family therapy.* New York: Brunner/ Mazel.

Kirschner, D. A., & Kirschner, S. (1990). Couples therapy: A new look. *Journal of Couples Therapy, 1,* 91–100.

Kris, E. (1951). On preconscious mental processes. In D. Rappaport (Ed.), *Organization and pathology of thought* (pp. 474–493). New York: Columbia University Press.

Mahler, M. (1980). On the first three subphases of the separation–individuation process. *International Journal of Psycho-Analysis, 53,* 333–338.

Mahler, M., Pine, F., & Bergman, A. (1975). *The psychological birth of the human infant: Symbiosis and individuation.* New York: Basic Books.

Stein, A. (1980). Comprehensive family therapy. In R. Herink (Ed.), *The psychotherapy handbook* (pp. 204–207). New York: New American Library.

# Chapter 11

# INDIVIDUAL CHANGE IN ORGANIZATIONAL SETTINGS

## Barbara Benedict Bunker and Jacqueline J. DeLisle

The rapid pace of technological change, the changing demographics of the American work force, and the competitive threat that results from a global economy are affecting organizational life in the United States in important ways. Specifically, this turbulence in the environment is creating pressures to change in those who work for organizations. Employees who assumed they had a lifetime commitment to Exxon, GE, or Ma Bell, to name only a few large and well-known companies, are finding themselves laid off, retired early, or working for a vastly different enterprise than the one that hired them. Even if they are currently making money, other companies are moving to redesign both technical and social work systems in the anticipation of competition from abroad. They know that within a few years they may be outpaced if they do not continually improve their productivity.

This changing and demanding environment is not only being experienced in the private sector. Public education is under both economic and consumer pressure to improve quality and expand services. Voluntary social service and cultural agencies are facing reduced govern-

BARBARA BENEDICT BUNKER AND JACQUELINE J. DELISLE • Department of Psychology, State University of New York at Buffalo, New York 14260.

mental support and increased regulation. Pressure from the external environment on organizations often creates an internal need for individuals within the organization to change.

Even without a pressing external environment, there are other sources of pressure for individuals to change from within organizations. Organizations have long been determining new directions and goals and expecting employees to bring their behavior in line with these goals. A new president or director, for example, is selected and announces a new program, changes in structure, goals, and people's roles. Planned organizational change that affects individuals is a long-standing and familiar aspect of work organizations.

In more subtle ways, all organizations have a culture (Schein, 1985) to which employees must adjust themselves. For some people the adjustment is small, for others more change is required. In the American business organization, for example, most often started by white males, the culture reflects the white male origins of the organization. Women, people of color, Spanish-speaking and Asian persons, and even some white men may find that the expected behavior, dress, and attitudes are different from their preferred style or culture of origin. Informal negotiations between individuals and organizations about how much they must adjust go on continuously in most organizations.

Consider how much time we spend at work and our dependence on these organizations for sustenance as well as self-esteem. Work organizations, like the family, are powerful forces in the lives of those they employ. Consciously or unconsciously, we are molded and changed by work roles that demand not only certain skills and behaviors, but also allegiance to the philosophy and values of the organization that employs us.

This chapter is an examination of individual change as it occurs in work settings. In the first section, we will discuss ways of thinking about how individuals and organizations interact. Then we will examine a variety of theories about how individuals are motivated to change in organizations. Following the theory section, we will consider the issue of resistance to change and what organizations are doing to work with this natural process. Toward the end of the chapter, we consider key internal processes of organizations that promote individual change.

## THE INDIVIDUAL AND THE ORGANIZATION

Theorists of work adjustment (Dawis & Lofquist, 1984) are interested in how people maintain correspondence between their own needs and desires and the demands of the major environments of their lives.

"Correspondence" is a dynamic state in which the individual fulfills the requirements of the workplace (satisfactoriness) and the work environment meets the individual's requirements (satisfaction).

In the interactionist perspective on work adjustment (Schneider, 1983), correspondence or the "goodness of fit" between a person's characteristics and the properties of his or her work environment (person–environment, or P–E fit) defines work adjustment (Kahn, 1981). When these characteristics are discrepant, strain is experienced. Note that strain may be created either by the actual situation or by perception of reality. Studies of job properties by proponents of P–E fit theory indicate that most people want more job complexity, more participation, and more clarity rather than less (Kahn, 1981). Thus, organizational theorists are providing an important corrective to the overly simple notions of organizations as demanding change and employees as adjusting. The interactionist perspective emphasizes that organizations themselves may change in response to their people.

Within all organizations, individuals are increasingly held accountable in two areas. They are expected to be able to do their jobs competently and they are expected to work effectively with others in the interest of the organization's goals. We know that job skills are changing with the accelerating pace of technological change. Some futurists are even saying that from now on much of the workforce will have to be retrained every five years. Organizations are increasingly becoming educational settings that require continuous learning and development.

Interpersonal competence (the skills to collaborate, coordinate work, contribute in groups, and get along with others) is becoming more important in organizations that are restructuring work and often forming self-managing teams to do it. In the many-layered organization of the past, the brilliant but corrosive personality (enfant terrible) or the passive–aggressive person may have been tolerated or isolated in some niche. Nowadays, as organizations trim hierarchical layers and jobs become more interdependent, there is less willingness and less capacity to tolerate people whose interpersonal competence is low.

The experience that individuals in organizations have of change can be conceptualized on two dimensions (see Fig. 1). First, the change may have either a short or a longer time frame. If the change is incremental, if it happens gradually over time, the person will probably feel more in control of it than if it happens abruptly or suddenly. On the other hand, the opportunities for resistance and even sabotage are greater in a longer time frame. If the change is sudden or abrupt, the probability that it will be experienced as demanding and arbitrary increases.

The second dimension is the degree of control over the change that

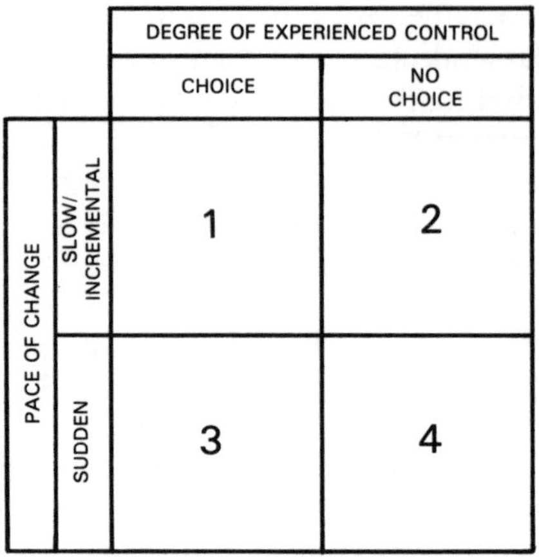

| DEGREE OF EXPERIENCED CONTROL | | |
|---|---|---|
| | CHOICE | NO CHOICE |
| PACE OF CHANGE — SLOW/ INCREMENTAL | 1 | 2 |
| PACE OF CHANGE — SUDDEN | 3 | 4 |

FIGURE 1. Dimensions of Change

the person experiences. Can people choose to change as compared with being required to change? The general assumption here is that the greater the choice and experience of control, the less resistance to the change.

These two dimensions create a matrix of four types of change experience (Fig. 1) that individuals in organizations may experience. When one has both choice and plenty of lead time in a change process, we expect that the change will occur naturally and without difficulty (Fig. 1, box 1). Personal career pathing and planning and individual management development are good examples. At the group level, some quality circles meet voluntarily and select their own change projects and time frames. There are, however, incremental change processes where individuals do not have a choice about the direction of the change and their participation in it (Fig. 1, box 2). Corporate changes in direction or culture may be a several-year process, but all employees are expected to support and become part of the new arrangements.

When the change happens quickly, as is sometimes the case in organizational life, choice provides some relief from the sense demand (Fig. 1, box 3). For example, a promotion may suddenly be offered and the decision time frame short. Yet the employee has some freedom to agree or decline. The financial picture in an agency may suddenly require reductions but managers are given some choice about who or what to reduce. The degree of choice may involve freedom to accept or reject a change or it may only involve some degree of control over the change, for example, how or when it is implemented. In general, participation in change processes is believed to facilitate change and lead to greater internalization (Zaltman & Duncan, 1977).

Finally, when the change is abrupt and employees have no choice about the change, we can expect the greatest degree of reaction and unwillingness to change (Fig. 1, box 4). In fact, Brehm (1976) describes a theory of "reactance" in which persons deprived of their freedom move to restore it that is quite useful in understanding this situation. Corporate mergers, a frequent and often difficult part of organizational life today, seem often to have these characteristics. A new CEO who is brought into an organization to "turn it around" may create this kind of situation. New pay plans and other structural changes inadequately introduced may fall into this category. From the standpoint of the employee, change that is demanded suddenly and without participation is the most difficult to willingly embrace.

## SIX FRAMEWORKS FOR CHANGE

Kurt Lewin once said that "nothing is so practical as a good theory" (Marrow, 1969). People who work as organizational change consultants ground their work in a variety of frameworks. None is really a full-blown theory in the scientific sense, but each framework seems to include some basic assumptions about human nature (i.e., how human beings are motivated to respond to the environment and thus to change), identification of the catalyst or forces in the environment that are apt to lead to change, and finally the process, condition, or phases that lead to the final outcome of behavior change.

We will discuss six frameworks (see Table 1) or sets of assumptions from the organizational psychology literature that are often cited by practitioners as the grounding ideas that support and define the activities of organizational change efforts. Such efforts are planned rather than spontaneous, though these frameworks are also used to explain changes that occur in unplanned ways. Most models are based on the premise that individual change is a precursor to organizational change.

Before moving to a discussion of the six frameworks, we will comment on two important issues that cut across all the frameworks. The first is the targeted levels of individual change, from the most internal levels that include feelings and values and are the most difficult to change, to the more external levels like skills and observable behaviors that usually change more easily.

There are several levels at which a person may be asked to change (Hornstein, Bunker, Burke, Gindes, & Lewicki, 1971). Some changes organizations ask their employees to make are relatively "superficial,"

TABLE 1. Comparison of Six Frameworks for Change

| Theory | Basic assumptions | Catalyst | Intermediate state | Final outcome |
|---|---|---|---|---|
| Socratic–rational | People are logical, rational, look out for self-interest | New information | Recognition that new information is better, makes more sense | Behavior change |
| Social psychological | Disequilibrium leads to tension. People are motivated to reduce this tension. | Information | Noticed discrepancy or disconfirmation | Behavior change |
| Normative–reeducative | People interact with and are influenced by social environment. Can use information to change, but are also strongly influenced by social norms, values, pressures. | Information Social interaction | Attitude change | Behavior change |
| Behaviorist | People respond to and are motivated by stimuli in the environment. Behaviors are part of an S–R chain or cycle. No internal cognitive processes. | Reinforcement | Shaping | Behavior change |
| Systemic | Human action is a product of both conscious and unconscious forces. | Events or processes in one part of the organizational system that have effects in other parts of the system. | Implicit assumptions, unconscious forces within individual create pressure for action that is expressed in behavior. | Behavior change |
| Power coercive | People with less power will change for those with more power. | Requirements, regulations, threats (fear, anxiety) | Cognitive assessment (cost-benefit analysis) Emotional reactions | Behavior change |

showing employees the "correct" way to do this (the "best" way for all involved since it places the least amount of strain on the back, is less likely to cause injury than other methods of lifting and carrying, and therefore should also reduce on-the-job injuries, sick leave, and compensation), it should naturally follow that employees will now lift and carry objects in the new manner.

## SOCIAL PSYCHOLOGICAL FRAMEWORK

The social psychological model of change, the second framework, originated in Kurt Lewin's work (Marrow, 1969). In his model a three-stage process is proposed: unfreezing, change, and refreezing. "Unfreezing," the first step in the change process, involves decreasing the forces that maintain the situation at its present level of equilibrium so that change is possible. Unfreezing is a state of disequilibrium in a normally balanced state. It can result from several different processes. One of the most common is disconfirmation or lack of confirmation, which may produce guilt or anxiety. Take the case of a worker who receives information that he or she is not engaging in certain behaviors that are a required part of the job. This information would likely cause some stress or anxiety, which would disrupt the comfortable assumption that all is well and would create an atmosphere of concern and tension.

From these early notions a group of widely accepted social psychological theories developed known as the consistency theories (cognitive dissonance theory, Festinger, 1957; balance theory, Heider, 1958; and congruity theory, Osgood & Tannenbaum, 1955). Although there are important differences among them, they all assume that human beings are motivated to change their cognitions and attitudes when they find themselves in a state of imbalance or dissonance in order to restore balance and an internal sense of harmony. In accordance with these theories, Leavitt (1978) states that tension and discomfort are produced when someone thinks there is a gap in their knowledge. He sees change as a very emotional process. Consequently, he emphasizes in this stage that it is necessary to increase psychological safety by reducing threat, removing barriers, and otherwise creating an acceptable climate for change.

Schein and Bennis (1965) also propose that psychological safety features in the environment will be necessary for the change to take place, because of the emotional nature of change. They go on to suggest that if these features are not present, the person will simply become defensive and resist change.

The next stage is the process of changing. New attitudes and values have already developed. Now new behaviors are learned and are tried out. This may occur at work with a role model who possesses the desired values or performs the desired behaviors or in a training program.

Refreezing is similar to the Kieslers' (1969) notion of private acceptance or Kelman's (1961) notion of internalization. This is the point at which the new response becomes integrated into the person's belief or value system, which locks the change into place. Although refreezing may occur solely within the individual, support mechanisms are often used to reinforce the new level the person has reached. At work this might involve incentives like stock ownership programs, profit sharing, bonuses based on productivity or performance, or public or private commendations. While the first two stages are necessary for change, the third, refreezing, is necessary to sustain the change.

## NORMATIVE–REEDUCATIVE FRAMEWORK

The normative–reeducative model (Chin & Benne, 1978), like the social psychological framework, emphasizes the power of disconfirming information at the beginning of the change process. It acknowledges, however, the strong impact of sociocultural norms and the commitment of individuals to these norms or patterns of behavior. These social forces can either support or hinder change and thus are factors in the change process.

In the work of Schein and Bennis (1965), the basic learning cycle consists of cognitive, emotional, and behavioral elements. The change process itself involves an interdependent cycle that begins with some dilemma or disconfirming information often from the social environment. One finds out, for example, that co-workers are reacting negatively to some actions or attributing hostile intent to you. This, in turn, leads to an attitude change, which leads to new behavior, which produces new information and/or an increased awareness.

This model stresses the active nature of human beings and the effect of this activity on change processes. Information serves as a catalyst for change in this model, but a person must participate in his or her own reeducation for change to be effective. Thus, one emphasis in this theory is on people's involvement in working out a program of change for themselves. As Kiesler and Kiesler (1969) note, this will increase the likelihood of private acceptance. Currently, for example, many organizations are trying to educate workers about the benefits of health and fitness programs. In order for this attempt at education to be successful, however, it requires active participation on the part of the employee, whether it be cutting down on foods high in cholesterol or starting to exercise more frequently. If strong cultural norms dictate that employees have a few drinks together after work, or that the lunch hour is spent playing cards rather than jogging, information alone will not be enough to effect the attitude change that is the necessary precursor to behavior change.

## BEHAVIORIST FRAMEWORK

Behaviorist theory provides a noncognitive view of the change process. In this model, observable behavior is the target for change, with little concern for internal or unconscious processes. According to London (1975), through the use of shaping and modeling one can "aim for precision in establishing the conditions that will work the desired effects without having to worry much about what is going on in that person that makes them work" (p. 47). Through such devices as behavior modification, the change agent attempts to alter a person's observable behavior or performance. While the social psychological model considers attitude change to be a prerequisite of behavior change, the behaviorist model ignores and discounts these internal processes. In Lofquist and Dawis's (1969) book, *Adjustment to Work*, they note that, "The employer specifies the behavior required in the achievement of the work organization's goals. He also determines the stimulus conditions in which this behavior will take place, and he sets up the reinforcements intended to stimulate and maintain appropriate behavior" (p. 33). At work, pay systems based on performance (or nonperformance) of a behavior are very obvious examples of how rewards shape behavior. To the degree that raises and promotions are contingent on specific behaviors, they are powerful. Sulzer-Azaroff and Mayer (1977) suggest that employers deliberately arrange salaries so that they are contingent upon employees performing at acceptable levels. For example, in one study a new payment system was developed for a group of hourly teenage workers with inadequate performance ratings (Pierce & Risely, 1974). Under this system a checklist of job performance items was created and payment was based on these ratings. Job performance subsequently improved to near perfect levels.

A major problem in many organizations that are trying to change employee behavior is that the management espouses its new program, for example, "Managers will devote more time to employee development this year," without changing the underlying organizational reward system. Then after managers have been exposed to training in employee career development, management wonders why "the training was not effective." The cynicism of many employees about change programs stems from this incongruence between what employees are told to do and what they are rewarded for doing.

In one setting, where the management was congruent about the expected employee behavior and the reward system, management not only urged greater productivity, but also posted data on a daily basis about how each unit was doing. In a period of months there was a marked improvement in productivity ("Emory airfreight," 1975).

There are also subtle reinforcement contingencies (informal norms) operating in organizations that affect behavior. Unlike those planned by management, these emergent reinforcers sometimes conflict with the stated goals of the organization. If bringing the organization's official reward systems into alignment with official policy is not easy, tackling the informal reward system is even more complex and difficult. Yet all impact behavior.

## SYSTEMIC FRAMEWORK

The systemic framework of individual change in organizations is different from those we have already discussed because it is not a theory of consciously planned change. Instead, individuals are viewed as changing their behavior in response to forces largely out of their awareness.

Some of the most useful work to have entered the organizational consultation literature comes from the systems notions that are especially well described in family therapy literature (Minuchin, 1974; Napier & Whitaker, 1988). Patterns of behavior in the family can be seen as responses to underlying pressures that need to be changed. For individual change to occur, the system must change since individual behavior is a response to the whole system. In organizational systems the work unit is the system that must be understood if individual change is to occur effectively. Dysfunctional patterns that are unrecognized must be brought into the awareness of system members. As they become educated about their own system, choice becomes possible. For example, a staff team realized that a series of people who had joined the team over the last several years had had a very difficult time being accepted and integrated. As they discussed the issue, it became clear that there was a strong pattern in this organization of there always being a person who was "out" (often the new person) while others were "in." They were able to trace this pattern back for more than ten years through widely different types of personalities who were given the "out" treatment. Gradually it became clear that an "out-person" served an important function in this system and so one usually "appeared." An analysis of this pattern led to understanding that this occurred as a result of other pressures and forces that were out of their awareness.

The notion that individual behavior is at the same time both the individual's own response and may also be in the service of the group or organization's dynamics is a notion that holds both the person and the group accountable for an individual's behavior. (Turquet, 1985; Wells, 1985). While not usually a part of the thinking about goal-oriented change problems, it is a very important set of concepts in analyzing dysfunctional organizational events. It helps prevent scapegoating, for example, or at least redressing that situation if it is recognized.

## POWER–COERSIVE FRAMEWORK

The final framework involves the use of power–coercive tactics (Chin & Benne, 1978; Hornstein *et al.*, 1971). Change occurs when individuals are forced to change by those with more power. This is similar to Kelman's (1961) idea of compliance and the Kieslers' (1969) notion of public performance without private acceptance. Compliance on the part of those with less power to the plans, directions, and leadership of those with greater power is less likely to lead to private acceptance on the part of the individuals involved, though it may happen. This strategy emphasizes political and economic sanctions in the exercise of power.

Mintzberg (1983) suggests that an individual in a system has three options when presented with a demand to change: stay and contribute as expected, leave, or stay and try to change the system. Although these *are* options, fear or other psychological processes that intervene when someone uses power–coercive tactics may make them unrealistic.

There are many bases of power: reward, coercive, legitimate, referent, expert, and information (French & Raven, 1959). While half of these focus on the power holder's ability to change the behavior of another person (reward, coercive, information), the other half place part of the responsibility for the success of the change effort on the perceptions of the power holder as held by a person who is the target of the change effort (Kakabadse & Parker, 1984).

The six frameworks discussed here focus on behavior change as the final outcome. It is, however, important to note that the process can be reciprocal. Changes in behavior may lead to changes in attitudes, as well as changes in attitudes leading to changes in behavior.

# RESISTANCE TO CHANGE

As noted earlier in this chapter, organizations experience pressures to change from any number of sources: global pressures, economic pressures, social pressures, productivity pressure, and technological advances. Since failure to change is costly, organizations are increasingly finding it necessary to change. They are also finding that many change programs fail. Resistance on the part of individuals to the change effort is the most common source of these failures.

Definitions of resistance vary. The most common view is that people who resist change oppose it or try to retard it. Resistance is "any conduct that serves to maintain the status quo in the face of pressure to alter the status quo" (Zaltman & Duncan, 1977, p. 63). Another view describes resistance as "multi-directed energy" and conceptualizes it as a useful, self-regulating facet of healthy systems (Nevis, 1987). No matter how it is defined, to effectively deal with resistance the primary basis for it must be understood.

While resistance has typically been conceived of as a problem to be surmounted, especially by those attempting to implement change, there can be benefits to resistance. It can highlight unanticipated consequences of change and call attention to forces and issues overlooked by change agents. As Zaltman and Duncan (1977) appropriately note, some resistance may be caused by errors made by the change agent! Whatever the cause, the system is providing us with important data that should be explored, including who the resisters are and why they are resisting the change effort (Klein, 1976).

Kotter and Schlesinger (1979) describe the four most common reasons why people resist change: a desire not to give up something of value, a misunderstanding of the change and its implications, a belief that the change does not make sense for the organization, and finally, a low personal tolerance for change. Change is often a uniquely individual process, and Dalziel and Schoonover (1988) theorize that a person's tolerance for change is connected to his or her personality. Notice that the first three reasons demonstrate that perceptions play a critical role in determining whether or not a person will resist change. Personality may play a role, but a less central one.

There are several other reasons why change might be resisted at the level of the individual (Harvey & Brown, 1988; Zaltman and Duncan, 1977). First, people are consciously and unconsciously selective in attending to and storing information. Thus, individuals may not realize that the current situation is not satisfactory. Even if the individual thinks that there is a problem, and therefore a need to change, he or she may not agree on the cause of the problem. Second, individuals generally find a comfortable level of arousal and try to maintain that level. The change process may create levels of stimulation well beyond the comfort zone of the individual, especially if there is uncertainty regarding the change or possible threats to the position or benefits of that individual. Third, people need to be liked, and conformity to norms and culture can be very strong. Social and psychological investments in the current situation may make it very difficult to "unfreeze" some people. Finally, any one of a number of personality factors such as low tolerance for change or fear of risk taking may cause a person to resist a change effort. Organizers of successful change efforts anticipate resistance, recognize it, and deal with it effectively.

Just as there are forces that hinder change efforts, there are also what Harvey and Brown (1988) call "motivating forces" (forces that help increase the likelihood of acceptance/implementation of the change program). These forces include dissatisfaction with the present situation, external pressures toward compliance, momentum toward the change, and motivation by the consultant.

Strategists want to have these forces on their side when attempting to implement a change effort. If strong motivating forces are not present, there are still several steps a change agent can take to help lessen resistance. First, Nevis (1987) suggests that the resistance must be respected. Attempts to overpower it, avoid it, or eliminate it are not effective methods. Working from the Gestalt tradition, he prescribes staying with the resistance in order to fully experience it and then moving on from there.

Other suggestions to lessen resistance and mobilize energy for change (Beer, 1988; Bunker, 1979; Harvey & Brown, 1988) include increased education and communication in order to provide information about the change and participation of members in the change process. Participation could mean working with others to decide what changes would solve a common problem or deciding how to implement a change that is mandated. There are several levels of involvement with varying degrees of control over the change process. In summary, information, education, and participation are listed as primary methods of dealing with resistance in much of the change literature.

Methods such as manipulation and co-optation, explicit and implicit coercion, and other power strategies are also included by some authors (Harvey & Brown, 1988) as alternatives for lessening resistance. Indeed, Nevis (1987) suggests that resistance really only has meaning when there are power differences among people. If the mandator of the change and the change target have equal power, the change target can simply refuse. Power strategies have some advantages if speed is essential or if an organization lacks the time and resources required for increased participation of the part of its members. As we indicated before, however, the use of these tactics may leave people feeling angry and manipulated. Thus, the likelihood of internalization is much lower than with other methods.

## ORGANIZATIONAL EVENTS AND INDIVIDUAL CHANGE

Some of the earliest writing in management speaks of the "implicit psychological contract" between management and employee (Barnard, 1938). As collectivities structured around a common purpose, organizations expect certain behaviors from their employees. In return, the employees expect to be compensated, respected, and rewarded. Organizations and those who work for them are interdependent; they need each other.

In this section, the chronology of an employee's career provides a framework in which to discuss the choice points where organizations ask or require their members to change. The entry process, performance appraisal of job skills and interpersonal competence, management training and retraining, employee assistance programs, retirement, or outplacement are all possible transition points in organizational life where change may be required. These changes may be at any level, from learning new skills to changes in attitudes and feelings.

### ORGANIZATIONAL SOCIALIZATION

The first months after joining a new organization are a time of heightened sensitivity and learning for most new employees. If the organization has an orientation program, the person is likely to be given some knowledge of the total organization, its history, values, and current goals and achievements. The implicit message is that the new recruit is expected to fit into this structure and further its purposes.

The official orientation program is only a small part of the data that new employees are taking in while trying to understand their new social reality.

From the perspective of the employing organization, the concern is to get the new person oriented and functioning as rapidly as possible. From the point of view of the person who is entering, the situation may be quite problematic even if one is well equipped to take on the assigned responsibilities. This is because each organization has its own culture, that is, assumptions about reality, ways of doing things, and values that are implicit and unstated (Schein, 1985). The new hire is always confronted with learning the culture along with learning the job. Van Maanen (1977) describes entry into a new organization as a crisis period or "breakpoint in which established relationships are severed and new ones forged, old behavior patterns forgotten and new ones learned, former responsibilities abandoned and new ones taken on. In short, breakpoints require the individual to discover or reformulate certain everyday assumptions about their working life" (p. 16).

Van Maanen (1977) and others working to understand organizational socialization begin with the assumption that all reality is created. Thus, new organizational members have the task of creating a situational identity. In dramatological terms, they must find their place upon the stage and their role in interaction with others in the cast. Since each person has a history in other settings, each brings certain assumptions with him or her to a new setting about what is normal and proper in their own and others behavior. Usually there is some type of reality shock (also called culture shock when one enters new cultures) when one's assumptions are disconfirmed. This prompts the individual to reconsider what has been taken for granted. "Normalizing the setting" (Van Maanen, 1977) is finding out what is normal and not normal in this new setting. This includes learning the labels or people categories used by the more experienced members of the culture. Negative labels are especially important to learn since they identify what is not normal and also what the newcomer should avoid. Another way to normalize the setting is to identify which of the many activities within a person's role should be considered most important.

Organizations also have different theories of socialization that affect the difficulty of the entry task. Schein (1968) discusses two types of organizational socialization processes that would impact new people very differently. The "self-destructing" philosophy sees the socializing process as a tearing down of old assumptions followed by a personal restructuring process. People need to go to "boot camp" in order to be initiated in depth into the culture. Socialization is seen as a traumatic event, though shared trauma may lead to future bonding. The other philosophy is a "self-enhancing" one where the core values are that people must find or create their niche rather than be forced to fit in. Either of these philosophies may fit well with or be uncomfortable for some personalities.

Obviously, the degree that the new organization differs from a new person's values or previous organizational experience will determine how much reality shock is experienced. Yet, recent theorists of organizational socialization have emphasized that the transaction is not one-sided. Although organizations do make great demands on their people, individuals also shape organizations. Definitions of reality are negotiated rather than imposed. Negotiations go on throughout careers, not just at the beginning. Interactionists (Jones, 1983; Toren & King, 1982) emphasize the role of individual values and differences as effecting the impact that the situation may have.

## JOB ROLE REQUIREMENTS

Three areas of the work role that can be the foci of needed change are the specific skills of a job or role, the employee's attitude toward work, and the person's interpersonal competence. In technical and service organizations today, the rapid development of new technology, and innovation require almost continuous learning and change. Rosow and Zager (1988) assert that most employers overestimate the difficulties and costs of retraining and grossly underestimate the costs of firing old and hiring new people. When we add to this picture the sad state of U.S. education and the probability that more and more entry-level employees will not be fully capable of functioning at work if they are able to get jobs at all, it becomes clear that American organizations are likely to be in the education and training business even more in the future than they are now.

In business organizations that produce products, a quiet revolution is currently taking place throughout the nation. Competition for worldwide markets, referred to at the beginning of this chapter, is causing many companies to redesign work in order to achieve greater efficiency. There are many ways to improve productivity. Total quality improvement (Ishikawa, 1985), sociotechnical redesign (Pasmore, 1989), and other methods, though different approaches, have some commonalities. For example, self-managing work groups often take responsibility for making and shipping a complete zero-defects product. The kinds of changes that workers in redesigned systems are experiencing involve job and interpersonal skills as well as work attitudes. First, they are expected to learn to do more than one job (cross-training) and are often paid for the number of skills acquired rather than what they are doing on any specific day. Second, they are part of a team that has much greater responsibility than workers in traditional plants. The team makes its own decisions about work scheduling, maintenance, deals with customers, maintains its own quality control, and even hires and fires its own members. Thus, they must be able to work with others in group settings.

These new team work groups may disrupt collusive old relationships because of the new expectations for performance. In traditional organizations, it is not uncommon to find workers who are illiterate or who cannot do part of what their job requires protected or "covered" by other workers. In some workplaces, these arrangements have gone on for years. Training programs that are offered are often refused if people feel their functional illiteracy will be exposed (Rosow and Zager, 1988). Yet, the new skill demands make these deficits in basic skills real impediments. Many plants are organizing special programs in job-related basic skills to help workers meet the new challenges. When technical training is combined with specific basic skill training, there seems to be more motivation to learn basic skills and the process is more efficient than when literacy training precedes technical training (Rosow & Zager, 1988). Nonetheless, these are very sensitive issues where self-esteem is often involved.

To participate in this kind of new workplace requires attitude changes that are far reaching for many. People no longer work alone on a production line just putting in their hours. They are expected to take responsibility for making the product better and improving productivity. One of the first steps in creating openness to these kinds of changes is often visits to other similar organizations where these systems are already in place. When workers see how much others like the new work setting and how productive they are, they may become more motivated to consider new work process organization.

Supervisors in these settings also find their jobs changing from maintaining close control to roles of coaching, counseling, and coordinating for which they have little preparation and experience. They are likely to experience a loss of power as it is traditionally conceived. Not only is their job changing, but an attitudinal paradigm shift is expected. A quick summary of this shift is to say that the central issue in traditional workplaces has been worker *control* whereas now the issue is worker *commitment*.

The need for new skills and changed attitudes in the American workforce is not limited to manufacturing businesses. Service industries are also experiencing this demand. As competition increases in the health care industry, for example, hospitals are beginning to look at patients as "customers" and study how the hospitals can become more attractive. Emergency rooms are reorganizing to reduce customer waiting time; maternity units are offering special services to attract expectant parents. To those of us who have become inured, though still resentful of long hours waiting for health care professionals, to be thought of as a customer who needs to be well served as well as kept happy is nothing short of startling. Imagine the attitude changes as well as the redesign of work process that must be required of these workers!

## CAREER DEVELOPMENT

As people progress in their careers, organizations continue to shape behavior and to motivate employees to channel their energies in organizationally appropriate directions. Sometimes what is asked of employees is incremental change, gradual improvement over time. Other times, especially when the organization itself faces a crisis, major change is required. The systems used by organizations to facilitate these changes, such as performance appraisal, are well known. More sophisticated forms of performance appraisal are developmental and collaborative rather than summative and evaluative. In many organizations, some form of collaborative goal setting occurs. After the top management clarifies the company's goals for the year, individuals have the opportunity to consider and commit to the ways in which their own work will forward these goals. Management by objectives and key results systems are examples of performance-guiding systems in which employees participate in setting their own goals (Beer, 1987). The assumptions of these systems are that greater participation will lead to greater motivation and that increased motivation will increase the effectiveness of role behavior.

Incentive systems also influence performance (Lawler, 1987). In some companies, several types of payment are received; for example, base pay for the job, additional pay for skills, group or organizational bonuses for performance, individual bonuses for reaching pretargeted goals. Performance appraisal and incentive systems are complex areas each with a substantial theoretical and research literature. It is beyond the scope of this chapter to do more than indicate their relevance to individual change.

## TRAINING IN THE ORGANIZATION

At lower levels of organizational functioning training is usually focused on technical skills. Advancing into middle management from some technical background, for example, managers may have had little practice at managing people, delegating work, or holding others accountable in ways that increase motivation. Their training for these new roles may be planned and run by their own company, purchased from a vendor who sells "training packages," or they may be sent to a public seminar.

Management training is also used by organizations to shape managerial awareness of new company goals and directions. As the new president of General Electric, Jack Welch put his entire management through a five-day training program whose purpose was to help them understand the change in direction that he was spearheading (as well as the implications for their behavior) and to motivate them to jump on the train before it left them behind. Of course, a critical question about the effectiveness of such programs is whether they achieve compliance or internalization (Kelman, 1961).

With the publication of the Hudson Institute report on Workforce 2000 (Johnston & Packer, 1987), management awareness of the changing demographics of the workforce is increasing. If only 15% of new hires by the year 2000 will be white and male, managers will need to be able to manage a diverse workforce with larger numbers of women, people of color, Asians, Spanish-speaking, and others.

The world of work has been a white male bastion in the United States for many years. When people of different cultures work together, the management of differences becomes critical. This means that whites who have been the establishment majority must come to understand the assumptions of their own culture (Katz, 1978) as they also seek to understand the culture of other groups. It means that men can no longer insist on the culture of the all-male group (Aires, 1987). It means that differences need to be embraced and seen as a resource rather than punished and eradicated (Bunker, 1990). To be a good manager in the future will require changes of attitudes and feelings as well as new knowledge and understanding. Some companies are already moving to begin this process with their employees. Corning, for example, is asking all management personnel to attend a seminar on gender and another on race in the next few years (*Wall Street Journal*, 1989).

The effectiveness of any training and change program is a complex assessment task. Training is often based on more than one of the change theories we presented in the theory section of this chapter. For the new employee, for example, new information that is job relevant is assumed to be easily internalized and motivating because people in new roles want to do well. It is assumed that the distress people feel about the new job requirements will make them eager to learn. Seminar methods often include active participation and feedback. There may also be incentives attached to attendance at the training program.

Four levels of assessment of training events are commonly discussed (Kirkpatrick, 1983; Robinson & Robinson, 1989): the trainee reaction to the training, what the trainee learned measured objectively, changed trainee behaviors back on the job (transfer of training), and the impact of changed trainee behavior on organizational measures, for example, turnover or absenteeism. The most commonly used is the trainee's reaction to the training program. This assessment gives data about what trainees think and feel about their experience but not what they do with it. Organizations are necessarily concerned with the transfer of training back into the work setting. Training programs today are being closely looked at for their contribution to organizational effectiveness (Robinson & Robinson, 1989).

## INTERPERSONAL COMPETENCE

People who have a strong and balanced set of interpersonal skills are usually seen as excellent employees assuming that their technical job skills are also in good order. Interpersonal skills are harder than job skills to define. Some performance appraisal systems describe them, some do not. Whatever the case, they are reflected in any employee's appraisal in most work settings.

Some employees never know that interpersonal skills are the reason that they are not promoted. This happens when the organization gives no feedback in this area or when the person has no awareness of their own interpersonal style. It is not uncommon to see one's personal style as something that is given and therefore not amenable to change.

There are several change technologies that focus particularly on interpersonal style. They begin by helping the person gain more awareness of that style and its impact on others. This is sensitive work that involves both the person's self-perception and his or her self-esteem. It is often done in human interaction laboratories, usually a week in length, in which "strangers" (people from different organizational settings) work together in three types of activities. The major activity is the sensitivity training group (T-group). After a group-building phase, people in T-groups have enough data about each other that they can exchange information about "how they come across" with each other. Managed by a properly trained social scientist, this process leaves the person with the freedom to choose whether any action on their part is warranted. The feedback process that is used requires participants to describe behavior and the feelings it creates in them rather than projecting interpretations, giving opinions, or attributing meaning to the behavior that they have observed (Bunker, 1979). These activities are supported by lectures about such topics as person perception, how people change, group dynamics and development, and interpersonal skills. Skill-practicing activities such as active listening, dealing with conflict, and group leadership are the third part of the workshop program.

We are no longer in the time when T-groups were part of a social movement (Back, 1973) and untrained leaders abounded. Several reputable organizations still offer this training on the public market (NTL Institute of Alexandria, Virginia; University Associates of San Diego, California).

Since the 1970s, it has been recognized by a number of practitioners that T-groups are less useful if the deficit in interpersonal functioning is in being able to stand up for and advocate one's own position. Assertiveness training that emerged in the 1970s as a result of the women's movement trains people in these specific skills. Using role-play, videotaping, and a range of situations, participants practice assertive behaviors and plan how they will incorporate them into their work roles. Other examples of training events that focus on interpersonal skills include conflict management, listening, and influencing skills.

## THE EMPLOYEE AS A PROBLEM

There are, of course, times when a person's job competence or interpersonal style are not acceptable and employees are told that major change is required. When this occurs, employees are usually expected to remediate their behavior within a specified time frame. Unfortunately, in too many organizations some employees are deprived of valid data about their inadequate performance for years. Then, when it becomes an organizational necessity to confront the performance problem, the situation is traumatic for the employee and difficult for the organization.

Individual problems of addiction, health, and family crises present an even more difficult dilemma for the organization when they affect work functioning. The individual needs to change but the problem may not be easily controlled voluntarily. Many companies now have Employee Assistance Programs (EAP), either by themselves or in federation with other organizations.

Between 6 and 20% of the workforce abuses substances at a high enough rate to hinder job performance (Harwood, Napolitano, Kristiansen, & Collins, 1985). Since the mid-1960s there has been a gradual shift in the perception of responsibility for these conditions that has been called the "medicalization of deviance" (Conrad & Schneider, 1980). What was once seen as completely under the employee's control is now understood to be the result of a complex of factors. For this reason, organizations take several approaches to the problem of substance abuse. They attempt to select nonabusers and to match people to jobs in order to increase satisfaction and productivity. Quality of working life programs may examine the stresses conducive to abuse that job conditions generate and attempt to change these conditions (Trice & Sonnenstuhl, 1988). Preventive wellness programs may offer employees opportunities for exercise, diet, and relaxation training to help deal with stress. The assumption is that prevention is less costly than remediation. Finally, for those employees with substance abuse problems that are affecting their work, the EAP program may be required. These programs are typically structured in a social learning framework where both confrontation and counseling are offered. Trice and Beyer's (1984) work, for example, demonstrates that constructive confrontation with counseling and group support are more effective than either separately.

## LEAVING THE ORGANIZATION

Organizations that are concerned about the people who spend years working for them are now offering help with the transitional process out of the organization. Retirement seminars are strategies to help people prepare for and move creatively into this next life stage.

If the transition out of the organization is imposed before the end of the career, for example by the closing of a plant or by a reduction in force, the psychological sense of loss (Marris, 1974) that must be dealt with can impede the transition process into the search for a new job. Where companies make no effort to help employees deal with the psychological issues of loss that are part of endings, such as the closing of a plant, employees have been known to show up at the closed plant for months and just stand around (Bunker & Williams, 1986). In addition to dealing with psychological processes, outplacement services can include office space from which to do a job search, help with resume writing and search processes, and self-help groups of persons in similar situations.

## SUMMARY

Throughout their careers, members of organizations are expected to change their knowledge, skills, and even attitudes and values. In this chapter, we have described the acceleration of change expectations in the 1980s and some of the theoretical notions that are the basis for programs of planned change. Organizations that are trying to meet the external press with internal actions that are humane and responsible often turn to social scientists to help them to plan, implement, and assess the effectiveness of programs. Since individuals are the critical ingredient in effective organizations, understanding the dynamics of individual change in the workplace is a topic that merits continued attention and importance.

## REFERENCES

Aries, E. J. (1987). Gender and communication. In P. Shaver & C. Hendrick (Eds.), *Sex and gender: Review of personality and social psychology*, vol. 7 (pp. 149–176). Newbury Park, CA: Sage.

Back, K. W. (1973). *Beyond words: The story of sensitivity training and the encounter movement.* Baltimore: Penguin.

Barnard, C. I. (1938). *The functions of the executive*. Cambridge, MA: Harvard University Press.

Beer, M. (1987). Performance appraisal. In J. W. Lorsch (Ed.), *The handbook of organizational behavior* (pp. 286–300). Englewood Cliffs, NJ: Prentice-Hall.

Beer, M. (1988). The critical path for change: Keys to success and failure in six companies. In R. H. Kilman & T. J. Colvin (Eds.), *Corporate transformation: Revitalizing organizations for a competitive world*. San Francisco: Jossey-Bass.

Brehm, S. S., & Brehm, J.W. (1981). *Psychological reactance*. New York: Academic Press.

Bunker, B. B. (1979). Using feedback to clarify important relationships. In L. C. Porter & B. Mohr (Eds.), *Reading book for human relations training* (Seventh edition, pp. 39–41). Arlington, VA: NTL Institute.

Bunker, B. B. (1990). Appreciating diversity and modifying organizational cultures: Men and women at work. In S. Srivastva & D. L. Cooperrider (Eds.), *Appreciative management and leadership* (pp. 126–149). San Francisco: Jossey-Bass.

Bunker, B. B., & Williams, H. (1986). Managing decline in organizational life. *Personnel*, American Management Association, New York.

Chin, R., & Benne, K. D. (1978). General strategies for effecting changes in human systems. In W. L. French, C. H. Bell, Jr., & R. A. Zawacki (Eds.), *Organization development: Theory, practice, and research*. Dallas, TX: Business Publications, Inc.

Conrad, P., & Schneider, J. (1980). *Deviance and medicalization: From badness to sickness*. Lexington, MA.: D. C. Heath.

Dalziel, M. M., & Schoonover, S. C. (1988). *Changing ways: A practical tool for implementing change within organizations*. New York: AMACOM.

Dawis, R. V., & Lofquist, L. H. (1984). *A psychological theory of work adjustment*. Minneapolis: University of Minnesota Press.

Emory airfreight: Positive reinforcement boosts performance. (1975). In K. N. Wexley & G. A. Yukl (Eds.), *Organizational behavior and industrial psychology* (pp. 560–568). New York: Oxford University Press.

Festinger, L. (1957). *A theory of cognitive dissonance*. Evanston, IL: Row, Peterson.

French, J. R. P., Jr., & Raven, B. (1959). The bases of social power. In D. Cartwright (Ed.), *Studies in social power*. Ann Arbor, MI: Institute for Social Research.

Harvey, D. F., & Brown, D. R. (1988). *An experiential approach to organization development* (3rd ed.). Englewood Cliffs, NJ: Prentice-Hall.

Harwood, H. J., Napolitano, D. M., Kristiansen, P. L., & Collins, J. J. (1985) Economic costs to society of alcohol and drug abuse and mental illness. Publication #RTI-2734/001FR. Research Triangle Park, N.C.: Research Triangle Institute.

Heider, F. (1958). *The psychology of interpersonal relations*. New York: Wiley.

Hornstein, H. A., Bunker, B. B., Burke, W. W., Gindes, M., & Lewicki, R. (1971). *Social intervention: A behavioral science approach*. New York: Free Press.

Ishikawa, K. (1985). *What is total quality control? The Japanese way*. Englewood Cliffs, NJ: Prentice-Hall.

Johnston, W. B., & Packer, A. H. (1987). *Workforce 2000: Work and workers for the 21st century*. Indianapolis, IN: Hudson Institute.

Jones, G. R. (1983). Psychological orientation and the process of organizational socialization: An interactionist perspective. *Academy of Management Review, 8,* 464–474.

Kahn, R. L. (1981). *Work and health*. New York: Wiley.

Kakabadse, A., & Parker, C. (Eds.) (1984). *Power, politics and organizations*. New York: Wiley.

Katz, J. (1978). *White awareness*. Norman: University of Oklahoma Press.

Kelman, H. C. (1961). Processes of opinion change. *Public Opinion Quarterly, 25,* 57–58.

Kiesler, C. A., & Kiesler, S. B. (1969). *Conformity*. Reading, MA: Addison-Wesley.

Kirkpatrick, D. A. (1983). *Practical guide for supervisory training and development* (2nd Ed.) Reading, MA: Addison-Wesley.

Klein, D. (1976). Some notes on the dynamics of resistance to change: The defender role. In
    W. G. Bennis, K. D. Benne, R. Chin, & K. E. Corey (Eds.), *The planning change* (3rd
    edition, pp. 117–124). New York: Holt, Rinehart and Winston.
Kotter, J. P., & Schlesinger, L. A. (1979). Choosing strategies for change. *Harvard Business
    Review*, March-April, 106–114.
Lawler, E. E. (1987). The design of effective reward systems. In J.W. Lorsch (Ed.), *The
    handbook of organizational behavior* (pp. 255–271). Englewood Cliffs, NJ: Prentice-Hall.
Leavitt, H. J. (1978). *Managerial psychology: An introduction to individuals, pairs, and groups in
    organizations.* Chicago: The University of Chicago Press.
Lofquist, L. H., & Dawis, R. V. (1969). *Adjustment to work: A psychological view of man's
    problems in a work-oriented society.* New York: Appleton-Crofts.
London, P. (1975). The end of ideology in behavior modification. In A. M. Graziano (Ed.),
    *Behavior therapy with children II.* Chicago: Aldine.
Marris, P. (1974). *Loss and change.* London: Mackay.
Marrow, A. J. (1969). *The practical theorist: The life and work of Kurt Lewin.* New York: Basic
    Books.
Mintzberg, H. (1983). *Power in and around organizations.* Englewood Cliffs, NJ: Prentice-
    Hall.
Minuchen, S. (1974). *Families and family therapy.* Cambridge, MA: Harvard University
    Press.
Myers, D. G. (1987). *Social psychology* (2nd ed.). New York: McGraw-Hill.
Napier, A. Y., & Whitaker, C. A. (1988). *The family crucible.* New York: Harper & Row.
Nevis, E. C. (1987). *Organizational consulting: A gestalt approach.* New York: Gardner Press.
Osgood, E. C., & Tannenbaum, P. H. (1955). The principle of congruity in the prediction of
    attitude change. *Psychological Review, 62,* 42–55.
Pasmore, W. A. (1988). *Designing effective organizations: The sociotechnical systems approach.*
    New York: Wiley.
Pierce, G. H., & Risely, T. R. (1974). Recreation as reinforcer: Increasing membership and
    decreasing disruptions in an urban recreation center. *Journal of Applied Behavior Analy-
    sis, 7,* 403–411.
Quinn, R. E., & Cameron, K. S. (1983). Organizational life cycles and shifting criteria of
    effectiveness: Some preliminary evidence. *Management Science, 19* 33–51.
Robinson, D. G., & Robinson, J. C. (1989). *Training for impact.* San Francisco: Jossey-Bass.
Rosow, J. M., & Zager, R. (1988). *Training—The competitive edge.* San Francisco: Jossey-Bass.
Schein, E. H. (1968). Organizational socialization and the profession of management.
    *Industrial Management Review* (Winter), 1–16.
Schein, E. H. (1985). *Organizational culture and leadership: A dynamic view.* San Francisco:
    Jossey-Bass.
Schein, E. H., & Bennis, W. G. (1965). *Personal and organizational change through group
    methods: The laboratory approach.* New York: Wiley.
Schneider, B. (1983). Interactional psychology and organizational behavior. In L. L. Cum-
    mings & B. M. Staw (Eds.), *Research in organizational behavior.* Greenwich, CT: JAI
    Press.
Sulzer-Azaroff, B., & Mayer, G. R. (1977). *Applying behavioral analysis procedures with chil-
    dren and youth.* New York: Holt, Rinehart and Winston.
Toren, N., & King, J. (1982). Scientists' orientation toward their work: The relative effect of
    socialization versus situation. *International Journal of Comparative Sociology, 23,* 34–46.
Trice, H. M., & Beyer, J. (1984). Work related outcomes of constructive confrontation strate-
    gies in a job-based alcoholism program. *Journal of Studies in Alcohol, 45,* 393–404.
Trice, H. M., & Sonnenstuhl, W. J. (1988). Drinking behavior and risk factors related to the
    work place: Implications for research and prevention. *Journal of Applied Behavioral
    Science, 24,* 237–346.

Turquet, P. M. (1985). Leadership: The individual and the group. In A. D. Coleman & M. H. Geller (Eds.), *Group relations reader 2* (pp. 71–87). Washington, D.C.: A. K. Rice Institute.

Van Maanen, J. (1977). *Organizational careers: Some new perspectives.* New York: Wiley.

*Wall Street Journal* (1989). One firm's bid to keep blacks and women. February 16, B1.

Wells, L. (1985). The group-as-a-whole perspective and its theoretical roots. In A. D. Colman & M. H. Geller (Eds.), *Group relations reader 2* (pp. 103–126). Washington, D.C.: A. K. Rice Institute.

Zaltman, G., & Duncan, R. (1977). *Strategies for planned change.* New York: Wiley.

CHAPTER 12

# CONFLICT, NEGOTIATION, AND CHANGE

## JEFFREY Z. RUBIN AND CAROL M. RUBIN

Although the history of social conflict is as old as humanity itself, the history of social psychological interest in the area is far more recent. The first experimental social psychologist was probably Kurt Lewin, and it was Lewin who first engaged in the social psychological study of conflict (compare Lewin, 1935, 1947, 1951).

Kurt Lewin was not only an important theorist but also a great teacher. Many of his students, in turn, went on to become some of the most important social psychologists to date. These intellectual progeny have had an abiding interest in conflict in its various manifestations. Leon Festinger, for example, did important theoretical and experimental work on the nature of intrapsychic conflict and its resolution, first with his "theory of social comparison processes" (Festinger, 1954), and then with his highly influential "theory of cognitive dissonance" (Festinger, 1957). If Festinger was Lewin's most distinguished student of intrapsychic or intrapersonal conflict, then John Thibaut and Harold Kelley were two of the most influential analysts of interpersonal and intergroup conflict. Their book, *The Social Psychology of Groups* (1959), provides a conceptual framework for understanding interpersonal and intergroup

JEFFREY Z. RUBIN • Department of Psychology, Tufts University, Medford, Massachusetts 02155.    CAROL M. RUBIN • Private Practice, 20 Claremont Street, Newton, Massachusetts 02158.

conflict that has remained, to this day, one of the most important contributions to the field. Finally, bridging the domains of intrapsychic conflict on the one hand, and interpersonal/intergroup conflict on the other, were a number of Lewin's students. The most important of these theorists is Morton Deutsch who, beginning with his "theory of cooperation and competition" (1949) and continuing to his present work on the motive of justice, has advanced a set of propositions that bear on conflict both within and between individuals.

During the 1950s, Lewin's intellectual progeny (in the form of "children," "grandchildren," and "cousins") turned much of their attention to the study of attitudes. Much of the earlier interest in conflict (in one form or another) shifted to include the study of the circumstances under which individuals can be persuaded to change their attitudes—where such change, it was conceived, often requires a three-stage process of "unfreezing" existing attitudes, putting new attitudes in their place, and then "refreezing" these new attitudes. Such models (see, for example, the writings of Hovland, Janis, & Kelley, 1953) assume the existence of intrapsychic conflict, a state of resistance to change that necessitates the three-stage process described above.

With the appearance of Luce and Raiffa's (1957) book, *Games and Decisions*, a provocative paradigm for the study of interpersonal conflict appeared on the social psychological scene: the Prisoner's Dilemma Game. This deceptively simple research paradigm, involving two players and a nonconstant sum conflict (in which both can win, both can lose, or one can win while the other loses), stimulated an enormous amount of laboratory research during the 1960s and early 1970s. Hundreds of experimental studies used the Prisoner's Dilemma to examine the conditions that are conducive to cooperative versus competitive behavior. Coupled with a few other simple research paradigms for understanding the nature of interpersonal conflict [notably Siegel and Fouraker's (1960) Bilateral Monopoly Game and Deutsch and Krauss's (1960) Acme-Bolt Trucking Game], the study of interpersonal bargaining and negotiation was given so large a boost that in their 1975 review of the experimental literature on bargaining, Rubin and Brown cite nearly 1,000 studies, most of them conducted by social psychologists.

The late 1960s and early 1970s proved to be the high-water mark in the social psychological study of interpersonal and intergroup conflict. Perusal of the major social psychological research journals today would rapidly lead the reader to conclude that psychologists no longer have much interest in the study of interpersonal conflict and negotiation.*

*Note that early research in this area tended to use the term "bargaining" to describe the joint decision making processes involved. In recent years the term has been supplanted by the more fashionable, if conceptually synonymous, term "negotiation."

Indeed, this is largely the case. While a few notable exceptions (e.g., Pruitt, 1981), social psychologists have turned their attention to other pursuits.

The field of conflict and negotiation studies has continued to flourish, however. Encouraged by a growing number of practitioner organizations—focusing on conflict and negotiation in such settings as the family, labor, business, organizations, and international relations—as well as the availability of increased external funding for theoretical work, conflict and negotiation studies are now the province of such far-flung disciplines as law, anthropology, international diplomacy, sociology, political science, communications, statistics, economics, and urban planning, to name but a few. In short, the field of conflict and negotiation studies is alive and well, only it has moved down the hall from the social psychologist's laboratory.

These, then, are a few of the strands of social psychological inquiry into the conflict and its resolution that have emerged over the last 50 years or so. Given this cursory and admittedly partial summary of major themes and trends, what are the major conclusions regarding *change,* which is the theme of the book? This chapter outlines a fourfold answer to this query.

## CONFLICT "RESOLUTION," SOCIAL INFLUENCE, AND CHANGE

Inspired by the work of Hovland's Yale group and its studies of attitudes and attitude change, the attention of conflict researchers and theorists was for many years directed to the laudable objective of conflict "resolution." This outcome denotes a state of attitude change that effectively brings an end to the conflict in question. In contrast, conflict "settlement" denotes an outcome in which the overt conflict has been ended, even though its underlying basis may not have been addressed.

The difference between the resolution and settlement of conflict is nontrivial, and is reminiscent of Herbert Kelman's (1958) distinction among three consequences of social influence: compliance, identification, and internalization. While conflict settlement implies the consequence of compliance (a change in behavior), conflict resolution instead implies internalization (a far more profound change involving underlying attitudes as well as behavior). The third consequence of social influence, identification, denotes a change in behavior that derives from the target of influence valuing his or her relationship with the source; identification thus serves as a conceptual bridge between behavior change and attitude change.

Kelman's trinity of compliance, identification, and internalization finds play in almost any situation in which one person wishes to influence (change) another. Efforts at socialization, for example, might be expected to move from compliance through identification to internalization—whether it is people being socialized into a fraternity or sorority, the military, life in prison or summer camp, the career of a first-year medical or law student, or whatever the socialization context may be. The socializing agent first induces the individual to change his or her overt behavior. When the socialized person values the relationship with the socializer, the conditions exist for internalization. This occurs when an outlook is "implanted" and subsequently takes on a life of its own for the individual—independent of the continued presence of the socializer.

French and Raven (1959), in their analysis of the bases of social power or influence, have developed a framework that meshes rather well with the Kelman conceptualization of influence. As elaborated by Raven and Kruglanski (1970), there are six bases of social power that can be used in an attempt to influence another: reward power (promises), coercive power (threats), expert power (appeals that derive from the source's apparently greater knowledge than that of the recipient), referent power (appeals that rely on the target of influence valuing his or her relationship with the source), legitimate power (influence attempts that work because the source has a legitimate right to make certain requests or demands), and informational power (appeals that rely on the intrinsic value of the information conveyed by the source to the target).

For example, a teacher who wishes to influence a grade-school child, Johnny, to stop disrupting the class by calling out, might try one or more of the following: (Reward) "If you raise your hand and wait to be called on, I will give you a gold star at the end of the day." (Coercion) "Unless you stop calling out, and start raising your hand, I will have you stay after school." (Expertise) "Raise your hand when you want to say something, Johnny. I'm the teacher, and I know how a class should be run." (Reference) "Raise your hand if you want to say something. All the other kids are doing that." (Legitimacy) "Raise your hand, Johnny. As the teacher, I have a right to set the rules, and *this* is a rule." (Information) "Perhaps it hasn't occurred to you, Johnny, but if everyone were to call out whenever they wished to say something, no one would be able to hear or understand anything that was going on, and no one would be able to learn. So please raise your hand."

Without elaboration, it can perhaps be argued that the use of reward and coercion is likely to produce the consequence of compliance; identification is likely to result from the use of expert, referent, and legitimate power; only informational power is likely to result in internalization. Depending on the kind of interpersonal change one wishes to instill—in the form of compliance, identification, and/or internalization—the change agent's influence efforts may be shaped by the typology outlined by Raven and Kruglanski (1970).

To return to the theme of conflict resolution, social influence, and change, much of the social psychological research on conflict in the 1950s and 1960s focused on *conflict resolution*: bringing about changes in the attitudes of the antagonists that would make conflict less likely to arise in the future. Only within the last decade or so has a subtle shift taken place, from a focus on attitude change to behavior change. Underlying this shift is the view that, while it is wholly desirable and laudable to aspire to the true resolution of conflict, the attainment of such an objective is often quite unrealistic. Merely getting two school children in a fist fight to stop pummeling each other is an accomplishment in its own right, even if the underlying concerns that gave rise to the fight in the first place are not addressed. Bringing a costly strike to an end is significant and meaningful, even if labor and management continue to despise each other. And getting Iran and Iraq, Contra and Sandinista, Israeli and Palestinian to lay down their weapons—even temporarily—is a considerable accomplishment, even in the absence of anything more lasting. Moreover, as Deutsch and Collins (1951) observed, in their research on the circumstances under which "stateways" (laws) can change "folkways," when simple acts of cessation of overt conflict are coupled with other such acts, the results may generate the momentum necessary to move antagonists out of stalemate toward a settlement of their differences. In other words, a string of behavioral changes may, over time, produce the basis for subsequent attitude change.

This shift from a focus on resolution to the settlement of conflict has had an important effect on the conflict field: it has increased the importance of *negotiation* as a field of study in its own right. Negotiation— defined as an approach to the settlement of conflict that entails the exchange of information in the form of offers and counteroffers, in pursuit of a mutually acceptable agreement—is, after all, concerned not with attitudes but with behavior. If some deeper understanding and appreciation of the issues and/or the other party should emerge from a negotiated settlement, that is well and good. The point of negotiation, however, is simply to move toward an agreement that all sides deem acceptable.

To reiterate, negotiation is a method of settling conflict rather than resolving it; the focus of negotiation is not attitude change per se but an agreement to change behavior in ways that make settlement possible. Two people with underlying attitudinal differences (for example, over the issue of school-ordered busing, abortion, or the existence of God) may come to change their views through discussion, but we would be hard pressed to describe such an exchange as "negotiation."

The net effect of the shift from conflict resolution to settlement thus has been to stimulate interest in the set of techniques that can be used to create a settlement through negotiation, as well as with the assistance of individuals (third parties) who are external to the conflict in some way. And with this shift toward the study of negotiation has come a parallel increase in attention to negotiation practice; countless professional organizations have sprung up over the last several years, devoted to assisting practitioners in such areas as labor negotiation, divorce mediation, international diplomacy, and so forth.

## CHANGE AND SELF-INTEREST

In his important book, *The Resolution of Conflict* (1973), Deutsch distinguishes between productive and destructive conflicts. Defining conflict as existing "whenever incompatible activities occur" (p. 10), he argues that destructive conflict is characterized by competition, misjudgment, and misperception, as well as (over) commitment; productive conflict, in turn, is characterized by creative thinking, cooperative problem solving, benevolent misperception, and cooperative commitment. While Deutsch acknowledges (following the earlier work of Coser, 1956) that conflict can have productive consequences and characteristics, as indicated above, much of his formulation is directed to the nether world of destructive conflict.

Building on his 1949 theory of cooperation and competition, Deutsch believes that the key to conflict resolution is movement from competitive behavior to cooperation. A cooperative relationship is characterized by some measure of trust in, and liking for, the other person, as well as a willingness to behave in trustworthy ways. A cooperative relationship is necessary if conflict is to be settled or resolved.

Over the last decade or so, this formulation—both of conflict and the motivation necessary to bring about settlement or resolution—has shifted. Thus, the critical element for effective conflict settlement may be not cooperation, but what may be described as "enlightened self-interest." According to this outlook, each side to a dispute is motivated primarily by efforts to do as well for oneself as possible (what Deutsch has characterized as an "individualistic orientation"). In addition, however, each side tries to remain open to the possibility that the other will also be able to do well. One's objective is not to cooperate with, trust, or be generous toward the other disputant—only to behave in ways that leave the door open to the other person finding an agreement that is attractive. One's objective is neither to help nor hinder the other person, only to be enlightened about the existence of agreements that work well for both sides. If ways exist that allow me to move toward my objective in negotiation, while at the same time making it possible for you to approach your goal, then why not behave in ways that make both possible? If the accomplishment of both our objectives can be furthered simultaneously, then you are less likely to stand in my way.

The earlier work of Deutsch and others, focusing as it did on the perils of competition and the seeming virtues of cooperation, made an important contribution to the field of conflict studies; in doing so, however, attention also shifted away from the pathway of individualism—a pathway that may, on occasion, provide a way out of conflictual stalemate and toward a settlement of differences. Thus, two people do not have to like or trust each other in order to negotiate wisely. Nor do they have to be driven by the passion of a competitive desire to beat each other. All that is really necessary is for each side to be clear about what it wants and to consider means of reaching its individual goals—while leaving the door open for the other to also do well. "Trust" and "trustworthiness," two concepts that are central to the development of cooperation, are no longer necessary, only the understanding of one's underlying interdependence with the other side, coupled with some appreciation of what the other side may want or need.

This point of view has been advanced by a number of negotiation scholars in recent years (for example, Fisher & Ury, 1981; Lax & Sebenius, 1986; Pruitt & Rubin, 1986; Raiffa, 1982; Susskind & Cruickshank, 1987). The key to understanding the other's point of view—a necessary ingredient if enlightened self-interest can be pursued—is operating not at the level of positions but interests. That is, instead of exchanging demands and offers in a negotiation, the parties need to move toward some understanding of the interests that underlie these demands.

An anecdote that clearly makes this point comes from the writings of Fisher and Ury (1981) and, before them, Follett (cited in Metcalf & Urwick, 1940). Two sisters are arguing over the division of an orange between them. Each would like to have the entire orange, and after a series of offers and counteroffers (e.g., "How about three-quarters for me, and one-quarter for you?" "No, how about three-quarters for *me*, and one-quarter for *you*?"), they eventually settle for a fifty–fifty split. At this point, one of the sisters peels her half of the orange and eats the insides, while the other proceeds to peel her half, throws away the fruit, and uses the peel to bake a cake. If only they had operated not at the level of positions (*how much* of the orange each wanted to have) but of interests (*why* each wanted some of the orange), each could have had all she wanted; instead, half of the orange was thrown away unnecessarily.

Like Jack Sprat and his wife, one of whom prefers lean meat while the other prefers fat, the two sisters in this anecdote are interdependent. For them to do well requires little or no trust per se, only a clear statement of individual interests and some understanding of what the other wants. Similarly, the United States and the Soviet Union, Iran and Iraq, two quarreling neighbors, or labor and management do not need trust to move out of stalemate toward agreement, but appreciation of their interdependence coupled with analysis of underlying interests.

Analysis of underlying needs and concerns, in the pursuit of enlightened self-interest, is no panacea, of course. Not all conflicts are amenable to settlement, let alone resolution. Nevertheless, this approach often helps to create the basis for agreement where such an arrangement might otherwise prove difficult or impossible. What is called for is less a matter of individual change per se and more a matter of flexibility of outlook—a way of thinking about one's objectives in a negotiation in ways that allow various approaches to be taken in pursuit of those objectives.

## CHANGE AND RIPENESS

Psychotherapists have long understood the simple fact that change can only take place in therapy if the client is motivated to embark upon such change. All the good ideas and interventions will prove useless in the absence of the readiness and willingness of the client to change.

This assumption, so obvious and integral a requirement for change in psychotherapy, has found its way into negotiation analysis only in recent years. The concept of "ripeness"—as advanced by scholars such as political scientist I. William Zartman (1981) and sociologist Louis Kriesberg (1987)—advances the view that, like the maturation of some fruit of the vine, there is a certain *best* or *right* moment to pluck a conflict or to wait. To pluck the fruit of a conflict too soon is to risk the greenness that comes from having insufficient motivation on the part of one or more of the interested parties; without the motivation to take their dispute seriously, and to do whatever may be necessary to bring about a settlement, the disputants are unlikely to engage in the exchange of views that can create a negotiated agreement. On the other hand, to wait too long, beyond some point of optimal ripeness, is to risk finding that one or more of the parties is by now so deeply entrenched in its position that there is little opportunity remaining to reach agreement. Positions may have been taken in public negotiation efforts, perhaps before the watchful eye of various constituencies, that are so extreme that their partisans believe that they are now locked into these positions, unable to budge without endangerment.

If there is a right, or "ripe," moment to pursue change, then, the question arises of how to *create* such conditions. One answer is simply to wait, deliberately to decide to do nothing. Often the passage of time has the effect of changing elements in such a way that a new reality emerges, one that may make negotiation appear more promising than before. If two sides are hurting, but not quite enough to take their conflict seriously, the passage of time may increase the cost to such a point that the equation changes in favor of negotiation.

Another way to create the ripe moment is by deliberately producing a "hurting stalemate." A third party, from the vantage point and legitimacy conferred by third-party status, can often do things that produce a situation so unappealing to each side that rather than continue in efforts to dominate the other each prefers the alternative of negotiated settlement. Each side is, in effect, led to the edge of a great abyss, shown where one's broken body would lie in the chasm down below, and chooses negotiated agreement instead. Henry Kissinger is alleged to have resorted to such moves in the opening few days of the 1973 Middle East War, in an effort to bolster Arab self-confidence and Israeli humility (Safran, 1978). As well, labor mediators, couples counselors, and other intervenors have been known to work to create a hurting stalemate, in order to motivate disputants.

There is another—often far better—way to create a situation that is ripe for settlement; namely, through the introduction of new opportunities for joint gain. If each side can be persuaded that there is more to gain than to lose through collaboration, that by working jointly, rewards can be harvested that stand to advance each side's agenda, then a basis for agreement can be established. Whether it is the two sisters and their orange, the Sprats, or two nations, one of the benefits of analysis of underlying interests may be to point the disputants toward overlooked opportunities for joint gain.

## CHANGE AND THE ROLE OF THIRD PARTIES

Whether it is a therapist vis-à-vis a couple, a mediator intervening in a labor dispute, or Kissinger engaging in shuttle diplomacy among the capitals of the Middle East, third parties have a potentially important role in the settlement of conflict. By virtue of their merely being "third," that is, not the first or second party, but someone additional, outside intervenors can often make a difference. A third party can help disputants analyze and understand the issue in conflict; he or she can also suggest ways of understanding, modifying, or packaging these issues so as to make agreements more likely.

Perhaps the most important service rendered by a third party emerges from the fact that this individual stands outside of or apart from the conflict, and is seen as endorsing qualities that make agreement more likely. Consider the situation that arises when two antagonists are locked in a stalemate. Neither may wish to make a concession, lest it be construed as a sign of weakness that invites efforts at exploitation and sets an undesirable precedent for future rounds of negotiation. Enter the third party. This individual is presumed to endorse norms of fair play, reciprocity, and so forth and to value behavior that makes agreement more likely. Thus, when this third party advances a proposal for settlement, it is likely to carry the weight of the third-party's reputation and expectations. Moreover, a concession requested by a third party (rather than one's adversary) eliminates the danger of future exploitation. Each negotiator can reason, in effect: "I am giving something up, not because my adversary made me, but because the third party requested it." If, as a result of such conciliatory behavior by the disputants, an unsuccessful agreement is produced, the third party can be blamed. If, instead, the result is a success, then the disputants can take credit for having had the good sense and temerity to do whatever was necessary to reach agreement.

Within the last several years, the literature on various forms of third-party intervention in conflict has grown dramatically. Research, theory, and practice have all burgeoned, spurred on by the prevalence of conflict in all aspects of American society, the spiralling costs of settling conflict through the court system, and the parallel growth in the general field of negotiation and conflict settlement. It is not possible to review this extensive literature here, but special attention should be paid to one major distinction that runs through much of the work. This is the difference between the third party who actively intervenes, suggests ideas for settlement, and oversees all aspects of the agreement-making process versus the third party who focuses on process considerations instead and tries whenever possible to encourage the disputants to devise the solutions that work best for them. This distinction is akin to Deborah Kolb's (1983) comparison of "dealmakers" and "orchestrators." Dealmakers are third parties of the first sort, individuals who figure out what sort of deal makes sense in a particular conflict, then help move the parties to accept that deal. Orchestrators, in contrast, are concerned less with the particulars of a particular deal than they are with the process that characterize the disputants' efforts to manage their conflict.

Disagreement exists in the field of conflict studies concerning which of these two intervention styles is more effective; more precisely, work continues to address the particular circumstances under which one style works better than the other. Underlying this work, however, is a continuing interest in the topic of change, and how one best brings change about. One school of thought argues for the use of whatever third-party tools, techniques, and power may be available: "Do whatever it takes to produce an agreement," this point of view reasons. In contrast, the second point of view contends that agreements are only of value if the disputants develop them for themselves. Agreements that are imposed from without may produce change, but it is the sort of change that produces compliance, rather than identification or internalization. Those that are developed from within (by and for the disputants) are agreements that may be more difficult to create, but which also have a far greater chance of enduring, precisely because they reflect an internalized change in underlying attitudes rather than behavior change alone.

## CONCLUSIONS

This brief overview of major themes and trends in the social psychological study of conflict and change leads us to the following observations.

First, it is very difficult, and often impossible, to create the basis for true change in a conflict between individuals, groups, or nations. Rather than "resolve" conflict, it often makes sense instead to aim toward "settlement." In any event, a series of settlements, strung together, may eventually succeed in bringing about the attitude change that is considered desirable.

Second, the kind of change that accompanies the settlement of conflict typically does not require cooperation, trust, and general benevolence. Instead, the literature points to the importance of self-interest, enlightened by a perspective that leaves room for the other side to do well.

Third, the best ideas in the world for dispute settlement and change will fail unless the parties are motivated. It is possible to create conditions that are "ripe" for settlement, and this can be accomplished in any of a number of ways. Perhaps the most constructive and valuable of these means calls for the disputants to understand some previously overlooked opportunities for agreement. Often such opportunities can be identified by moving from a statement of positions in conflict to some analysis of underlying needs and interests.

Finally, third parties can help promote change. As intervenors in conflict, they can introduce new ideas, increase motivation to work toward agreement, and most importantly they can help make it possible for concessions to be made with reduced risk of losing face and/or inviting exploitation in the future.

## REFERENCES

Cosler, L. (1956). *The function of social conflict*. New York: Free Press.

Deutsch, M. (1949). A theory of cooperation and competition. *Human Relations, 2,* 129–152.

Deutsch, M. (1973). *The resolution of conflict: Constructive and destructive processes*. New Haven: Yale University Press.

Deutsch, M., & Collins, M. E. (1951). *Interracial housing: A psychological evaluation of a social experiment*. Minneapolis: University of Minnesota Press.

Deutsch, M., & Krauss, R. M. (1960). The effect of threat upon interpersonal bargaining. *Journal of Abnormal and Social Psychology, 61,* 181–189.

Festinger, L. (1954). A theory of social comparison processes. *Human Relations, 2,* 117–140.

Festinger, L. (1957). *A theory of cognitive dissonance*. Stanford, CA: Stanford University Press.

Fisher, R., & Ury, W. L. (1981). *Getting to YES: Negotiating agreement without giving in*. Boston: Houghton Mifflin.

French, J. R. P., Jr., & Raven, B. H. (1959). The bases of social power. In D. Cartwright (Ed.), *Studies in social power* (pp. 150–167). Ann Arbor, MI: Institute for Social Research, University of Michigan.

Hovland, C. I., Janis, I. L., & Kelley, H. H. (1953). *Communication and persuasion*. New Haven, CT: Yale University Press.

Kelman, H. C. (1958). Compliance, identification, and internalization: Three processes of attitude change. *Journal of Conflict Resolution, 2,* 51–60.

Kolb, D. M. (1983). *The mediators*. Cambridge, MA: MIT Press.

Kriesberg, L. (1987). Timing and the initiation of de-escalation moves. *Negotiation Journal, 3,* 375–384.

Lax, D. A., & Sebenius, J. (1986). *The manager as negotiator: Bargaining for cooperation and competitive gain*. New York: Free Press.

Lewin, K. (1935). Psycho-sociological problems of a minority group. *Character and Personality, 3,* 175–187.

Lewin, K. (1947). Frontiers in group dynamics: I. Concept, method and reality in social science: social equilibria and social change. *Human Relations, 1,* 5–41.

Lewin, K. (1951). *Field theory in social science*. New York: Harper & Row.

Luce, R. D., & Raiffa, H. (1957). *Games and decisions: Introduction and critical survey*. New York: Wiley.

Metcalf, H. C., & Urwick, L. (Eds.). (1940). *Dynamic administration: The collected papers of Mary Parker Follett*. New York: Harper & Row.

Pruitt, D. G. (1981). *Negotiating behavior*. New York: Academic Press.

Pruitt, D. G., & Rubin, J. Z. (1986). *Social conflict: Escalation, stalemate, and settlement*. New York: Random House.

Raiffa, H. (1982). *The art and science of negotiation*. Cambridge, MA: Harvard University Press.

Raven, B. H., & Kruglanski, A. W. (1970). Conflict and power. In P. Swingle (Ed.), *The structure of conflict* (pp. 69–109). New York: Academic Press.

Rubin, J. Z., & Brown, B. R. (1975). *The social psychology of bargaining and negotiation*. New York: Academic Press.

Safran, N. (1978). *Israel: The embattled ally.* Cambridge, MA: Harvard University Press.

Siegel, S., & Fouraker, L. E. (1960). *Bargaining and group decision making: Experiments in bilateral monopoly.* New York: McGraw-Hill.

Susskind, L., & Cruickshank, J. (1987). *Breaking the impasse: Consensual approaches to resolving public disputes.* New York: Basic Books.

Thibaut, J. W., & Kelley, H. H. (1959). *The social psychology of groups.* New York: Wiley.

Zartman, I. W. (1981). Explaining disengagements. In J. Z. Rubin (Ed.), *Dynamics of third party intervention: Kissinger in the Middle East* (pp. 148–167). New York: Praeger.

PART III

# INTEGRATION AND CONCLUSIONS

# CHAPTER 13

# HOW PEOPLE CHANGE WITH AND WITHOUT THERAPY

## ALLAN COOPER AND JOEL COOPER

New situations require new behaviors. New roles require change in ways of relating to others. Sometimes the change is made easily, sometimes it seems impossible to change. Sometimes people manage to change on their own or with the help of friends. Sometimes people need psychotherapy before they are able to change. How people make behavioral and attitudinal changes in or out of psychotherapy is the subject of this chapter. We will approach this goal by melding insights from the interpersonal view of psychoanalysis with the theoretical constructs of social psychology.

An ideal time to study change is when the interpersonal situation changes. A new situation, such as a job promotion, marriage, or the birth of a child, brings a change in the role people are expected to play. In turn, the new role alters expectancies about the ways of relating to the significant people in the environment.

Consider Ms. M. She enjoys warm and friendly relationships with others. She knows how to maintain relationships and will often sacrifice some of her immediate desires in order to preserve relationships. She is usually pleasant and will go along with suggestions made by her

ALLAN COOPER • William Alanson White Institute, New York, New York 10023.    JOEL COOPER • Department of Psychology, Princeton University, Princeton, New Jersey 08544.

friends, such as to where they will have dinner or which movie to see. She is regarded as the "flexible" type. She is also an intelligent, well-trained professional. At work her superiors like her and she is promoted. However, she begins to have trouble with senior management when her clients complain about not receiving their material on time. The problem is identified as her not staying on top of her clerical and support staff. Her boss points out that her secretary spends more time making personal calls than getting the work done and that this pattern is continued down the line with others of her support staff. The solution seems easy to her boss. Simply be firmer with her subordinates. She agrees that it would be in her best interest to change her behavior but finds it difficult to do so. She becomes anxious, with sweaty palms and a rapid heart, when she tries to tell the secretary to get off the phone. When she finally does say something it sounds more like she is asking a favor than setting limits. Her boss is perplexed since he gets her verbal agreement about what has to be done, but finds that she does not do it.

Ms. M is in jeopardy of losing her job. This will have major ramifications at home where she is expected to earn some of the family income and where her professional status is important both to her and her family. A simple shift of behavior on the job will accomplish what seems to be required. Be firm and set limits. Yet, Ms. M is in the midst of a crisis in which the option of changing and the options of remaining the way she has always been both seem untenable. Why is it so difficult for her to change?

Some behavior can be shifted easily and with little change to one's sense of self. Other behaviors are intimately entwined with feelings, perceptions, needs, beliefs, and other interlocking facets that make up the person's character. An observer, such as the boss, cannot predict if a "simple" change in behavior will or will not require some fundamental change in character for the subject. From the observer's perspective the change may seem to be a minor and simple change. For the person who has to change, the shift may feel completely contrary to his or her sense of self.

Our "flexible" woman is not flexible when the change interferes with the primary way that she relates to others. That is, she gets along by being friendly and accepting. She overlooks small faults in others and gracefully covers up for their limitations. It makes her feel good to be liked, and she gets uneasy when people are annoyed at her. Reprimanding others and seeing that rules are followed does not fit with her character. At this point in her story we could not predict whether she wants the job badly enough to try to change. If she does, we cannot predict if she will be successful. The number of factors involved makes prediction difficult. We can, however, try to establish some of the issues that we believe are important for her to decide to change, and what some of the consequences are of that decision.

## CHANGING ATTITUDES AND BEHAVIORS

What do we really mean when we refer to "change?" From the observer's point of view, the way the person behaves with others is the only change he sees. From Ms. M's point of view, the new behaviors are inextricably intertwined with fundamental attitudes and values. We know, further, that attitudes and behaviors are related to one another. To change one affects the other. And herein lies both the potential and the difficulty for change.

Laboratory research in social psychology and a long tradition of theory and observation in clinical psychology merge to create an understanding of the change process. Both disciplines have studied the possibilities and the limitations of change. We shall consider first the insights from social psychological theories, and then the insights of clinical psychology as we assess the change process.

### The Social Psychology of Change

Attitudes are related to behaviors. We would all be surprised if people consistently and reliably behaved in ways that contradicted their attitudes. Generally, people who have favorable attitudes toward an object, person, or issue, act positively toward the object, person, or issue. We would find it surprising if people who favored the Republican party consistently voted for Democrats. Similarly, we would find it surprising if, in our previous example, Ms. M believed it was best to act warmly to people, yet consistently behaved in a cold and aloof fashion.

It would be tempting to argue that attitudes always and accurately predicted behavior. If it were so, then we would understand why Ms. M acted as she did before her employer criticized her. We would also be able to predict whether Ms. M would change her behavior toward her staff on the basis of whether her boss had been successful in changing her attitude. If Ms. M believed that it was best to please her boss or that her boss's view was the right way to run her department, then we would know what her behavior would be.

Since La Piere's (1934) classic study of the relationship of behaviors to attitudes, we know that the issue is not so straightforward. La Piere traveled across the United States with a couple of Chinese origin. Later, La Piere wrote to each of the restaurant and hotel owners asking if they would serve a Chinese couple. Overwhelming, the owners expressed negative attitudes about serving a Chinese couple. Yet only one restaurant owner *behaved* consistently with that attitude. All of the other owners served the couple despite their attitude to the contrary.

Research during the ensuing decades has been devoted to understanding the conditions under which attitudes are related to behaviors. People tend to behave consistently with their attitudes when they have had direct experience with the attitude object (Regan and Fazio, 1977) and when the behavior in question is at the same level of specificity as the attitude (Ajzen and Fishbein, 1980). More accessible attitudes also lead to more consistent behaviors while attitudes that are more difficult to bring to consciousness do not as often lead to consistent behaviors (Fazio, 1986).

Changing an attitude, then, may or may not lead to behavior change depending on such issues as accessibility and direct experience. Let us look, instead, at the other direction. Do changes in behavior lead to changes in attitudes? The theoretical concept that has had most to contribute to the relationship of behavior to attitudes is the theory of cognitive dissonance (Festinger, 1957). Dissonance theory holds that people experience tension when they perceive an inconsistency among their cognitions. Cognitions are "pieces of knowledge" about the environment, about behavior, about attitudes and feelings. Thus, if one behaves discrepantly from one's attitudes, an uncomfortable tension state ensues. That tension state leads to a motivation to change any of the cognitions in order to restore consistency. If a person has a pro-Republican attitude but makes a public statement endorsing Democrats in a congressional election, the psychological tension of dissonance ensues, and the person experiences a need to change a cognition. The cognition least resistant to change is the attitudinal cognition. The behavior, after all, was public and difficult to deny. If the attitude changed, however, then the behavior and the attitude would no longer be inconsistent and tension would be reduced. It follows, then, that if Ms. M could make a change in her behavior, for example, to be more firm with her secretary there would then be pressure to change her attitude about the way that she relates to people.

The story becomes more complicated, however. Research has shown that there are some very important qualifications on this effect. For example, dissonance is greatest if counterattitudinal behavior is engaged in for very little incentive. Giving someone an extraordinary amount of money, for example, to vote Democrat will probably elicit the behavior, but will not be effective in obtaining attitude change (Festinger & Carlsmith, 1959). In addition, the behavior must be engaged in freely (Linder, Cooper, & Jones, 1967), and is most effective when it relates to basic attitudes about the self (Aronson, 1969; Cooper & Fazio, 1984; Steele & Liu, 1983).

Can Ms. M change her behavior and can she sustain the change? We propose that the first question involves behavioral change and the second involves attitudinal change. We are looking for the ways that people change their behaviors that can be buttressed by changes in attitudes. Dissonance theory, as a theory that relates behavioral to attitudinal changes, suggests that there are conditions under which Ms. M can change her behavior and that such changes can produce shifts in fundamental attitudes, which in turn can sustain the new behavior. We will return to this later.

## PSYCHOANALYTIC INTERPRETATIONS OF CHANGE

There are divergent views about how people change stemming from different branches of the psychoanalytic study of human behavior. One comes from Freudian psychoanalysis, a second from interpersonal psychoanalysis and other contemporary views of therapy, and a third from social psychology. The Freudian position is very different from the other two. The Freudian would say that character problems are formed very early in childhood (LaPlanche & Pontalis, 1973). They postulate that these problems have their origin in early childhood desires and the defenses erected against them. According to this view, only depth analysis with the uncovering of the repressed wishes will allow for a change in character. Psychoanalysts holding this belief will regard any change that is made outside of analysis as superficial, and would predict that the change would not be long lasting. The variables that the Freudian's deal with are concepts such as oral aggressiveness, penis envy, castration anxiety, and anal retentiveness. These variables are believed to represent wishes and fears that arise from the biology of human beings and represent "human nature." They explain the fact that these ideas are not present consciously in the minds of most people through the concept of psychological defenses. They propose that these defenses, such as repression, are developed naturally to protect against feeling or acting on the infantile impulses. These defenses are also thought to be part of "human nature," and do not need to be learned from other people.

The interpersonal analysts postulate that character is formed through the interaction with significant people in one's life, from birth and continuing throughout one's life. The people who help form a person's character include more than the father and mother, that is, peers, teachers, clergymen, aunts and uncles, siblings, lovers, marriage partners, and so forth (Thompson, 1964). The list of significant people is long and varied. The list is different and unique in the life of each individual. Biological impulses are modified and shaped through the specific and unique interactions with the mothering people during infancy. The biological areas (oral, anal, phallic) in Freud's system were seen by Sullivan (1953) as zones of interaction. It is the *learning* that takes place in the *interaction* that shapes the meaning of the biology. From infancy onward it makes no sense in this system to imagine an unaltered biological impulse hiding under the mountain of repression and still affecting a person's character. The variables that make up character in the interpersonal system include attitudes, feelings, beliefs, and perceptions of self and others. It often focuses on the way people relate to others and includes how one relates sexually, but is not limited to this one facet of life. The variables outlined are similar to those that social psychology would examine when studying the process of change in the laboratory. These variables are not arcane. They are described in simple English, and we are used to seeing them change during the life cycle.

In the case of our young professional woman, the Freudian's would diagnose her as an oral dependent character. They would expect that until the infantile impulses to be fed were brought into the open, along with repressed hostility toward the mother, any changes would be superficial.

Interpersonal analysis postulates that character development does not end at age five, with the resolution of an Oedipus conflict. They believe that there is significant molding of character by the culture and the subculture the person grows up in. That there are people in addition to the parents who strongly influence a persons' character development. The list is different and unique in the life of each individual. For this reason it is not possible for the interpersonal analyst to state in simple schematic terms which attitudes or feelings will undergo change and cause the person to behave differently (Cooper, 1987).

Attitudes about how to relate to the significant people in one's life are not formed in one stage of life. They can begin very early in life, and then are modified in succeeding eras. Different people influence these attitudes during different eras. Changes in cultural attitudes along with the person's own ingenuity and reflections will affect the person's attitudes. From this perspective it does not make sense for the analyst to attempt to find the point in time when the attitude was formed. A current attitude has evolved and changed over time.

Freudian theory postulates a single and primary cause for a person's problems, such as maternal deprivation or castration anxiety. Every other influence on the development of character is seen as secondary, and rather inconsequential. The combination of a primary cause and the use of universal variables lends itself to simple schematic explanations. That is how the Freudian analyst can reduce the problem to an oral dependent character problem.

Interpersonal theory, postulating a multidetermined character development cannot so simply diagnose the "problem" or "prescribe" the cure. Is the woman's problem really a function of dependency and did it develop in the oral stage? It could be that the woman comes from a subculture in which causing someone to "lose face" is regarded as inflicting a deep narcissistic wound. It could be that she comes from a family in which subservient and self-effacing behavior was considered appropriate for women, and martyrdom was the accepted role in life. It could be that women were supposed to be caretakers, and any sign of strength or forcefulness was seen as "being like a man."

## CHANGING ATTITUDES AND BEHAVIOR

For our hypothetical Ms. M, change can take many forms. She might change her *attitudes* about what she is entitled to from others. She may come to *feel* differently about people who like her only when she serves them and people who are concerned about her needs as well as their own. She may learn to *perceive* a difference between a temporary, surface injury to someone's feelings, and a deep and destructive wound to their self-esteem. She may come to *feel* less sorry for people who take advantage of her, when she causes them a minor and temporary "loss of face." She may come to *believe* that temporary pain will teach a useful lesson and is therefore a "good" thing to do. The change in her character will involve similar variables whether it takes place in or out of therapy. The techniques that bring about change will be different in the two settings but the nature of the internal variables that undergo change will be the same. The ease with which we change does not necessarily indicate a "better" character structure, nor does it indicate a healthier one. It simply means that the required change is more in keeping with one's existing character. A more manipulative woman who had learned implicitly from her family to be ingratiating to authorities but demanding toward servants might have had an easier time with her promotion than our young woman did.

According to interpersonal theory, change will occur when the person becomes aware of her attitudes, has a good reason to question them, and allows herself to reconsider her position. Her inner resources are activated and some change may take place. We cannot watch this part of the process any more than we can observe the process of creation of a new idea. Even in therapy we cannot predict what her inner resources will do to her attitudes. She may change or she may reaffirm her position. This process is the same for her feelings, beliefs, perceptions, and the other internal variables that underlie a behavioral change.

## THE DILEMMA

Attitudes that are part of a person's character are difficult to change. They do not exist in isolation as mere intellectual opinions. As we have seen in the case of Ms. M, they are linked to the person's self-image, his family's views about relationships, and his culture's prescriptions about how to treat people. They are intimately linked to other beliefs, passions, hopes, and fears. Thus, when there is a strong conflict between behavior change and existing character, change will be very difficult (Cooper, 1987).

When faced with this conflict, the person must make a decision. Does he or she want to try to change? What consequences is he or she willing to pay for not changing? What happens if the person changes because of social pressure and the change conflicts with values that are important to him?

If we decide to change there are many directions the change can take. It would be a rare situation that had only one solution. We are actually confronted with several choices when we are confronted with the need to change. We choose whether to change or to resist change. We choose the type of change we will make. Sometimes a person sees a change that would resolve a predicament, but decides the remedy is something he cannot use. If the change conflicts with characteristics that are important enough to his sense of self, he may be unable or unwilling to make the change. In such a circumstance he will have to take the responsibility for choosing to remain static in the face of environmental pressures to change.

Ample research has demonstrated that there are significant cognitive and emotional consequences for both changing and not changing, given the inducement and the opportunity. If a person decides to change the way in which she behaves, there are many immediate consequences. Many of the values, beliefs, and attitudes that had been built up over the course of a lifetime now stand at variance with the new behavior. If Ms. M were to decide to take a firmer approach with her subordinates, so many of her self-relevant attitudes about friendliness, conflict, and being liked would be contradicted. If she does not change her way of behaving in the interpersonal arena with her subordinates, she stands to lose her job, and thus suffer a potentially severe loss of self-esteem.

As the pressure increases, there are several different resolutions that can be chosen. If a person is very creative he may come up with a solution that meets the demands of the new situation without conflicting with his or her fundamental attitudes and values. Ms. M for instance, could find a way of improving her persuasive capacities so that she is able to encourage her subordinates to do a better job without trying to be "tougher." Increasing her persuasiveness would fit better with her existing character and sense of self than learning how to be tough. Learning to be more persuasive will involve change but does not require a broad range of other fundamental changes. This change will be fairly easy and adaptive.

Let us imagine, however, that Ms. M is a person who cannot find an adaptive, compromise solution. She is now in the dilemma of deciding whether or not to change her behavior as demanded by her boss. We have noted that a change in her behavior will lead to major inconsistencies with her previous self-attitudes. If she does undergo behavioral change, she will immediately plunge herself into an uncomfortable tension state that we have referred to earlier as dissonance. If she were to adopt the firm, tough approach suggested by her boss, then her behavior is at variance with her gentler, conflict avoidant character.

The resolution of the dissonance reducing situation should be a change in attitude. Research from experimental social psychology laboratories has made it clear that behavioral change is followed by changes in attitude. So, our advice to Ms. M might *seem*, at first glance, to be to have her follow her boss's advice. Evidence that we presented earlier, however, places major qualifications on this advice.

A change will have disastrous results if the woman simply yields to external demands. In order for behavioral changes to lead to dissonance, a person must choose to engage in the behavior. She must take personal responsibility for acting, without casting that responsibility to others (Cooper, 1971; Cooper & Axsom, 1982). If she does not accept personal responsibility, but rather sees the boss's demands as the sole reason for her tougher, firmer behavior, she will not change her internal attitudes. Her concept of her self will not change and she will remain in internal conflict. If she does not resolve the conflict it might eventually lead to depressive reactions or anxiety attacks. If in addition she does not take responsibility for yielding to social pressure, she may look for a scapegoat. Her friends and her family might become likely targets, for she might see them as the reason that she had to stay in her job. The regard that she needs from her friends and the finances she contributes to the family may be seen as the ultimate "causes" of the behavior and her relationships may deteriorate accordingly. In effect she would say to herself that she never really changed. For the same reason, it is crucial that Ms. M not attribute her new behavior to external inducements. If she decides that she has changed her behavior only to obtain a raise or to avoid being fired, then, as we have seen previously (Festinger & Carlsmith, 1959), both responsibility and dissonance will be lowered. She will think that the only reason she changed her behavior was to please her friends and family, and the conflict, anxiety, and scapegoating will persist.

Ms. M will do better if she accepts responsibility for changing, rather than blaming others. In this case, as she copes with change, dissonance will put pressure on her to change the network of attitudes, values, beliefs, and values that are not consistent with the new behavior. She will recognize that old attitudes, coping strategies, cognitive conceptualizations, and interpersonal relationships will not support her new approach. Clinical experience shows that she may have to accept living with some anxiety until she learns new ways of relating to others, until she develops new internal and external means of support, but change will come.

Consider the very real possibility that Ms. M decides not to change. Suppose that, despite all of the very good reasons she has for adopting a new behavior pattern at work, she decides to behave the way she formerly did. We have already discussed the reason that change is difficult and to the degree that previously learned ways of interacting are important and imply more changes than Ms. M is willing to make, she may indeed decide to remain as she was. However, there are genuine emotional consequences to this decision as well. She had good reason to change and did not do it. This apparent discrepancy also produces dissonance and is likely to lead to attitudinal changes that will strengthen the original set of attitudes.

In a laboratory study, Darley and Cooper (1972) asked students to write an essay with which they disagreed. They were provided with a monetary inducement to write the essay but were given freedom to decide if they wished to engage in the counterattitudinal task. The results showed that for subjects who chose not to behave in a way that was discrepant from their attitudes, the greater the incentive magnitude, the more they changed their attitudes to make them even more extreme in the direction they originally believed. In other words, as a way of justifying turning down a large amount of money, the students became more extreme in their original position.

A person whose life circumstances gives them very good reason to change but who makes the difficult decision to avoid the change, may also become more extreme in his or her original convictions. In the case of Ms. M, the decision not to change her behavior toward her staff may result in her becoming more extreme in her deferential orientation toward others. She may elevate her attitude to a new height, making it more rigid and more doctrinaire than it was previously. Not only will she suffer from the anxiety of being unable to perform the necessary supervisory tasks in the present situation, but her more rigid attitude may make it still more difficult for her to perform well in subsequent situations.

## SUSTAINING CHANGE

We take the position that people live in a continuously changing interpersonal environment, that they continuously need to reorganize internal values, perceptions, desires, and coping strategies. They especially need ways of maintaining support in relationships while they undergo change.

This view is in contrast to an older psychoanalytic belief that if people proceed successfully through the early stages of psychosexual development they can deal with any problem that develops later in life. If a person has trouble resolving current conflict, and if symptoms appear, it was once assumed that a problem from early childhood must be the cause. This view does not take into account the problem of the compatibility between character and the social situation. In earlier writings when analysts spoke about character they always referred to character pathology. Analysts like Fromm (1947) and Sullivan (1953), however, began to talk about people's character without focusing solely on the pathological side. They put more emphasis on how a person's character fits in with the culture and subculture the person lives in. This new way of looking at character implies that people who have been showing positive development, and who appear to have a healthy character, can be in serious trouble when their situation changes and their character is not suited to the new condition. Take the example of a teenage boy who has developed a positive attitude toward others and is prepared to give and take with them in a reasonable manner. He is liked and respected by his peers. He is a good student and is well liked by his teachers. The teenager has grown up in a solid middle-class family. His family has serious financial reversals, and they have to move to a lower-class neighborhood where the teenagers pride themselves on being tough. The boy's cooperative attitude will be less useful than the ability to fight and "take care of himself." He becomes despondent when he finds that he is bullied and pushed around unfairly. He has neither the character orientation nor the skills to fight back. He begins to live in a state of anxiety about going to school and facing another day of being bullied. His way of relating does not lend to his being liked and he finds it impossible to make friends. He develops symptoms of insomnia, anxiety attacks, and depression. Would the outbreak of symptoms mean that he "must" have had a developmental flaw that we had not realized? It seems likely that the boy would have continued on his positive developmental trajectory if he had been able to remain in his middle-class environment. It seems unreasonable to conclude that he had a developmental flaw that simply had not shown up yet. It is clearly more parsimonious to conclude that when a person's character does not fit with his social situation, serious psychological problems can develop. There is certainly face validity to this position, while the hypothetical flaw that "must" always be there represents a tautology. The tautology maintains that people with good character will survive their circumstances. If the person does not survive, then he "must" have had a character flaw. It seems more likely that even a healthy person will have problems in a sick society, or one to which he is not suited. There is no way that the theory of "there must have been a flaw" can be tested. It does not lend to predictions that can be proven true or false.

There are difficulties in studying some of the Freudian beliefs, but some psychoanalytic hypotheses about development have been compared with the results of the natural observations of children. Chess and Thomas (1984) have done a 20-year follow-up on children's development. One of the more important findings was that there is no consistency between problems at one age and problems or the lack of them at later ages. The study also suggested that the nature and degree of pathology is less important than the parent's reaction to the child's problem. These studies indicate that different parents define "pathology" differently. What one parent cannot live with another parent enjoys. Pathology is seen as less clear-cut than in the medical model. It suggests that the ability of the parents, and other significant figures, to accept and enjoy the child is more important than the type and nature of the "pathology." This "goodness of fit" between the child and significant others is crucial for the self-esteem of the child. We suggest that the same holds true during adulthood, in slightly different form. The "goodness of fit" between a man and his family, his friends, and his colleagues is crucial when he is under pressure to change. If he goes into therapy he will hopefully receive this support in the therapeutic relationship.

When early analysts spoke about the need for change, they were always speaking about the need to give up irrational childhood desires. For Freud (Fenichel, 1945), it was the Oedipal desires. For Klein (Segal, 1964) and others it was the longing for the breast. Thus change always meant giving up an irrational desire of childhood. The analyst "knew" that the trouble *always* came from early childhood. The analyst "knew" *which* change had to be made. However, empirical research suggests that what is "normal" is hard to define. What may be as important as any concept of health is the "goodness of fit" between people and their interpersonal situations. When interpersonal circumstances change, a change is also needed in the way they deal with their new situation. The need for change is not only brought on by lack of mental health but by the demands of new situations. There are many possible changes that would solve the problem and the individual must accept the responsibility choosing one of them. If the person feels coerced he will resist the change. If he blames others for forcing him to change, he will not find his own solution, and the problem will not be resolved.

In Freudian therapy, if the patient interfered with the process of recalling the postulated unconscious infantile desires, the analyst "knew" the patient was resisting. If the patient did not accept the "correct" interpretation, the analyst "knew" that the patient was resisting the process of making a change. Existential dilemmas in a person's life were seen as derivatives of early childhood problems and the nature and direction of "change" was known by the analyst. Looking at the therapy situation from the current prospective, the analyst, however well meaning, may be pushing the patient in a direction that the person feels he must resist. Resistance from this perspective is not the patient's unconscious refusal to give up infantile wishes. The resistance is in response to an interpersonal threat from the analyst. The patient's goal, conscious or unconscious, may be to protect his sense of self.

Newer psychoanalytic theories postulate that character development does not end at age five with the resolution of the Oedipus conflict. Especially within the interpersonal school there is belief that there is significant molding of character by the culture and the subculture in which the person develops. There are people in addition to the parents who strongly influence a person's character development. The list of people is different and unique in the life of each individual. Development is thought by some to continue throughout the life cycle. For this reason it is not possible to state in simple schematic terms the attitudes, feelings, beliefs, needs, or perceptions that lead to the development of a person's character. For the same reasons it is not possible to say whether any given change in a person's situation will lead to difficulty or to an ease of "changing."

Sometimes a good friend can help a person make and sustain changes. It needs to be the kind of friend who can listen carefully and patiently. This friend would probably indicate that he could be accepting and nonjudgmental about any of the solutions he chose. At the same time the friend would still raise relevant questions in a nonjudgmental manner. He would probably offer his own ideas without insisting that he had the "right" solution. This good friend does not have a vested emotional or financial interest in seeing that the man change in a particular way. He will be interested and concerned. He will be interested in hearing the full story from his friend. He will use his own ingenuity in asking relevant questions that may foster new ideas in the troubled man. He will automatically protect the self-esteem of the man he is trying to help.

He should be able to ask relevant questions and offer suggestions. This process should help reduce the person's anxiety and tension, which should make his own mental resources more available. High anxiety does not lead to productive thinking. Having people who are interested in sharing the problem usually creates a sense of confidence and often stimulates a better use of the person's faculties such as his own ingenuity. Most people feel more confident when they have allies and function better with this feeling. If the friend is sensitive and thoughtful, his questions and suggestions may stimulate the person's thinking about the changes he might make. The suggestions may be directly useful or they may act as a stimulus for the person to change attitudes and feelings about the situation. It may stimulate the person to see the possible changes from a new perspective.

The friend is also in a unique position to help a person take responsibility for change. The friend will not be seen as coercive or in any way undermining the dissonance process. By helping the person clarify his values and attitudes, the friend helps the person choose, and choosing is essential for accepting responsibility. Thus, the sympathetic friend may consistently reinforce the notion that the person has acted in a new way because he or she chose to do it, and may be able to help the person with the consequent changes in self-relevant attitudes.

## CHANGING IN PSYCHOTHERAPY: POSSIBILITIES AND DIFFICULTIES

The changes that take place with the help of a friend are not different in type from the changes made in psychotherapy, though the changes made in psychotherapy may be more extensive. In some cases the help of a friend might not be effective where therapy could be effective. The therapist makes use of training and experience in dealing with people. He or she is skilled in interviewing techniques, and will be able to ask about sensitive topics in an empathic way. He or she will also make use of the patient's reactions to him, and will use his own reactions to better understand the person. He will not consciously manipulate the person into doing what he thinks is best for him. The therapist uses all of the skills he has learned to help the person make a decision about change for which the patient can assume responsibility.

However, having said all this about the ideal therapist, we must bear in mind that in addition to the problem of the transference–countertransference reactions, the therapist brings his own bias into the therapy situation. In the case of the woman who risked her job because she could not be sufficiently firm, the therapist might accept the woman's giving back the promotion because of his own views on the roles of men and women. He might see a woman's place as "in the home," and therefore respond encouragingly for a decision *not* to change. The therapist's own sexist attitudes might cause him to insist that a man, in the same position, change his behavior to act as his boss required. The therapist might be very conventional in his thinking, and being part of our culture might automatically assume that people should move up the ladder to success and happiness. This attitude might be implicit and never even rise to the therapist's consciousness. Therefore, he will formulate the problem from a certain perspective without being aware of it. A therapist who responds from his own set of preconceptions is not likely to foster the kind of behavioral change that comes with personal responsibility. As we have developed it, this kind of behavioral change will not produce supportive changes in attitudes. To the contrary, this patient is likely to develop "resistance." As the therapist puts more pressure on the patient, the patient will "resist." The therapist might point out the resistance, and the patient may become "unable" to overcome it. The patient may even consciously agree with the wisdom of the therapist, the spouse, the boss, and the majority of the culture, but is still likely to "resist." If coercion is perceived, no matter how well intentioned, it leads to no change at all, or to the kind of resistance (reactance) that results in greater rigidity instead (e.g., Brehm, 1972).

The individual as well as those around him may agree on the area where change is necessary. However, it may be counterproductive for other people to prescribe which of the many possible changes a person should chose.

One legitimate choice might be to relinquish a promotion altogether. A person's true ambition might be to become a very good line worker rather than an administrator. A doctor for instance might want to improve his or her skills and work well with patients rather than becoming the administrator in charge of the department. Another legitimate choice, described above, would be to take the position and to learn new ways of motivating the workers through friendly persuasion rather than being the "tough" boss.

A therapist will be willing to engage in the long process of "working through," which will result in a more extensive change in character (Cooper, 1989). We think of character as a large group of relatively autonomous but interlocking sets of variables such as attitudes, beliefs, feelings, needs, and perceptions. Sometimes a person can manage to change some important piece of behavior by changing just a few of the key variables. This may leave internal disharmony and result in a low-level continuing feeling of tension and anxiety. The long process of working through will be necessary to develop a new internal balance or a truly meaningful "attitude change." This means that a greater number of variables will be examined and undergo change resulting in a new internal balance, a new sense of "self," and a new "character."

If a person cannot change on his own and he does not have a good friend, psychotherapeutic intervention may be helpful. When a person attempts to change, whether in psychotherapy or not, it is crucial that he feels that he is responsible for the change. He should not be coerced into the change or the change will not be relatively enduring in his character. Evidence from research demonstrated that personal responsibility for changes of behavior is crucial if the change is to create a successful and enduring cognitive restructuring.

## CONCLUSION

This has been a discussion of attitudes and behaviors. True "change" involves both concepts. We have argued that people whose social milieu changes are sometimes confronted with a dilemma. The new social environment will be coped with best by a change of behavior, but that change in behavior may run contrary to a system of interlocking attitudes we have called character, or self. Behavioral change, in that context, is difficult. We have presented a model in which both character development and behavior are determined with an interaction with the environment. In contradistinction to Freudian psychoanalytic views, we have looked at the interpersonal environment for both the generating of the attitudes (character) and the potential for change.

## FOR THE FUTURE

The variables we have identified need to be tested by empirical research. Concepts from interpersonal theory that form the basis of our analysis can be tested and analyzed in both the psychological laboratory and the therapy office. Such synergistic but systematic research is the next step in understanding the process of change.

# REFERENCES

Ajzen, I., & Fishbein, M. (1980). *Understanding attitudes and predicting social behavior.* Englewood Cliffs, NJ: Prentice-Hall.

Aronson, E. (1969). The theory of cognitive dissonance: A current perspective. In L. Berkowitz (Ed.), *Advances in experimental social psychology,* Vol. 4 (pp. 1–34). New York: Academic Press.

Brehm, J. W. (1972). *Responses to loss of freedom: A theory of psychological reactance.* Morristown, NJ: General Learning Press.

Chess, S., & Thomas, A. (1984). *Origins and evolution of behavior disorders.* New York: Brunner/Mazel.

Cooper, A. (1987). Transference and character. *Contemporary Psychoanalysis, 23,* 502–513.

Cooper, A. (1989). Working through. *Contemporary Psychoanalysis, 25,* 34–62.

Cooper, J. (1971). Personal responsibility and dissonance: The role of foreseen consequences. *Journal of Personality and Social Psychology, 18,* 354–363.

Cooper, J., & Fazio, R. H. (1984). A new look at dissonance theory. In L. Berkowitz (Ed.), *Advances in experimental social psychology,* vol. 17 (pp. 229–266). New York: Academic Press.

Cooper, J., & Axsom, D. (1982). Effort jurisdiction in psychotherapy. In G. Weary & H. Mirels (Eds.), *Integrations of clinical and social psychology* (pp. 214–230) New York: Oxford University Press.

Darley, S. A., & Cooper, J. (1972). Cognitive consequences of forced non-compliance. *Journal of Personality and Social Psychology, 24,* 321–326.

Fazio, R. H. (1986). How do attitudes guide behaviors? In R. M. Sorrentino & E. T. Higgins (Eds.), *The handbook of motivation and cognition: Foundations of social behavior* (pp. 204–243). New York: Guilford.

Fenichel, O. (1945). *Psychoanalytic theory of neurosis.* New York: Norton.

Festinger, L. (1957). *A theory of cognitive dissonance.* Stanford, CA: Stanford University Press.

Festinger, L., & Carlsmith, J. M. (1959). Cognitive consequences of forced compliance. *Journal of Abnormal and Social Psychology, 58,* 203–210.

Fromm, E. (1947). *Man for himself.* New York: Holt, Rinehart and Winston.

La Piere, R. T. (1934). Attitudes vs. actions. *Social Forces, 13,* 230–237.

LaPlanche, J., & Pontalis, J. B. (1973). *The language of psychoanalysis.* New York: Norton.

Linder, D. E., Cooper, J., & Jones, E. E. (1967). Decision freedom as a determinant of the role of incentive magnitude in attitude change. *Journal of Personality and Social Psychology, 6,* 245–254.

Regan, D. T., & Fazio, R. H. (1977). On the consistency between attitudes and behavior: Look to the method of attitude formation. *Journal of Experimental Social Psychology, 13,* 28–45.

Segal, H. (1964). *Introduction to the work of Melanie Klein.* New York: Basic Books.

Steele, C. M., & Liu, T. J. (1983). Dissonance process as self-affirmation. *Journal of Personality and Social Psychology, 45,* 5–19.

Sullivan, H. S. (1953). *The interpersonal theory of psychiatry.* New York: Norton.

Thompson, C. (1964). Transference and character analysis. In M. R. Green (Ed.), *Interpersonal psychoanalysis* (pp. 23–31). New York: Basic Books.

# CHAPTER 14

# TOWARD AN INTEGRATIVE THEORY OF PSYCHOLOGICAL CHANGE IN INDIVIDUALS AND ORGANIZATIONS
## A COGNITIVE–AFFECTIVE REGULATION MODEL

### REBECCA CURTIS

The authors in this volume describe change processes both inside and outside therapy. Although reaching consensus on the change process in therapy is difficult enough, the present chapter will look at psychological change in general, including ideas from social and organizational psychology. Space does not allow for a full explication of this model, so I shall focus on the convergencies in cognitive–behavioral, social-organizational, and psychodynamic–developmental theories.

This chapter will present a model in which cognitive–affective regulation leads to change. The term "self-system" will be used to refer both to a person or a group in order to discuss simultaneously change involved in both individual and relational psychotherapy, as well as change in organizations. The chapter will present ideas regarding

REBECCA CURTIS • Derner Institute of Advanced Psychological Studies, Adelphi University, Garden City, New York 11530.

(1) how the change process starts, (2) how normal self-regulatory change processed go awry, (3) how change agents intervene to focus attention on factors to which the person or groups are not adequately attending on their own, and (4) how new experiences and a new organization of experience occur to the extent that the self-system is able to tolerate unpleasant experiences or the expectation of unpleasant experiences and is aware of this capability. That is, a person or group is able to cope with unpleasant experiences to the extent that the self-system has no question about its self-preservation, either physically or symbolically, whichever is more valued.

This model differs from cognitive–behavioral models of self-regulation (Bandura, 1977, 1989; Carver & Scheier, 1981, 1990; Kanfer & Hagerman, 1987; Scheier & Carver, 1988) in three ways. First, the role of affect is primary; it is assumed that human beings feel and that these feelings signal the need for the self-system to continue current efforts toward reduction of the discrepancy between actual and desired experiences or to disengage from such efforts. In short, it postulates that change is affect-driven (see Dahl, 1979; Westen, 1985, Chapter 2). It is assumed that people are motivated to attain positive affect and to avoid negative affect. It is postulated that it is the motivation to avoid negative affect that leads to dysfunctions in the self-regulation system. Second, it is assumed that selective inattention, both motivated and unmotivated plays a crucial role in maladaptive self-regulation. Third, meaning, symbolic images, and metacommunications are considered to be central to the change process in humans. This model allows for consideration of implicit (McClelland, Koestner, & Weinberger, 1989) as well as explicit cognitive–affective processes, making possible a model not only compatible with theorists and practitioners who have examined change from a cognitive–behavioral viewpoint, but also to observers of the change process, especially those with a psychodynamic perspective, who have insisted that this viewpoint neglects important factors.

"Self-system" is not used to denote the whole person or organization, nor a constellation of representations or schemas. Instead, the self-system is conceived of as a process (see Chapter 5, Greenberg and Rhodes's analysis of emotion in this volume) in which feelings, thoughts, and behaviors are recognized by the person or the group as differentiated from those of another person or group. Goals provide organization to the self-system. The self is dependent upon an *awareness* (cf. Gallup & Suarez, 1986) of "sameness," as the origin of the word implies. Therefore, a person may have no sense of self, that is, no "self," as may have been the case in early *Homo sapiens* (cf. Jaynes, 1976) or in non-"modern" cultures (cf. Baumeister, 1987; Westen, 1985). Obviously, a group of people observed by others may not consider itself to be a group and therefore would not possess a sense of self or constitute a self-system. The self-system in individuals is composed of a rational conceptual (cognitive) system that is verbal and symbolic, an experiential (affective) system that is nonverbal, and connections between the two. Such simultaneous processing systems have been postulated by Epstein (1990, 1991), Paivio (1978a, b, 1986), and Bucci (1985, 1989) (cf. Curtis & Zaslow, 1991). Carver and Scheier (1990) have recently proposed simultaneous systems of "action-loops" and "meta-loops," but these loops do not represent a separation of the cognitive and affective systems. Although a dual processing system is assumed in the present model, it is not essential to the other arguments regarding how normal change processes go awry or how change agents intervene.

Within a person or a group the goals vary in the degree to which they are independent, cooperative with, or competitive with one another. Therefore, goals may conflict with one another. The goals of the system also vary in the extent to which they are independent of, cooperative with, or competitive with those of other systems [see Deutsch's (1973) analysis of goal structures]. There are three separate dimensions characterizing the self-system's interrelationship with other people or groups: (1) the degree of differentiation, that is, the degree to which the system is able to recognize its own needs and goals as different from those of other systems; (2) the degree of interdependence of the goal structure with that of another system or systems, that is, the degree to which the system's attainment or failure of attainment of goals is dependent upon the attainment of goals of another system; and (3) the type of interdependence that exists with other systems, namely, cooperative, competitive, or mixed. In this regard, Deutsch has described a purely cooperative relationship as one in which a system can attain its goals only if another system attains its goals as well. A purely competitive relationship is one in which a system can attain its goals only if another system fails to attain its own goals. An individualistic reward structure is one in which the attainment of goals by the two systems is independent.

## HOW THE CHANGE PROCESS BEGINS

As people engage in goal-directed behavior, external events sometimes impinge upon the self-system, leading to a momentary interruption in the goal-directed activity and arousal. The change process in a self-system (that is, an individual or a group) begins when a discrepancy is perceived between actual experiences and desired experiences (see Curtis, 1989). This happens (1) when new external realities impinge upon the system, as social and organizational psychologists have frequently noted (see Cooper and Cooper, Chapter 13, this volume); (2) when an event leads attention to be focused upon different aspects of the current realities or upon a discrepancy between outcomes and goals; (3) when an event leads to an increased sense that the discrepancy can be reduced so that defensive avoidance of perceiving the discrepancy is less likely to occur; or (4) when former goals are attained and new goals emerge. When goal-directed activity is interrupted, arousal leads simultaneously to both a perceptual search and to affect if the experience is incongruent with (better or worse than) the anticipated progress toward the goal. Some affective responses are innately wired (Plutchik, 1980) but others require a cognitive labeling of the arousal (Schachter & Singer, 1962). Although the self-system is motivated to achieve pleasure and avoid pain, pleasure involves maintaining an optimum level of arousal (Berlyne, 1960). If the arousal is too great or small, behavioral adjustments are attempted. Carver and Scheier (1990) have recently described in greater detail how disruptions in goal-directed activity lead to arousal (Mandler, 1984; Mandler & Watson, 1966), which creates the potential for emotion (Schachter & Singer, 1962). From a psychodynamic point of view, Stern (1985) and developmental researchers have demonstrated how the lack of emotional attunement in infants' caretakers leads to disruption of the infants' goal-directed activity and inadequate affective regulation.

## SELF-REGULATION MODELS AND NORMAL CHANGE PROCESSES

Cybernetic models of regulation are generally associated with electromechanical devices, such as thermostats, missiles, and computers (Scheier & Carver, 1988). Similar models have been generated to explain human behavior in the areas of cognitive processes (Festinger, 1957; Miller, Galanter, & Pribram, 1960), physiological functioning (Schwartz, 1977), and attentional processes (Carver & Scheier, 1981, 1990). According to the Carver and Scheier model of self-regulation, people monitor their present activities and states by comparing them to a reference value that is synonymous with a goal or standard. If the person perceives a discrepancy between the present behavior and the reference value, a behavioral adjustment is made. If obstacles to goal attainment are encountered, the person evaluates the situation and derives "an outcome expectancy—the subjective likelihood of successful discrepancy reduction, given continued effort" (Scheier & Carver, 1988, p. 321). If a person perceives that an adequate amount of progress is being made toward the goal, that is, toward a reduction in the discrepancy between the present state and the desired outcome, attempts to achieve the goal are continued. On the other hand, if a person perceives that an inadequate amount of progress is being made toward the goal, the person will assess the likelihood of attaining the goal and will engage in new behaviors to attain the goal, ruminate about the goal (Martin & Tesser, 1989), withdraw behaviorally from the attempt to attain the goal, or withdraw mentally if there are constraints upon overt behavior.

Scheier and Carver (1988) point out that goals vary in their level of abstraction (Powers, 1973; Rosenbaum, 1987; Schank & Abelson, 1977; Vallacher & Wegner, 1985, 1987). According to Powers's view of superordinate and subordinate goals, there are nine levels of control inherent in human action, the highest level dealing with goals such as one's idealized sense of self or of interpersonal relationships and the lowest level dealing with muscle tension in the body. Psychological change may involve behavioral changes at low or intermediate levels of control or may require changes in the highest level of abstraction—those of the person's sense of self and others.

The concept of comparisons to standards or "set goals" in self-regulatory theory described by Carver and Scheier and recently by Bandura (1989), Kanfer and Hagerman (1987), and Kuhl (1987) is not limited to cognitive or cognitive–behavioral models of motivation. It is also important in the traditional psychoanalytic conceptualization of "superego" functions, in self-psychology's formulation of the idealized self-object (Kohut, 1971), in the humanistic concern with discrepancies between the actual and ideal self (Rogers, 1959, 1961; Rogers & Dymond, 1954), and in experimental social psychological theory on cognition and motivation (Festinger, 1954; Higgins, 1987; Walster, Walster, & Berscheid, 1978). Furthermore, the concept of self-regulation is essential to psychoanalytic "self psychology" and Stern's (1985) theory of infant development. According to Stern's theory, the caretaker regulates the infant's own "self-experiences," including arousal, affect category and intensity, sense of security, and experiences of somatic states (1985, pp. 102–103). Kohut (1977), the founder of the "self-psychology" approach, has contended that people use aspects of another person throughout their lifetimes in order to stabilize themselves against the disintegrating potential of stimulation and affect. He refers to these self-regulating others as "self-objects." People internalize the self-regulating techniques they learn from others.

## DYSFUNCTIONS IN THE SELF-REGULATION PROCESS

When a goal is extremely important, the person will persist in attempts to achieve the goal even when the probability of success is low. Therefore when the unattained goals involve the system's idealized sense of self and relationships, the system will pursue an unrealistic goal even when disengagement is the more rational behavior, with failure to achieve or to expect to achieve the desired outcome leading to the experience of unpleasant affect. Pyszczynski and Greenberg (1987) and Kuhl and Helle (1986) have used this reasoning in their recent theories of depression (cf. Klinger, 1975).

Experimental research by Wicklund and Gollwitzer (1982) has shown that people will persist in attempts to attain goals related to their self-definitions in ways these authors label acts of "symbolic self-completion." Arguing that recognition from others is necessary for self-definition, they demonstrated that people who were committed to self-defining goals that they had not yet attained engaged in more of a variety of symbolic self-completion behaviors, such as refusing to admit to failure, attempting to influence others, and displaying more symbols of the desired self-definition in their outward appearance than did people who had attained their self-defining goals.

Two goals identified by many personality theorists necessary to the self-definitions of most people are that they are lovable and competent. In this volume the Kirschners have discussed the goals of mastery and belonging in family systems (see Chapter 10). Bales (1958) had identified two similar requirements for effective leadership in groups: leaders must satisfy work groups' task needs and socioemotional needs. Regarding organizations, Bunker and DeLisle (see Chapter 11, this volume) have discussed the necessity for workers to be competent in their job requirements and in interpersonal relations as well as the necessity for the organization to bring satisfaction to its work force.

To the extent that the attainment of such highly valued goals is incomplete or disrupted by changes in external realities (as, for example, might occur in the case of a corporate takeover of an organization), the person may fail to disengage from certain goals and persist in attempts to attain them. If alternative strategies are apparent in the context of new external realities, the self-system can regulate itself in the normal process. The system will have difficulty self-regulating, however, if the alternative behaviors led to failure or anxiety in the past, especially if the system had difficulty tolerating and integrating such anxiety, and/or if the dominant responses for previously achieving one of these goals provided relief from anxiety in the past, as in the case of phobic and masochistic behaviors. In these situations, failure to engage in the well-learned behavior results in intolerable anxiety.

Research in at least five different areas of psychology provides information about the processes that ensue when the self-system is frustrated in goal-attainment and people become aroused or anxious: (1) arousal leads simultaneously to a narrowing of attention and greater distractibility (Kahneman, 1973; Wachtel, 1967); (2) anxiety leads to persistence of dysfunctional cognitive solutions (Cowen, 1952); (3) frustration of goal attainment leads to lower constructiveness and greater repetition (Barker, Dembo, & Lewin, 1941); (4) behaviors that have eliminated pain in the past will be repeated even when they are the very behaviors producing pain in a new situation (Mowrer, 1950); and (5) arousal facilitates performance of the dominant or well-learned response and inhibits performance of nondominant or novel responses (Eysenck, 1975a, b; Mandler & Sarason, 1952; Spence, 1956; Taylor, 1956; Zajonc, 1965; Zajonc & Sales, 1966). Research on attitude change processes also demonstrates that arousal related to cognitive dissonance results in the bolstering of the original attitude when the attitude is central to the self-definition (Sherman & Gorkin, 1980) and that commitment to a goal leads to a "defensive bolstering" of attitudes (Tetlock, Skitka, & Boettger, 1989) associated with less integratively complex and more evaluatively consistent thinking. These research findings all suggest that when the self-system is unable to tolerate the failure to attain an important goal, inattention to alternative aspects of the current situation occurs and the system repeats behaviors that were effective in the past, but are no longer adaptive. A "vicious circle" (Horney, 1939; Mowrer, 1950) then ensues as the system attempts to avoid the anticipated painful experience.

Although the Carver and Scheier model of self-regulation takes into account the importance of achieving the goal attempted, it does not give adequate attention to the importance of the failure to attain adequate progress toward the desired outcome and the affect associated with such a failure. The model of motivation formulated by Atkinson (Atkinson, 1957; Atkinson & Birch, 1978; Atkinson & Feather, 1966; McClelland, Atkinson, Clark, & Lowell, 1953), however, postulates that the tendency to engage in an action is a function of the tendency to achieve success minus the tendency to avoid failure, with the tendency to achieve success being determined by the expectancy (or probability), the value of success and the motive for achievement, and the motive to avoid failure determined by the expectancy and value of failure, or anxiety. The current model of change presented in Figure 1 makes explicit the role of the *value* (importance) of both achieving success and avoiding failure. Importance is, of course, a continuous variable, but is presented as a dichotomous one in the figure, for simplicity's sake.

The model of change presented in Figure 1 is therefore similar to the control model of Carver and Scheier until the point of assessing the

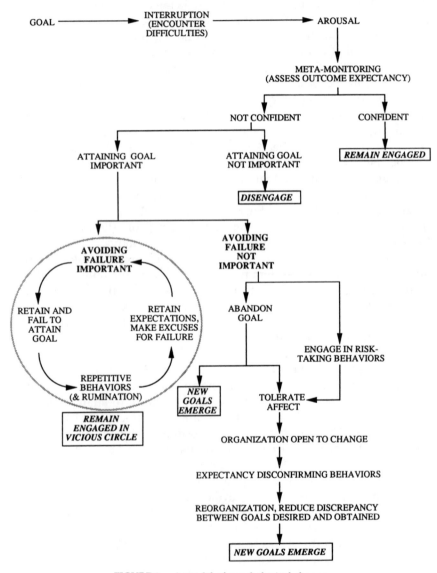

FIGURE 1.   A model of psychological change.

importance of avoiding failure. The current model, however, does make explicit that the arousal-regulation processes learned beginning in infancy will affect the choice made at this point. That is, the avoidance of painful affect related to disengagement from the attempt to attain a goal will lead to a maintenance of the current organizational system and, if unsuccessful, make more likely a vicious circle of self-defeating behaviors. The decision to avoid risking failure, to maintain the current organization, and to increase effort may work successfully, however. The system may even bolster its current organizational system (Tetlock, *et al.*, 1989). Block and Block (1980) have called such a process of becoming highly organized and even obsessive in a particular circumstance "'progression in the service of ego'" (p. 48). On the other hand, if the person or group is willing to risk enduring a painful experience, the goal system becomes more permeable and elastic (see Lewin, 1935, 1936, 1951) in relation to other goal systems and a new Gestalt can emerge. The change then may be simply a change in the perception of the situation. From a psychodynamic perspective, this process is similar to what Kris (1952) labeled a "regression in the service of the ego."

From the cognitive–behavioral perspective, Carver and Scheier (1990) have recently included the possibility of the avoidance of anxiety-provoking experiences in their consideration of a discrepancy "amplifying" loop in which a system attempts to move as far away as possible from the reference value, but they have not described the relationship of such a loop to the overall regulation process. The model in Figure 1 makes explicit such a relationship.

## THE POSSIBILITY OF GIVING UP

The adaptive function of knowing when to give up in order to maximize achievement in work and relationships has been emphasized recently by Janoff-Bulman and Brickman (1982) and by Feather (1989). Atkinson and Birch's (1986) model of action has stressed the fact that the system compares the value of particular desired outcomes against those available through alternative allocations of time and effort. The organism makes an assessment of the value of these particular outcomes against what Thibaut and Kelley (1959, p. 81) called a "comparison level for alternatives." Feather's (1989) analysis of trying and giving up based upon Atkinson and Birch's expectancy value theory makes possible testable predictions from a mathematically based model that has been studied both experimentally (Kuhl & Geiger, 1986) and in computer simulations (Kuhl & Atkinson, 1986).

The model presented in Figure 1 thus extends Carver and Scheier's model of self-regulation and Curtis's (1989) model of the development and maintenance of self-defeating and self-enhancing behaviors to include the explicit assessment of the *importance* (value) of attaining the desired outcome and of avoiding failure. These assessments do not require, however, that the system be fully aware of desired or feared outcomes consciously. The assessment of the importance of attaining the desired outcomes and avoiding the feared ones is likely experienced along a pleasure–pain dimension of what Epstein (1990, 1991) has called the experiential as opposed to the rational conceptual system. The assessment and risk-taking phases of the model presented here correspond to what Prochaska and DiClemente (1983) have called the "contemplation" and "change" stages of the change process.

The role of the change agent is to facilitate in attaining an alternative principle of organization. This is accomplished, as Goldfried (Chapter 5) and others have noted in the present volume, by focusing attention upon neglected aspects of the situation and the organization's experience of it. The role of the change agent will be discussed further in the following section.

## THE ROLE OF CHANGE AGENTS

At least three aspects common to the change agent's role regarding both therapeutic and organizational change are apparent in the discussions in this volume: (1) the increase in perceived capability (confidence) generated by consultation with an expert; (2) the refocusing of attention upon aspects of a situation to which the self-system is not adequately attending; and (3) the facilitation of the perception that the system can cope with the worst possible outcomes, that is, the failure to attain goals central to the self-system's construction of reality.

The first aspect of the change agent's role has been discussed by Goldfried and by Bunker and DeLisle (see Chapters 4 and 11, respectively, this volume). Goldfried has described the sense of hope as the first essential component of the therapy process. Frank (1973) has also emphasized this aspect of the change process. In Bunker and DeLisle's discussion of organizational change (Chapter 11, this volume), the consultant is able to increase the perceived sense of control. In other words, consultation with an expert increases the perceived capability of reducing discrepancies between desired outcomes (goals) and actual outcomes or the perceived capability of relinquishing unrealistic goals and formulating new ones.

The second aspect, the *refocusing of attention*, was pointed out explicitly by Goldfried and is inherent in Aronson's emphasis upon attention to details (Chapters 4 and 8, respectively, this volume). Inattention may result from learning, as in the literature on cognitive sets and functional fixedness (Luchins, 1942), generalized anxiety (see the research on cognitive narrowing referred to in the previous section), or specific anxiety, as in the case of motivated selective inattention. In both individual and organizational change, the change agent points out behaviors that were adaptive in a previous situation that are not adaptive in a current situation. Much of the work involves articulating the goals of the client and the strategies for attaining these goals. This is the process referred to as the verbal labeling of unconscious wishes and impulses by psycho-analytically oriented change agents (see McCullough, Chapter 4, this volume). In therapeutic work, the change agent also may need to validate the affect elicited when unattained goals are clarified in order for the affect to be integrated into the self-system (see Greenberg & Rhodes, Chapter 5, this volume; Socarides & Stolorow, 1984/85).

There are many aspects of the current situation and the client's experience of it to which the change agent may refocus attention. The change agent may focus attention on informational or cognitive aspects of the situations as suggested in the rational model of change described by Bunker and DeLisle (Chapter 11, this volume). The change agent also may focus attention on the existing reinforcers of behaviors the client desires to acquire, as suggested by the behavioral model of change. In addition, change agents may focus attention specifically on affect, as described by McCullough and by Greenberg and Rhodes (Chapters 6 and 5, respectively, this volume). The focus on affect will be discussed more thoroughly shortly. Change agents intervene at all stages in the process depicted in Figure 1 not only to focus attention on neglected aspects of the external situation but also to focus attention on *how* the system selectively inattends to experience and how it organizes itself. The change agent may validate the system's experience and, if necessary, even "join" the resistance (Spotnitz, 1985) or *prescribe* the current organization by use of paradoxical techniques in order to heighten the focus on the system's current organization or mode of organizing experience (see Selvini-Palazzoli, Cecchin, Prata, & Boscolo [1978] and Swann, Pelham, & Chidester [1988] for a description of this technique in family therapy and attitude change research, respectively). The technique of validating the client's experience is also used in organizational change (Harwood, 1990). Westen (1986) has enumerated five of the ways change agents intervene in the therapy process: (1) uncovering and altering dysfunctional goals and making conflicting goals conscious; (2) reworking maladaptive cognitions and expectations; (3) uncovering and re-working anachronistic affects; (4) uncovering and reworking maladaptive compromises between multiple cognitive–affective schemas; and (5) uncovering and reworking dysfunctional control mechanisms. Change agents in other settings make use of similar interventions. According to the Carver and Scheier control process model, the focus of attention leads to activation of the relevant goal hierarchies.

## FOCUS UPON AFFECT

Affect is experienced as a consequence of the fulfillment of goals or the expectation of their fulfillment, the lack of fulfillment of goals, or the expectation of their lack of fulfillment, or a conflict in the goals desired (see Bandura, 1989; Higgins, Tykocinski, & Vookles, 1990). When attention is focused on this affect, as Greenberg and Rhodes have argued, grief and frustration related to unmet goals or fear or anger related to the expectation of their lack of fulfillment are experienced. When these goals are central to the system's construction of reality, that is, at the highest level of Powers's (1973) hierarchy of organization, the system has experienced the worst possible outcomes imaginable, and is able to relinquish the former goal. This can happen if, as described in Strupp's (1988) formulation, the painful affect, the desired outcome or wish, the faulty belief, and the current internal experience come together. The self-system is then ready to begin a process of setting goals derived from the existing perceived realities and integrating them into a coherent reorganization of the self-system.

Thus, the refocusing of attention by the change agent may lead to the exploration of the worst outcomes imaginable. The change agent's refusal to avoid the aspects of the situation eliciting painful affect gives the client hope that the affect can be tolerated. Socarides and Stolorow (1984/85) and Stolorow, Brandchaft, and Atwood (1987) have argued that validation of affective experiences is necessary in order for these affective experiences to be integrated into the self-state and for developmental maturation to progress. From a very different perspective, Wicklund and Gollwitzer (1982) have also asserted that acknowledgment by another is necessary for self-definition and symbolic self-completion. The refocusing of attention by the change agent may lead then to the toleration of unpleasant experiences, or the toleration of such experiences may occur as a consequence of naturally evolving processes without the presence of a change agent. The following section will discuss this experience more fully.

## THE TOLERATION OF UNPLEASANT EXPERIENCES OR THE EXPECTATION THAT SUCH EXPERIENCES CAN BE TOLERATED AS ESSENTIAL TO THE CHANGE PROCESS

Crucial to Bandura's self-regulation model is the concept of self-efficacy defined as the conviction that one can successfully execute the behavior required to produce an outcome (1977, p. 193). Efficacy expectations determine how long people will persist in the face of obstacles and aversive experiences. Central to psychoanalytic theory is the idea that the ego must be capable of tolerating anxiety without disintegrating (Fenichel, 1945; Wachtel, 1977, 1987). The religious conversions or "counterconversions" described by William James (1961) provide examples of changes in the highest level of goals, in which the converts come to their new realizations after surviving intense emotional pain. These stories involve either the experience of sadness or depression. James reports that John Bunyan was "struck into a very great trembling" for days; Henry Alline, a Nova Scotian evangelist, became "one of the most unhappy creatures on earth," the French philosopher Jouffroy spent "the saddest days of his life," a man who fell violently in love became "so nervous and sleepless that he thought he should become insane," and a Frenchman wrote that he became like an epileptic patient he had seen in an asylum, "with greenish skin, entirely idiotic." Martin Luther also experienced a depression close to insanity (Erikson, 1962). A new organization of the person's beliefs and values then emerged in all of these examples. Such intense affect is only experienced in the change process when a person or people in a group are making changes in fundamental assumptions and superordinate goals.

In the therapy process as described by McCullough and by Greenberg and Rhodes (Chapters 6 and 5, respectively, this volume), intense pain is tolerated before the person makes observable changes. In families the Kirschners have described this process of regression and progression (see Chapter 10, this volume). In organizations, the risk of failure in giving up the security of old scripts is also necessary for change to take place. In our economic system, at least in the past, such risks of loss of capital were potentially highly profitable.

The toleration of the failure to achieve goals and the prospect of disintegration allows for a reorganization of the system. New goals, appropriate to the current realities, then emerge as the former goals recede into the background.

The question of what leads a person or individuals in a group to be able to tolerate such pain or, in Bandura's model to have high feelings of self-efficacy, is an important issue for which space in the current volume does not allow discussion. The literatures on "self psychology," object relations, and ego resiliency (Block & Block, 1980) have attempted to address this question. Certainly, a system must have some reason to feel hopeful that there is still something good possible after disintegration of the present organizational system; to the extent that this experience was provided early on and repeatedly in life, it should occur again. For others, a religious belief, or a glimpse of rejuvenation in the experience of another, may provide such hope [cf. Kierkegaard's (1941, p. 15) concept of the "leap of faith"].

Tolstoy's conversion (reported in James, 1961) provides an example of someone who had found contentment by attaining his goals, only to find himself in the depths of despair. He came to feel that he had nothing left to hold on to and driven to leave life when, as far as his outer circumstances went, he "ought to have been completely happy." He expressed his feelings as akin to those of the traveler in the oriental fable hanging onto a bush being eaten by mice on the side of a well into which he has fallen. At the bottom of the well is a devouring monster. Tolstoy concluded that to go on living was meaningless and absurd. In spite of all this, he still hoped to gain something from life. Eventually, a new meaning in life emerged to him.

The model of psychological change presented in this chapter does not predict that a low motivation to avoid failure will result in greater attainment of valued goals (cf. Atkinson, 1987). Instead, the model predicts a greater flexibility in problem solving, such as the perception of new strategies for goal attainment or psychological disengagement from a difficult-to-attain goal. Analyses of psychotherapy transcripts and reports of the therapy experience can provide data to test further the hypothesis that acceptance of the possibility of failing to attain goals (or to gratify wishes) leads to new strategies for goal attainment or disengagement from goals and the emergence of new ones.

## EXAMPLES OF THE APPLICATION OF THE INTEGRATIVE THEORY IN INDIVIDUAL AND ORGANIZATIONAL CHANGE

Two examples of the integrative theory of change depicted in Figure 1 should help make the model clearer.

### EXAMPLE OF INDIVIDUAL CHANGE IN THERAPY

A young man entered therapy with the goals of becoming more self-confident and having better social and intimate relationships. Although he wished to be more assertive and "manly," he also had the goal of avoiding being like his cruel father who had abandoned his family, embezzling the mother's money, or like his "macho," alcoholic stepfather. My job as the therapist, as far as refocusing attention was concerned, was simply to point out occasionally that the young man was trying to take care of me, as he had done with his mother who had become alcoholic after her first husband's departure. What seemed to be needed from me was availability without impingement.

When the client had accepted his failure at being his stereotype of a healthy "man," he was then able to find his own way of being a "man" and improve his intimate relationships. In regard to becoming more assertive, it seemed that the client was afraid that by standing up for his rights he would become overbearing and cruel. By chance, on a vacation, an older sibling recognized the natural father working in another country. My client then decided to go meet his father to talk with him. He realized that the father would likely be unkind to him, but wished to confront him. When my client found his father, the father denied knowing my client and requested that the police remove him from his property. Before this happened, however, my client had heard his father speak of an airline reservation to this country. The young man called home, had his father arrested at the airport, and brought to trial. Once my client accepted the failure of his goal of having a good relationship with his father and mourned his loss, he was able to feel much more self-confident. He then became more assertive in his career and in interpersonal situations.

## EXAMPLE OF ORGANIZATIONAL CHANGE

A European company had a goal of maintaining its license as the sole distributor of a type of machinery. Because of its internal organizational structure, the company was likely going to be in the position of adding less value to the distributor's operation when common market economic changes took place. It was very important for the families who owned the company to avoid losing their lucrative economic outcomes in return for minimal work. The change agents focused the attention of the owners on the inequitable financial distribution between owners and management. Once the families faced the prospect of losing their license to more efficient competitors, they were able to deal with their feelings related to their failure of maintaining the status quo within the company. They were then willing to contribute more alongside their hardworking management of traditionally lower social status and take a lower percentage of the profits within the company in order to compete better internationally.

# SUMMARY

A model of psychological change is described in which people formulate a goal and change either their strategies for achieving it or the goal itself if they perceive that an inadequate amount of progress is being made. Dysfunctions in this process occur when the goal is highly valued and the expected consequence of failure to attain the goal is intolerable pain or anxiety. In such a situation, people fail to disengage appropriately from attempts at goal attainment and are less likely to attempt alternative strategies for attaining the goals. Change agents are useful in that they provide (1) a sense of hope for an alternative perspective—either new strategies for achieving unmet goals or the capability of relinquishing unrealistic goals and formulating new ones; (2) a refocusing of attention on neglected aspects of the situation; and (3) the perception that people can cope with the failure to achieve a current goal.

It is asserted that change involving goals central to the self-definition of a system occurs only when the affect associated with the failure to achieve highly valued goals is assimilated into the self-system. New goals, appropriate to current realities, then emerge. This model is drawn not only from the contributions of cognitive–behavioral and psychoanalytic models of change, but also from the traditions of field theory, Gestalt theory, and experimental psychology.

## ACKNOWLEDGMENT

I wish to express my appreciation to Michael Leippe, Joel Weinberger, and Drew Westen for their helpful comments on an earlier version of this chapter.

# REFERENCES

Atkinson, J. W. (1957). Motivational determinants of risk-taking behavior. *Psychological Review, 64*, 359–372.

Atkinson, J. W. (1987). Michigan studies of fear of failure. In F. Halisch & J. Kuhl (Eds.), *Motivation intention and volition* (pp. 47–60). New York: Springer-Verlag.

Atkinson, J. W., & Birch, D. (1978). *An introduction to motivation.* New York: Van Nostrand.

Atkinson, J. W., & Birch, D. (1986). Fundamentals of the dynamics of action. In J. Kuhl & J. W. Atkinson (Eds.), *Motivation, thought, and action* (pp. 16–48). New York: Praeger.

Atkinson, J. W., & Feather, N. T. (Eds.) (1966). *A theory of achievement motivation.* New York: Wiley.

Bales, R. F. (1958). Task rules and social roles in problem-solving groups. In E. E. Maccoby, T. M. Newcomb, & E. L. Hartley (Eds.), *Readings in social psychology* (3rd ed., pp. 431–447). New York: Holt, Rinehart and Winston.

Bandura, A. (1977). Self-efficacy. Toward a unifying theory of behavior change. *Psychological Review, 84*, 191–215.

Bandura, A. (1989). Human agency in social cognitive theory *American Psychologist, 44,* 1175–1184.

Barker, R. T., Dembo, T., & Lewin, K. (1941). Frustration and regression: An experiment with young children. *University of Iowa Studies in Child Welfare, 18,* No. 386.

Baumeister, R. F. (1987). How the self became a problem: A psychological review of historical research. *Journal of Personality and Social Psychology, 52,* 163–176.

Berlyne, D. E. (1960). *Conflict, arousal, and curiosity.* New York: McGraw-Hill.

Block, J. H., & Block, J. (1980). The role of ego-control and ego-resiliency in the organization of behavior. In W. A. Collins (Ed.), *Development of cognition, affect, and social relations, Minnesota Symposium on Child Development,* Vol. 13 (pp. 39–101). Hillsdale, NJ: Erlbaum.

Bucci, W. (1985). Dual coding: A cognitive model for psychoanalytic research. *Journal of the American Psychoanalytic Association, 33,* 571–608.

Bucci, W. (1989). A reconstruction of Freud's tally argument: A program for psychoanalytic research. *Psychoanalytic Inquiry, 9,* 249–281.

Carver, C. S., & Scheier, M. F. (1981). *Attention and self-regulation: A control-theory approach to human behavior.* New York: Springer-Verlag.

Carver, C. S., & Scheier, M. F. (1990). Origins and functions of positive and negative affect: A control-process view. *Psychologic Review, 97,* 19–35.

Cowen, E. L. (1952). Stress reduction and problem-solving rigidity. *Journal of Consulting Psychology, 16,* 425–428.

Curtis, R. C. (1989). Integration: Conditions under which self-defeating and self-enhancing behaviors develop. In R. C. Curtis (Ed.), *Self-defeating behaviors: Experimental research, clinical impressions, and practical implications* (pp. 343–361). New York: Plenum.

Curtis, R. C., & Zaslow, G. (1991). Seeing with the third eye: Cognitive–affective regulation and the acquisition of self-knowledge. In R. Curtis (Ed.), *The relational self* (pp. 138–159). New York: Guilford.

Dahl, H. (1979). The appetite hypothesis of emotions: A new psychoanalytic model of motivation. In C. E. Izard (Ed.), *Emotions in personality and psychopathology* (pp. 201–225). New York: Plenum.

Deutsch, M. (1973). *The resolution of conflict: Constructive and destructive processes.* New Haven, CT: Yale University Press.

Epstein, S. (1990). Cognitive–experimential self-theory. In L. Pervin (Ed.), *Handbook of personality theory and research* (pp. 165–192).New York: Guilford.

Epstein, S. (1991). *Cognitive–experiential self-theory: An integrative theory of personality.* In R. Curtis (Ed.), *The relational self* (pp. 111–137). New York: Guilford.

Erikson, E. H. (1962). *Young man Luther: A study in psychoanalysis and history.* New York: Norton.

Eysenck, M. W. (1975a). Arousal and speed of recall. *British Journal of Social and Clinical Psychology, 14,* 269–277.

Eysenck, M. W. (1975b). Extraversion, arousal, and speed of retrieval from secondary storage. *Journal of Personality, 43,* 390–401.

Feather, N. T. (1989). Trying and giving up: Persistence and lack of persistence in failure situations. In R. C. Curtis (Ed.), *Self-defeating behaviors: Experimental research, clinical impressions and practical implications* (pp. 67–95). New York: Plenum.

Fenichel, O. (1945). *The psychoanalytic theory of the neuroses.* New York: Norton.

Festinger, L. (1954). A theory of social comparison processes. *Human Relations, 7,* 117–140.

Festinger, L. (1957). *A theory of cognitive dissonance.* Stanford, CA: Stanford University Press.

Frank, J. D. (1973). *Persuasion and healing: A comparative study of psychotherapy.* Baltimore, MD: John Hopkins University Press. (Original work published 1961)

Gallup, G. G., Jr., & Suarez, S. S. (1986). Self-awareness and the emergence of mind in humans and other primates. In J. Suls & A. G. Greenwald (Eds.), *Psychological perspectives on the self* (vol. 3, pp. 3–26). Hillsdale, NJ: Erlbaum.

Greenberg, J. R., & Mitchell, S. A. (1983). *Object relations in psychoanalytic theory.* Cambridge, MA: Harvard University Press.

Harwood, D. (1990). *Personal communication.* Hanover, MA: Situation Management Systems.

Higgins, E. T. (1987). Self-discrepancy: A theory of relating self and affect. *Psychological Review, 94*(3), 319–340.

Higgins, E. T., Tykocinski, O., & Vookles, J. (1990). Patterns of self-beliefs: The psychological significance of relations among the actual, ideal, ought, and future selves. In J. M. Olson & M. P. Zanna (Eds.), *Self-interference processes: The Ontario Symposium* (vol. 6, pp. 153–190). Hillsdale, NJ: Erlbaum.

Horney, K. (1939). *New ways in psychoanalysis.* New York: Norton.

James, W. (1961). *The varieties of religious experience.* New York: MacMillan Publishing Co. (Original work published 1901/1902)

Janoff-Bulman, R., & Brickman, P. (1982). Expectations and what people learn from failure. In N. T. Feather (Ed.), *Expectations and actions: Expectancy—value models in psychology* (pp. 207–237). Hillsdale, NJ: Erlbaum.

Jaynes, J. (1976). *The origin of consciousness in the breakdown of the bicameral mind.* Boston: Houghton-Mifflin.

Kahneman, D. (1973). *Attention and effect.* Englewood Cliffs, NJ: Prentice-Hall.

Kanfer, F. H., & Hagerman, S. (1987). A model of self-regulation. In F. Halisch & J. Kuhl (Eds.), *Motivation, intention, and volition* (pp. 293–307). New York: Springer-Verlag.

Kierkegaard, S. (1941). *Concluding unscientific postscript* (David F. Swenson, Trans.). Princeton, NJ: Princeton University Press.

Klinger, E. (1975). Consequences of commitment to and disengagement from incentives. *Psychological Review, 82*, 1–25.

Kohut, H. (1971). *The analysis of the self.* New York: International Universities Press.

Kohut, H. (1977). *The restoration of the self.* New York: International Universities Press.

Kris, E. (1952). *Psychoanalytic explorations in art.* New York: International Universities Press.

Kuhl, J. (1987). Action control: The maintenance of motivational states. In F. Halisch & J. Kuhl (Eds.), *Motivation, intention and volition* (pp. 293–308). New York: Springer-Verlag.

Kuhl, J., & Atkinson, J. W. (Eds.) (1986). *Motivation, thought, and action.* New York: Praeger.

Kuhl, J., & Geiger, E. (1986). The dynamic theory of the anxiety–behavior relationship. In J. Kuhl & J. W. Atkinson (Eds.), *Motivation, thought, and action* (pp. 76–93). New York: Praeger.

Kuhl, J., & Helle, L. (1986). Motivational and volitional determinants of depression: The degenerated-intention hypothesis. *Journal of Abnormal Psychology, 95*, 247–251.

Lewin, K. (1935). *A dynamic theory of personality.* New York: McGraw-Hill.

Lewin, K. (1936). *Principles of topological psychology.* New York: McGraw-Hill.

Lewin, K. (1951). *Field theory in social science.* New York: Harper & Row.

Luchins, A. S. (1942). Mechanization in problem solving: The effect of Einstellung. *Psychological Monographs,* No. 248.

Mandler, G. (1984). *Mind and body: Psychology of emotion and stress.* New York: Norton.

Mandler, G. & Sarason, S. B. (1952). A study of anxiety and learning. *Journal of Abnormal and Social Psychology, 47*, 166–173.

Mandler, G. & Watson, D. L. (1966). Anxiety and the interruption of behavior. In C. D. Spielberger (Ed.), *Anxiety and behavior* (pp. 263–288). New York: Academic Press.

Martin, L. L., & Tesser, A. (1989). Toward a motivational and structural theory of ruminative thought. In J. Uleman & J. Bargh (Eds.), *Unintended thought.* New York: Guilford.

McClelland, D. C., Atkinson, J. W., Clark, R. A., & Lowell, E. L. (1953). *The achievement motive.* New York: Irvington.

McClelland, D. C., Koestner, R., & Weinberger, J. (1989). How do self-attributed and implicit motives differ? *Psychological Review, 96,* 690–702.

Miller, F. A., Galanter, E., & Pribram, K. H. (1960). *Plans and the structure of behavior.* New York: Holt, Rinehart and Winston.

Mowrer, D. H. (1950). *Learning theory and personality dynamics.* New York: Ronald Press.

Paivio, A. (1978a). A dual coding approach to perception and cognition. In H. L. Pick & E. Saltzman (Eds.), *Modes of perceiving and processing information* (pp. 39–52). Hillsdale, NJ: Erlbaum.

Paivio, A. (1978b). The relationship between verbal and perceptual codes. In E. C. Carterette & M. P. Friedman (Eds.), *Handbook of perception: Perceptual coding* (pp. 375–397). New York: Academic Press.

Paivio, A. (1986). *Mental representations: A dual coding approach.* New York: Oxford University Press.

Plutchik, R. (1980). *The emotions: A psycho-evolutionary synthesis.* New York: Harper & Row.

Powers, W. T. (1973). *Behavior: The control of perception.* Chicago: Aldine.

Prochaska, J. O., & DiClemente, C. C. (1983). Stages and processes of self change on smoking: Toward an integrative model of change. *Journal of Consulting and Clinical Psychology, 5,* 390–395.

Pyszczynski, T., & Greenberg, J. (1987). Self-regulatory perseveration and the depressive self-focusing style: A self-awareness theory of reactive depression. *Psychological Bulletin, 102,* 122–138.

Rogers, C. R. (1959). A theory of therapy, personality and interpersonal relationships, as developed in the client-centered framework. In S. Koch (Ed.), *Psychology: A study of a science, Vol. 3. Formulations of the person and the social context* (pp. 72–224). New York: McGraw-Hill.

Rogers, C. R. (1961). *On becoming a person.* Boston: Houghton Mifflin.

Rogers, C. R., & Dymond, R. (1954). *Psychotherapy and personality change.* Chicago: University of Chicago Press.

Rosenbaum, D. A. (1987). Hierarchical organization in motor programs. In S. Wise (Ed.), *Neural and behavioral approaches to higher brain function: Recent explorations of the brain's emergent properties* (pp. 45–64). New York: Wiley.

Schachter, S., & Singer, J. E. (1962). Cognitive, social, and physiological determinants of emotional state. *Psychological Review, 69,* 379–399.

Schank, R. C., & Abelson, R. P. (1977). *Scripts, plans, goals and understanding.* Hillsdale, NJ: Erlbaum.

Scheier, M. F., & Carver, C. S. (1988). A model of behavioral self-regulation: Translating intention into action. In L. Berkowitz (Ed.), *Advances in experimental social psychology* (Vol. 21, pp. 303–346). New York: Academic Press.

Schwartz, G. E. (1977). Psychosomatic disorders and biofeedback: A psychobiological model of disregulation. In J. D. Muser & M. E. P. Seligman (Eds.), *Psychopathology: Experimental models* (pp. 270–307). San Francisco: Freeman.

Selvini-Palazzoli, Cecchin, G., Prata, G., & Boscolo, L. (1978). *Paradox and counterparadox* (E. V. Burt, Trans.). New York: Jason Aronson. (Original work published 1975)

Sherman, S. J., & Gorkin, L. (1980). Attitude bolstering when behavior is consistent with central attitudes. *Journal of Experimental Social Psychology, 16,* 388–403.

Socarides, D., & Stolorow, R. (1984/85). Affects and self-objects. *Annual Psychoanalysis, 12-13,* 105–119.

Spence, K. W. (1956). *Behavior theory and conditioning.* New Haven: Yale University Press.

Spotnitz, H. (1985). *Modern psychoanalysis of the schizophrenic patient: Theory of the technique.* New York: Human Sciences Press.

Stern, D. (1985). *The interpersonal world of the infant.* New York: Basic Books.

Stolorow, R., Brandchaft, B., & Atwood, G. (1987). *Psychoanalytic treatment: An intersubjective approach.* Hillsdale, NJ: Analytic Press.

Strupp, H. H. (1988). What is therapeutic change? *Journal of Cognitive Psychotherapy: An International Quarterly, 2,* 75–82.

Swann, W. B., Jr., Pelham, B. W., & Chidester, T. R. (1988). Change through paradox: Using self-verification to alter beliefs. *Journal of Personality and Social Psychology, 54,* 268–273.

Taylor, J. A. (1956). Drive theory and manifest anxiety. *Psychological Bulletin, 53,* 303–320.

Tetlock, P. E., Skitka, L., & Boettger, R. (1989). Social and cognitive strategies for coping with accountability: Conformity, complexity, and bolstering. *Journal of Personality and Social Psychology, 57,* 632–640.

Thibaut, J. W., & Kelley, H. H. (1959). *The social psychology of groups.* New York: Wiley.

Vallacher, R. R., & Wegner, D. M. (1985). *A theory of action identification.* Hillsdale, NJ: Erlbaum.

Vallacher, R. R., & Wegner, D. M. (1987). Action identification theory: The representation and control of behavior. *Psychological Review, 94,* 3–15.

Wachtel, P. L. (1967). Conceptions of broad and narrow attention. *Psychological Bulletin, 68,* 417–429.

Wachtel, P. L. (1977). *Psychoanalysis and behavior therapy: Toward an integration.* New York: Basic Books.

Wachtel, P. L. (1987). *Action and insight.* New York: Guilford.

Walster, E., Walster, G. W., & Berscheid, E. (1978). *Equity: Theory and research.* Boston: Allyn & Bacon.

Westen, D. (1985). *Self and society: Narcissism, collectivism, and the development of morals.* Cambridge: Cambridge University Press.

Westen, D. (1986). What changes in short-term psychodynamic psychotherapy? *Psychotherapy, 23,* 501–512.

Wicklund, R. A., & Gollwitzer, P. M. (1982). *Symbolic self-completion.* Hillsdale, NJ: Erlbaum.

Zajonc, R. B. (1965). Social facilitation. *Science, 149,* 269–274.

Zajonc, R. B., & Sales, S. (1966). Social facilitation of dominant subordinate responses. *Journal of Experimental Social Psychology, 2,* 160–168.

# HOW PEOPLE CHANGE
## A BRIEF COMMENTARY

### GEORGE STRICKER

It is possible to argue that change lies at the heart of psychology. Certainly, for clinical psychology, a discipline devoted to selected effective interventions that are designed to produce salutory change, the course and nature of change is a central issue. Before we examine how people change, we might address the question of whether they change at all. Certainly, people do change their behaviors and their attitudes, but do they change feelings, values, character traits, or other more substantial features? Probably, at times, but not easily and not quickly. What we have in this volume is a series of accounts of change, where it occurs, under what circumstances, and how it is best understood and explained. I would like to indicate the conclusions I have drawn from the chapters in this volume, not necessarily the conclusions they have drawn, or even would agree with, but the thoughts stimulated in me by exposure to this spectrum of presentations:

1. There are no general rules other than the need to attend to the specifics of each situation. This recognition of lack of generalizations leads to one important generalization: any attempt to impose our predetermined structure on a situation runs the risk of failing dismally. It is

GEORGE STRICKER • Derner Institute of Advanced Psychological Studies, Adelphi University, Garden City, New York 11530.

only through recognizing how little we know that we can make effective use of how much we know.

2. An understanding of the conditions of a particular situation will allow us to design an intervention appropriate to changing that situation. The details will vary from situation to situation, but there are always details and we always need to attend to them.

3. Change always disrupts an equilibrium. When it occurs, there often are pressures, arising both from within and without, to undo the change and restore the equilibrium. If equilibrium can be reestablished at a new and higher level, however, forces then will act to maintain this new and more favorable position. Until this stage is reached, the change agent cannot rest, but must work with the sequelae of the change in order to assure that the change will be maintained.

4. Change is rarely purely volitional. That is why "Just say no" is both simplistic and ineffective. People behave in the way they do for good, if idiosyncratic reasons. Perhaps the reasons are not constructive or enhancing, but they can be recognized as good ones if we understand the personal terms of each of the individuals. If they are to change, we must recognize that they are giving something up and therefore they have every reason to expect something in return for what they are being asked to give up. Robert Ruark once wrote a book entitled *Something of Value*, about changing customs and relationships in modern Africa. In the introduction, he said that if you ask someone to give up a way of being that is dear to them, you had better replace it with something of value. In planning intervention for change, we should keep this in mind. The something of value may initially be provided by the therapeutic relationship, but it must be supported by the world in which the patient functions.

5. The volitional issue also suggests an additional issue. Some people do not change despite their wish to do so; others do change, despite a wish not to do so, or a lack of recognition that they may be changed. People who wish to change do not pose any problem other than taxing our skills. But what are the ethical implications of instituting a change process when the changee is an unwilling or unknowing subject? I have no answer to the question, but I do want to raise your consciousness about the problem that can arise when we do not have a contractual relationship or we deviate from the contract that has been established.

6. Therapeutic learning is not restricted to therapy. This is why both social and clinical psychologists have something to teach us and each other. This is sometimes obscured because they study different problems in different laboratories, and the problem studied often structures the answer that is derived. The major source of variance leading to

change may differ from problem to problem, but we should not be so intrigued by the variance we study that we ignore other sources of variance.

7. Is the appropriate focus on how *people* change or how *we* can induce them to change? Is it the person to be changed or the process by which the change occurs? This may be the crucial line of demarcation between social psychologists and clinical psychologists. Should we focus on external reality, as social psychologists are wont to do, or internal change, as is the preference of clinical psychologists? This is reminiscent of the person–situation debate, one that seems most parsimoniously decided in favor of an interactionist solution. A social psychologist who ignores the dynamics of the individual or who overlooks the active response of the person on whom the intervention is practiced is doomed to fail with some of the people some of the time. A clinical psychologist who seeks to change the intrapsychic without regard to whether reality will support the change is unlikely to accomplish a great deal that is of lasting import. The recognition of a transaction between the internal and external, rather than an inclination to choose between them, seems critical.

8. If one is to design a lasting influence process, the value of external interventions lies in their impact on internal structures. We seek to change feelings, cognitions, knowledge, expectations, and motivation. By doing so, we empower the person to respond differently to his environment. If the environment does not support the resulting changes, they are unlikely to last. Again, we see the need to broaden, rather than narrow, our perspective.

9. Education is the primary vehicle for the production of change, but education is a great deal more than the transmission of information. The necessity for experiential learning was repeated over and over again. Along with this, the key role of the educator is underlined. Who the person is, as well as what the person does, is crucial to the success of the efforts. Contact is established in an intense relationship, but resistance, often not conscious, interferes with the cooperative pursuit of a mutual goal. The skill of the change agent is to promote and preserve the relationship, allowing the development of the matrix within which change can be facilitated.

10. In light of the key role of the change agent, it is important to know whether a therapist is born or made. There are some qualities, such as the capacity for human sensitivity, relatedness, and connectedness, that are absolutely necessary, but not sufficient, for change to occur, and these are not readily taught. However, there are some techniques we can teach, some skills we can hone, and some information,

theory, and understanding that can guide the process of change. To use another book title, Bettelheim wrote *Love Is Not Enough*.

In light of the dazzling array of examples and explanations to which we have been treated, how do we decide which one is correct? We must remember that theories are not true or false; rather, they are helpful or not helpful in promoting our understanding and appreciation. Rather than seek the one true explanation, I would encourage you to hold them all in mind, to pick and choose, and to develop a coherent and veridical explanation that will help you to understand change and to produce it. Some explanations will be more comfortable for some people than for others; some will fit some situations better than others. Many variations can be developed, and creatively integrated versions may be most compelling as we move toward a greater understanding and a more empowering approach to the mission of helping people to change.

## REFERENCES

Bettelheim, B. (1950). *Love is not enough: The treatment of emotionally disturbed children.* Glencoe, IL: Free Press.
Ruark, R. (1955). *Something of value.* Garden City, NY: Doubleday.

# INDEX